New York
Offbeat Walks

POCKET GUIDE

New York
Offbeat Walks

BY STEPHEN MILLAR

MUSEYON, NEW YORK

Published in the United States and Canada by:
Museyon Inc.
333 East 45th Street
New York, NY 10017

Museyon is a registered trademark.
Visit us online at www.museyon.com

Library of Congress Cataloging-in-Publication Data available.
ISBN 978-1-940842-55-4

Printed in China

Dedicated to the memory of Oney Judge and Jane Jacobs

ACKNOWLEDGMENTS

I dedicate this book to all the wonderful people in New York who have made this Scot feel welcome over the years. I first visited in 1990 and decades later still remain of the opinion that New York is the most exciting city in the world. It never stands still, even though that can often infuriate many of even its most loyal residents who prefer the past.

Most specifically, I would like dedicate this book to Monica, who let me stay at the wonderful Ansonia (that certainly beat the hostel with no ceiling), and my dear American friends Rachel and Nicole who I met by chance in Edinburgh while researching another book.

My thanks also to Akira and Janice at Museyon who helped me get this book over the line

TABLE OF CONTENTS

When I set out to write this book, my goal was to provide walkers with an alternative view of Manhattan. The book is not the typical guide to trendy restaurants or the most well-known attractions, but instead is a vision of New York City seen through a rather personal blend of history, architecture, and popular culture.

Along the way, you will visit the locations of lost canals, slave markets, and where mobsters were assassinated. You will pass pencil-thin towers where billionaires live in the early 21st century and where the city's elite rub shoulders in anonymous, exclusive clubs that have existed for generations. You will see where the Beat poets used to live and drink, where jazz reached its zenith and Elvis and the Beatles changed the world. In this book, the Westies gang and Jane Jacobs are as worthy of inclusion as George Washington, Andy Warhol, or Jackie Kennedy.

For simplicity, each walk concentrates on a particular district, or sometimes districts, but they do not attempt to be definitive guides in each case. For example, there is a single Upper East Side walk, but given its size and diversity, it would have been possible to include several walks covering that district.

I encourage you to take your time and take a few hours just to meander. Look up and down and resist the pressure most New Yorkers feel to get from A to B as quickly as possible. These walks should take hours, and you should take detours of your own. Try a new bar, restaurant or café you have never been to before, and talk to locals—everyone has their own fascinating story if you try and find it. If you see someone wandering the streets with this book—I would hope with a smile on their face—say hello or wave.

Over the past few years, I have written other walk books, including four covering London. I have always encouraged walkers to get in touch and let me know how they have got on. My contact email is ***stephenwmillar@hotmail.com***. Inevitably the city changes, so if you find things that need to be updated, or a direction is unclear, please let me know.

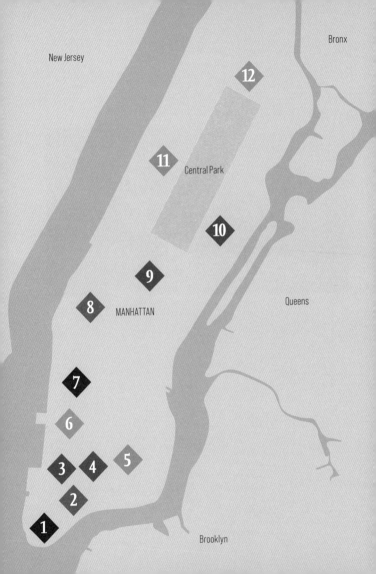

"The Purchase of Manhattan Island by Peter Minuit in 1626," William T. Ranney, c. 1855

1

COLONIAL NEW YORK WALK

START AND FINISH: Peter Minuit Plaza in front of Staten Island Ferry Terminal
SUBWAY STATIONS: Whitehall St **R**, **W**
South Ferry **1**, Bowling Green **4**, **5**

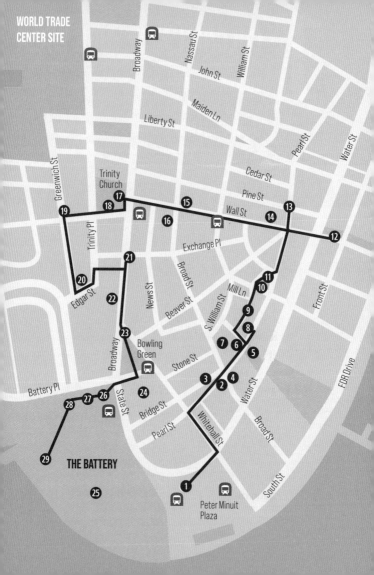

SOUTH ST
SEAPORT

FDR Drive

South St

Fulton St

BROOKLYN BRIDGE

EAST RIVER

COLONIAL NEW YORK WALK

Distance: 1.8 Miles

❶ Castello Plan
❷ Broad Street
❸ Bridge Street
❹ Fraunces Tavern
❺ Coenties Slip
❻ Site of the Stadt Huys
❼ 85 Broad Street
❽ 81 Pearl Street
❾ Stone Street
❿ Hanover Square
⓫ The Queen Elizabeth II
   September 11 Garden
⓬ Mannahatta Park
⓭ Pine Street
⓮ 60 Wall Street
⓯ Federal Hall National
   Memorial
⓰ The New York Stock Exchange

⓱ Trinity Church
⓲ Alexander Hamilton's Tomb
⓳ Greenwich Street
⓴ 67 Greenwich Street
㉑ Exchange Place
㉒ The site of George Washington's
   Home at 39-41 Broadway
㉓ Bowling Green
㉔ The Alexander Hamilton U.S.
   Custom House
㉕ The Battery
㉖ the Netherlands Memorial
   Flagpole
㉗ The Salvation Army Monument
㉘ Sculpture of Giovanni da
   Verrazzano
㉙ Castle Clinton

Brief Timeline of New Amsterdam/New York

- **1609** Henry Hudson sails past Manhattan while working for Dutch East India Company
- **1610** & **1613** Dutch ships explore further interest in beaver skins and trading opportunities
- **1624** Dutch West India Company moves 30 families to live on Nut Island (Governor's Island today)
- **1625** Settlers moved to southern tip of Manhattan and the beginning of Fort Amsterdam and New Amsterdam
- **1626** "Purchase" of Manhattan from Lenape by Peter Minuit
- **1643-45** Disastrous Kieft's War against Native Americans—colony almost fails
- **1647** Peter Stuyvesant arrives as leader of Dutch colony and it begins to recover
- **1650** Population: c. 1,000
- **1653** New Amsterdam became first legally chartered city in America; a fund is raised to pay for the building of fortification along the route of Wall Street
- **1654** Sephardic Jews arrived and began first Jewish community and Shearith Israel congregation
- **1655** Peach War
- **1664** English take over New Amsterdam and it becomes New York
- **1665** Official government language changes to English from Dutch
- **1673** The Dutch briefly take back New York, renaming it "New Orange"
- **1698** First Trinity Church organized; city's population 5,000
- **1699** Wall Street fortification torn down

- **1733** Common Council authorizes enclosure of land to create Bowling Green
- **1765** Stamp Act protests
- **1776** Declaration of Independence read out in New York, statue of George III torn down
- **1783** British finally leave
- **1789** Washington sworn in as President in New York
- **1792** Foundation of New York Stock Exchange through Buttonwood Agreement

This walk is an attempt at time travel, impossible of course, but hopefully, by the end you will have a sense of just how small the city used to be during the days of Dutch and then British rule between 1625 and 1783.

From the subway station, walk to the most southern point, the Staten Island Ferry Terminal. You'll find a green square in front of the terminal. This is Peter Minuit Plaza, and ❶ look for a waist-high artwork which depicts the famous **Castello Plan**—one of the earliest maps of New Amsterdam as it appeared in 1660. It shows the city stopping at Wall Street on the north side with less than a dozen proper streets and three canals. The southwest corner is dominated by Fort Amsterdam.

The Englishman Henry Hudson sailed here in 1609, and the reports he brought back to his Dutch paymasters of trading opportunities in beaver skins encouraged others to come. In 1625 The Dutch West India Company formally decided to start settling this part of Manhattan through the construction of Fort Amsterdam and several farms. Ironically it was the Pilgrims of the Mayflower landing in what they called Plymouth in 1620 that also sealed the fate of Manhattan. The Pilgrims had intended to come here but got a little lost, and the Dutch were worried that if they did not create a colony here first, the English would.

Peter Minuit (1580/5-1638) was the third director-general of the new Dutch colony of New Netherland and was a critical figure in making New Amsterdam the colony's main settlement. He arrived here in 1626, and soon "bought" Manhattan from the Lenape Native Americans for "60 guilders worth of trade." It is a great story, but nobody really knows what happened. Minuit's career with the Dutch West India Company ended badly, although he later returned to found another colony—New Sweden—which was centered around Fort Christina, the site of modern-day Wilmington in the state of Delaware (about 120 miles from here).

While New Amsterdam was on its way, the first few years of its existence were perilous—under threat from the English and Native Americans, disease, and bitter disagreements between residents about how the settlement should be run. It struggled on to become a city in 1653 even though the number of residents—then around 2,000 people—was still modest.

From the Plaza, walk up Whitehall Street, one of the oldest in the city and recorded by 1658. It is named after a large white house that was occupied by Peter Stuyvesant (1610-72), the most famous governor of New Netherland (incorporating New Amsterdam) and in charge when the British took over in 1667. The British gave his house the nickname Whitehall after the palace and surrounding district in London.

Turn onto Pearl Street, named by the Dutch for the oyster shells left here by the Lenape people on the river bank (the Dutch called it Paerel Straet). At the time it may have been the largest oyster field in the world. It is hard to imagine today as you walk along, flanked by boring office blocks, but in 1650 this was the commercial heart of New Amsterdam and the East River lapped against the shoreline, which was

to your right. The land from here all the way to the current shoreline of the river has appeared through land reclamation. Mid-17th century maps overlaid over current maps show about half of Manhattan south of Wall Street simply did not exist in the time of Peter Stuyvesant. Over the years, plots of land were reclaimed from the rivers on all sides, extending Lower Manhattan significantly. On this walk, you will keep mainly to the landmass residents during the Dutch and British periods would have known.

Stop at ❷ the corner of **Broad Street**. It was so named because by the standards of the 1600s, it was very . . . broad. Before the Dutch arrived a brook ran along the route. The Dutch then decided to build a grand canal—named The Heere Gracht—down the middle of what is today Broad Street and right down to the East River. It was used from 1646 to 1676, when the British—having taken over the city and not willing to keep its canals maintained—filled them in. Another reminder of this lost canal age is just a stone's throw away at ❸ **Bridge Street**, named for one of the three crossings built by the Dutch over their canal.

Continue across Broad Street where on the right ❹ is **Fraunces Tavern**. The building, originally a private home, was built for the prominent De Lancey family in 1719. It later became a tavern and was acquired in 1762 by Samuel Fraunces (1722/3-1795), a West Indian. Originally called the Sign of Queen Charlotte, it later was named the Queen's Head. During the Revolutionary War, secret meetings of the Sons of Liberty and other anti-British groups met here.

This spot is best known for being where General George Washington made an emotional farewell speech to his fellow officers on December 4, 1783. He left on the ferry and into retirement, although history would have one more important role for him. Samuel Fraunces would later become Washington's chief steward. Some government departments were situated in the building when New York was the national capital. Today this block is home to the Fraunces Tavern Museum, where visitors can learn about everything from George Washington to the Sons of Liberty.

Continue along Pearl Street, stopping at the corner of the ❺ curiously named **Coenties Slip** on the right. It gets a mention at the start of Herman Melville's classic American novel *Moby Dick*: "Circumambulate the city of a dreamy Sabbath afternoon. Go from Corlears Hook to Coenties Slip, and from thence, by Whitehall, northward. What do you see?"

If you could stand here in Colonial times looking towards the East River, you would see an inlet of water—or "slip"—with ships and small boats being unloaded. It may also have smelled a little—in 1691 the Common Council designated a number of markets in New York, one of which was the Coenties Slip fish market. The slip was drained and filled in during 1835.

"Coenties" is thought to be a corruption of the names Coenraet and Antje Ten Eyck. Coenraet Ten Eyck (1617–1686) arrived from the Netherlands in the mid-1600s and was a tanner, shoemaker and landowner. As with several other original Dutch settler families, later generations of the Ten Eyck dynasty become prominent businesspeople, artists and politicians in the city. In the 21st century, The Ten Eyck Group is an insurance firm founded by family members.

Now walk to the north side of Pearl Street opposite Coenties Slip. Look down to roundels on the ground that show the remains of an old well, cisterns and other foundations beneath your feet. This ❻ area was once **the site of the Stadt Huys**, a tavern built in 1641 that became the first City Hall in New Amsterdam in 1653.

The Stadt Huys was the hub of civic life for Dutch and other settlers in New Amsterdam, containing a jail, a school, and courts, all the while remaining a tavern that then stood by the edge of the East River. When the British took over, they used the building and a tavern

next door, built in 1670 and owned by Colonel Francis Lovelace (c. 1621-75), the second English governor of New York. Lovelace's tavern was used as the City Hall by the British after 1697 because the old Dutch Stadt Huys had become structurally unsafe.

If you look down, you will see grey-colored stones showing the outline of Lovelace's Tavern and cream stones representing the Stadt Huys.

Lovelace had quite an impact on New York, including overseeing a new postal service to Boston. However, he was punished after the Dutch briefly took back the city from August 1673 to December 1674. He died in the Tower of London in 1675. The tavern named for him burnt down in 1706 and these foundations were uncovered in 1979 during construction of a new building for Goldman Sachs. They represent the oldest visible remains of Colonial New York.

Follow the map, passing ❼ **85 Broad Street** on the left. Pearl Street is associated with oysters, and long ago the water of the East River lapped against the shoreline around here. This building also has links with another creature living in the depths as it used to be home to Goldman Sachs, described in 2009 by *Rolling Stone* journalist Matt Taibbi as a "great vampire squid wrapped around the face of humanity." Outside the entrance of 85 Broad Street is a roundel with a map of early New York. You can see how close City Hall and Lovelace Tavern were to the water.

Walk a little farther along Pearl Street to ❽ **No. 81** on the left (look for a plaque). This is the site of the first printing press in the city,

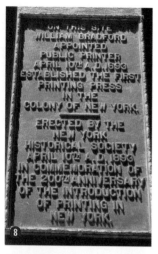

established in 1693 by Englishman William Bradford. Given how influential New York's publishing and newspaper industry would go on to become in later centuries, Bradford deserves to be remembered.

Retrace your steps and turn right (with 85 Broad Street on your left) and then right again to enter Stone Street. However, before you do, look back to 85 Broad Street. Stone Street used to continue right through what is now the lobby of the building.

Walk down Stone Street, one of the most attractive in Lower Manhattan. It is named for the cobblestones laid here in the mid-1600s after locals petitioned for what would become the first paved thoroughfare in the city. Earlier names include Straet van de Graft—Dutch for "street by the canal." It was also called Stony Street and Brewer or Brouwer Street, given its proximity to a brewery founded in the early

years of Dutch settlement. Today beer remains important in narrow
❾ **Stone Street**, and during the week, it is full of thirsty Wall Street
workers visiting the many bars here.

Walk on, stopping at the entrance to Mill Lane on the left. This
street existed by 1657, and connected South William Street (originally
Mill Street) to Stone Street. Its name recalls a horse-powered mill used
to process bark, the product of which was used for tanning leather.

By the 17th century, many Spanish and Portuguese Sephardic Jews
had settled in the Netherlands to escape the Catholic Inquisition at
home. Some emigrated to an area of Dutch-controlled Brazil, but when
that was returned to the Portuguese, most of the Jewish community
tried to get back to the relative safety of the Netherlands. One ship carrying Christian and Jewish refugees was captured by Spanish pirates
who were in turn caught by the French. The French offered to sail the
refugees to New Amsterdam for 2,500 guilders.

This was a crucial moment in the history of the Jewish community
in New York as the French brought 23 Jews here in 1654. These new arrivals, no doubt traumatized by their experiences, would form the first
Jewish community in America, the Congregation Shearith Israel. It
almost did not happen, as Peter Stuyvesant—an anti-Semite—wanted
to expel the new arrivals. However, pressure from other residents and
the Dutch West India Company forced him to relent. He grudgingly
permitted them to worship above an old horse mill that had previously
been used by early Christian settlers years before. No trace remains
today of the mill, but Mill Lane would have led up to it on what is today
South William Street.

For many years after that the Congregation met discreetly in private houses and temporary buildings in this area. It was not until 1730

that the Congregation Shearith Israel founded the first permanent synagogue in the city and North America on Mill Street (the site of 26 South William Street today—there is a plaque). Congregation Shearith Israel would go on to thrive and today, after many moves, is based on 71st Street and Central Park West.

Continue along Stone Street to reach William Street on the left and **Hanover Square ❿** on the right. The first is most likely named for William of Orange (1650-1702). He is an important figure in Dutch and British history because he married Mary, the daughter of James II of England. His father-in-law James (1633-1701) was the Duke of York (hence New York) before becoming King James II. It was James who sent the British fleet that arrived in New Amsterdam and forced Peter Stuyvesant to hand over the city.

However, James's Catholicism did not sit well with Britain's ruling classes who were staunchly Protestant. They got rid of James in the so-called Glorious Revolution of 1688 and his daughter Mary, and Dutch husband William of Orange, became co-rulers. So, the Dutch had some measure of revenge after losing control of New Amsterdam.

There is another British link here if you cross over to ⓫ **the Queen Elizabeth II September 11 Garden**. This commemorates the people of the British Commonwealth who were victims of the September 11, 2001 terrorist attack. The Queen only rarely visited the city, but came here to open the garden on July 6, 2010. George III was her third great grandfather.

Hanover Square's name is a reminder that the British have often felt they had no choice but to bring in a leader from abroad rather than rely on home-grown talent (Winston Churchill, of course, had an American mother). German-speaking George I began his reign as

British monarch in 1714, at which point he was already the ruler of Hanover in what is now north-western Germany. Like William of Orange, George was chosen as British ruler because he was a staunch Protestant. His grandson, King George III, would rule over Britain's American Colony when the Revolutionary War broke out.

If you look on the memorial plaque in the garden, you will see a reference to the St. George's Society of New York. Although it may seem any links today with the era of British colonial rule are long gone, this Society is an exception. St. George is the patron saint of England and the Society was founded on St. George's Day in 1770. The second oldest charity in New York, it was formed to help English settlers who had immigrated here.

The Scots and Irish did their own thing and today the St. Andrew's Society of New York (founded 1756) and The Society of the Friendly Sons of St. Patrick in The City of New York (founded 1784) are still going strong.

There is even a bit of Scotland right here in the garden—a stone that comes from the Queen's Royal Estate at Balmoral. The inscription reads, "New York to Aberdeen 3281 Miles."

Continue along Pearl Street until it joins up with Beaver Street on the left. This was originally the Dutch Bever Straat, named for the animal whose fur was critical to the foundation of New Amsterdam.

The original settlement was very much a "company town," with nearly everyone working for, or controlled by, the Dutch West India Company. Fur had traditionally been supplied from Russia, but an increase in prices in the 17th century, plus the fact that beaver fur was regarded as waterproof (useful for hats), gave imports from the New World tremendous value. Just ahead, you reach Wall Street.

Turn right down Wall Street, crossing over Water Street and stopping by **⓬ Mannahatta Park** on the other side, named for the word the Lenape used for Manhattan.

There is an information board here telling the chilling history of this spot when it was a slave market from 1711 to 1762. Slavery was introduced by the Dutch in the very earliest days of New Amsterdam and much of the city—its churches, roads and even the wall that gave Wall Street its name—was built through the misery and exploitation of people from Africa and Native Americans.

The importance of slavery to the growing city was also an indirect one because the trade in slaves was taxed, and so helped provide income to the civic authority that could be invested in developing infra-

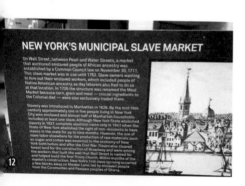

NEW YORK'S MUNICIPAL SLAVE MARKET

On Wall Street, between Pearl and Water Streets, a market that auctioned enslaved people of African ancestry was established by a Common Council law on November 30, 1711. This slave market was in use until 1762. Slave owners wanting to hire out their enslaved workers, which included people of Native American ancestry, as day laborers also had to do so at that location. In 1726 the structure was renamed the Meal Market because corn, grain and meal — crucial ingredients to the Colonial diet — were also exclusively traded there.

Slavery was introduced to Manhattan in 1626. By the mid-18th century approximately one in five people living in New York City was enslaved and almost half of Manhattan households included at least one slave. Although New York State abolished slavery in 1827, complete abolition came only in 1841 when the State of New York abolished the right of non-residents to have slaves in the state for up to nine months. However, the use of slave labor elsewhere was essential to the economy of New York both before and after the Civil War. Slaves also cleared forest land for the construction of Broadway and were among the workers that built the wall that Wall Street is named for and helped build the first Trinity Church. Within months of the market's construction, New York's first slave uprising occurred a few blocks away on Maiden Lane, led by enslaved people from the Coromantee and Pawpaw peoples of Ghana.

12

structure and institutions. Less well known is that white people were also traded here—indentured servants, debtors, orphans and other unfortunates who had fallen on hard times.

In the 1750s, twenty percent of the city's residents were slaves and slavery was only completely abolished in New York in 1841.

Retrace your steps back up to Wall Street. Water Street dates from 1696 and was first recorded with this name in 1736. Part of it was also called Little Dock Street—another reminder of how close the East River was to here.

When you reach the intersection of Wall Street and Pearl Street, take a small detour right along Pearl Street and stop at the next street on the left— ❸ **Pine Street**. This used to be called King Street, but after the British left New York, many streets like this were soon re-named after Revolutionary War heroes or to be uncontroversial (Hanover Square is an exception). Pine Street—also once called French Church Street—is unremarkable, but it does lie on the north side of Wall Street so when the Dutch settled here, this was outside of the defensive wall they built. If you had been a settler in the 1660s, all the area to the north of Pine Street was potentially dangerous to enter. For some New Amsterdamers, this spot represented the outermost physical limit of their American experience.

Retrace your steps and continue walking along Wall Street, named for the wooden defensive wall constructed in 1653. Why did the Dutch need such protection? The main threat came from the English who were envious of the Dutch colony. Other threats came from pirates and Native Americans. "De Wal Straat" was the path that ran inside the southern side of the wooden wall that stood nine feet high. It ran from one river to the other, from this point in the east by the water right along to what is now the graveyard of Trinity Church on the west (seen later). It also cost 5,000 guilders—considerably more than Minuit is said to have paid the Lenape for the rights to Manhattan.

How was New Amsterdam governed? Not easily. From the start, there were tensions between those who settled here in a Dutch colony and the Dutch West India Company. Settlers often saw the future of the colony differently than the company and its governors. Some of the earliest settlers were not even Dutch, such as 32 Belgian Huguenot families known as Walloons who wanted to escape religious persecution. In 1624 they came with the Dutch on the ship *Nieu Nederland* ("New Netherland") sent to help form the new colony.

When peg-legged Peter Stuyvesant arrived as the new governor in 1647, the town was home to tough slavers, farmers, artisans, tavern owners, sailors and tradesmen, many of whom were not Dutch. About a quarter of all businesses were "grog shops" catering to thirsty sailors, and many different religions were tolerated.

Stuyvesant was puritanical and domineering, leading to tensions with many residents who wanted a more relaxed approach. They tried to have him removed, and the dispute, together with war with England, led to the Dutch allowing New Amsterdam to become a chartered city in February 1653. Stuyvesant was still the top man, but he now had to rule with aldermen, chief magistrates, and a sheriff and district attorney. This new civic body met in the Stadt Huys (the site of which you passed earlier). When the British arrived, Stuyvesant wanted to put up a fight but most people (including his own son) wanted to avoid conflict and without their support Stuyvesant bitterly had to accept British rule.

Shortly, you pass ⓮ on the right, **60 Wall Street. A buttonwood tree once grew near this site**, and in 1792 men who stood under the tree to trade in securities came together to agree on rules on how to regulate the market they were already informally creating. The arrangement became known as the Buttonwood Agreement. The group would form the New York Stock & Exchange Board—the forerunner of the mighty New York Stock Exchange (seen shortly). Trading moved from the open air to the nearby Tontine Coffee House from 1792 to 1817.

During this time, and when the British ruled the city, the coffee house was a de facto exchange for everything that could be bought and sold. It was full of smoke, spies, politicians, brokers, insurance underwriters, merchants and other men of commerce—legitimate or otherwise—trying to make a profit on everything from sugar, slaves to stocks. You may be forgiven for thinking little has changed except these activities are hidden away inside office buildings or coworking spaces.

Wall Street has long been a byword for the most powerful financial services center in the world. It shares the same ethos as New Amsterdam as the original settlement was not founded to advance Dutch values or spread high ideals, but to make a buck on beaver skins. The defensive wall had fallen into disuse by the 1690s, then was briefly restored when the English feared a French invasion. It was finally pulled down in 1699.

Continue along. Try to imagine when Wall Street was lined with pretty Dutch-style houses, surrounded by gardens and favored by merchants and the wealthy, with plenty of taverns and coffeehouses nearby. As the city developed, this stopped being a residential area, and those who could afford it moved farther and farther north.

Soon you reach ⑮ at No. 26 the historic **Federal Hall National Memorial**. This was the site of New York's second City Hall, with construction taking place under British rule between 1699 to 1703, using stones taken from the demolished defensive wall.

Many events in early American history took place here, including a meeting of delegates from several colonies in 1765 to oppose the British Stamp Act. City Hall was later rebuilt and renamed Federal Hall when it became the new country's first seat of government in 1789. The First Congress met here, and the inauguration of George Washington as President took place on the balcony on April 30, 1789.

The current structure opened in 1842 as the Customs House and later served as part of the U.S. Sub-Treasury. It is now a museum (see current visiting times at www.nps.gov/feha/planyourvisit/index.htm)

On the other southwest side is ⑯ **The New York Stock Exchange building**—the most famous exchange in the world and one that owes its existence to the traders who stood under a buttonwood tree centuries ago.

Look down Broad Street. Before the Dutch arrived, a brook ran along here all the way to the East River. It connected to a marshy area near where you are now, later called the Sheep Pasture (approximately where Wall Street is today). There was also another small tributary known as the Beaver Path than ran approximately over the site of today's Beaver Street. The Dutch called the route of what is now Broad Street the Common Ditch.

In the 1640s the Dutch built three canals routed on these existing streams and an inlet. The biggest was the Heere Gracht (or Gentleman's Canal), that you crossed the route of earlier. This ran from the East River up to what is now the intersection of Broad and Beaver Streets. North of this ran in the same direction a second, shorter canal, the Prinzen Gracht (or Prince's Canal), that stopped by what is today Exchange Place. A third canal—the

Begijn Gracht—was the smallest. It ran westwards from the intersection of Beaver Street and Broad Street and joined the two larger canals at a right angle. All three were named after canals in Amsterdam and were crossed by three bridges.

The British were not keen on Dutch canals when they took over and had filled them in by 1680. However, the Dutch influence lives on in the appropriately named Broad Street. You'll notice a number of panels on the ground providing more information about markets and other institutions that stood near here in colonial times.

Continue to reach Broadway, and cross over to ⓱ **Trinity Church**. In the mid 17th century, New Amsterdam was struggling as a trading venture designed to make money for the Dutch West India Company. To encourage growth, the Company allocated plots of land to those willing to invest in development. However, many sat on their land hoping prices would rise, which led to disputes. Records show the names of those who owned plots along Broadway in the 1640s, with good solid Dutch surnames such as Van Dyck, Stuyvesant, Volkertsen, and Vandiegrist.

The church you see today is the third building on this site and is part of the Episcopal Diocese of New York. The original Trinity Church was built in 1698 on the site of the Dutch burial ground. Its founders were English Anglicans, a sign of how much the city was changing after New Amsterdam became New York.

Queen Anne of Great Britain (whose father was the Duke of York, later James II), gave Trinity substantial landholdings in Manhattan. Today Trinity controls assets worth several billion dollars, making it probably the richest church in America. Any Episcopalian church traces its heritage back to the Anglican Church of England that was established in every British colony. Today this church is part of the worldwide Anglican Communion and so it maintains links with similar denominations around the world and the colonial era.

The first church building was just one of up to 500 buildings destroyed in 1776 during the Great New York City Fire. The fire is said to have begun in the Fighting Cocks Tavern near Whitehall Slip. As it took place during the British occupation of the city, the fire may have been started deliberately.

The next Trinity Church was consecrated in 1790, and this is where George Washington worshipped when in New York. Alexander Hamilton (1755/7-1804) was a parishioner and is buried in the graveyard. The current Gothic Revival style church was completed in 1846. If you look around, you will notice how small this church seems compared to neighboring buildings. Then imagine how different the city must have

appeared when the church was built as this was the tallest building in the United States until 1869.

When you finish admiring Trinity Church, turn down Rector Street (on the south side of the Trinity graveyard). If you stop about half-way down on the right, you can see ⓲ **Hamilton's tomb**. English-born William Bradford (1663-1752), founder of the first printing press in the city (the site of which you saw earlier), is also buried here.

Why is New York not the capital of the United States? You might blame (or possibly thank . . .) Alexander Hamilton. At a dinner party on June 20, 1790, Thomas Jefferson (then secretary of state), James Madison, and Alexander Hamilton (then secretary of the treasury) discussed Hamilton's desire that New York would be the nation's capital, as well as his plans for a central bank and other financial innovations. They did not agree, and so Hamilton compromised, trading his dreams for New York in return for Jefferson and Madison removing their opposition to his financial plans. And so, at Jefferson's house on nearby Maiden Lane, the future of New York was sealed. Some would say that was a lucky break—had New York become the capital it may never have become the maddening, exciting city it is today.

Trinity Church had a major influence on the development of the city, from the names of its surrounding streets (several are named after vestrymen and rectors) to Columbia University, which began in 1754 as King's College on the grounds of the church (look for a plaque on Rector Street with some history).

Cross over Trinity Place to reach ❶ **Greenwich Street**. Just as Pearl Street faced onto the East River, Greenwich Street faced directly onto the waters of the Hudson. It was created out of landfill beside the high watermark of the Hudson River in the 1730s. In those days, if you wanted to travel from here to Greenwich Village, you took this street.

Greenwich Street used to be lined with townhouses for the city's elite. The Castello Plan of 1660 also shows a fortification wall ran along the south-north route, a little farther inland than Greenwich Street, that joined up with the fortification wall along what is today's Wall Street. This would have protected the Dutch settlers from an attack from the Hudson side.

Turn left (south) down Greenwich Street, trying to imagine tall-masted ships that would once have been docked at wharves all along the west side of the street in the mid-18th century when Hamilton would have been studying nearby at King's College, and visiting local taverns to stir up revolutionary debate.

Stop outside ❷ **No. 67 Greenwich Street**, which dates from 1810. While it wasn't built during the Colonial age, it is a rare survivor of the early Republic and the days when this street would have been thronged by wealthy and fashionable New Yorkers.

Now turn left up Edgar Street, left onto Trinity Place and almost immediately right up the narrow (and easy to miss) Exchange Alley. William Edgar was a wealthy merchant in the early 1800s who lived near here. At the end, you reach Broadway—another street Stuyvesant would have known the outline of.

If you had walked along Broadway in New Amsterdam c. 1660 what would you see? Surprisingly little. Behind the detached two-story Dutch-style houses facing onto the street lay gardens and open land, so the interior of what we now call blocks were fairly empty. On the west side of Broadway, before Trinity Church was built, you would see the Dutch burial ground and the large gardens of the Dutch West India Company. On the west side there was a small road and then the Hudson River.

In New Amsterdam, the Dutch built a fort (the site of which is seen shortly), and the open ground in front was the start of "The Broad Way"—or "De Breede Wegh." The thoroughfare ran to a gate in the fortified wall of Wall Street. It was also called by different names over the years, from The Gentlemen's Way to the Great Highway. It's unlikely those early settlers could have dreamed Broadway would become one of the best-known streets in the world.

Stop on the left ❹ at **Exchange Place**. Relations between European settlers and Native American people were often fraught. In 1655 Hendrick van Dyck shot a Native American woman stealing a peach from his orchard near this spot, triggering off a mass rising that had already been planned by a coalition of Native American tribes from surrounding areas. They ransacked New Amsterdam and then moved onto New Jersey where they murdered perhaps up to 100 colonists and took women and children as prisoners. The so-called Peach War brought New Amsterdam to its knees, and terrified settlers. If Stuyvesant had not taken measures to discourage settlers from fleeing the colony, New Amsterdam may have gone under (and who remembers New Sweden?).

Continue along Broadway, passing ❷ **the site of George Washington's home at 39-41 Broadway** (there is a plaque). This served as the second US Presidential Mansion between February to August 1790. The President had first moved to Cherry Street in April 1789, but it was not to Washington's liking so he moved here. Also in residence were

Oney Judge, William Lee, Christopher Sheels, Giles, Paris, Austin, and Moll, Washington's slaves from his home at Mount Vernon. Sadly, the Alexander Macomb House (named for the merchant who built it) was demolished in 1940.

Continue down Broadway, looking down to see inscriptions on the sidewalk marking the Canyon of Heroes, commemorating those who have been celebrated by a ticker-tape parade along Broadway. Soon you reach ❷❸ **Bowling Green** with its now-famous statue of the Charging Bull. In the 17th century, this area of New Amsterdam was an open public space used for a variety of purposes, from a cattle market to military parades. In 1733 it was turned into a park, and today is the oldest public park in New York. Its name refers to green lawn bowling, a recreational sport imported by the British.

Walk past the Bull to the park surrounded by railings.

In 1770, a gilded lead equestrian statue of King George III was erected in the center of the park, the monarch depicted in the style of the famous Marcus Aurelius statue in Rome. Throughout history, statues with a political significance have become the target of protes-

tors. On July 9, 1776 the statue of George III became a victim of anti-British sentiment after the Declaration of Independence was read to the soldiers in Washington's army.

After the reading, an excited mob rushed here from Broadway and pulled the statue down. The image of the destruction was captured in sketches and paintings and symbolized the dramatic end of colonial rule. The remains of the statue were melted down to make bullets used in the fight against the British. Some remains of the statue can be seen in the New-York Historical Society museum on the Upper West Side.

The railings are original, dating from 1771, and you can see where the mob sawed off symbols of the British monarchy.

Continue along the south side of the park to stand outside ㉔ **The Alexander Hamilton U.S. Custom House**, an imposing Beaux-Arts style building completed in 1907. It was, as its name suggests, a custom house for many years. Today it houses the George Gustav Heye Center of the National Museum of the American Indian which is well worth a visit, and admission is free.

The building is significant in that it stands approximately on the site of Fort Amsterdam. This was the main fortification built by the Dutch when they first arrived. On maps of the mid-1600s, the distinctive shape of the fort is the most recognizable and largest structure, with diamond-shaped bastions on each of the four corners.

The first fort began to be constructed in 1625, and played a crucial role in the city's daily life and development over many decades. For nervous settlers worrying if their move here was a bad decision, some comfort at least was supplied by having a strong fortification next to them. Run by the Dutch West India Company, it housed a church, warehouses, barracks for soldiers and accommodation for the Company's director.

The British kept the fort after it was surrendered by the Dutch in 1664. The British renamed both the city and the fort—it became Fort James (King James II was the Duke of York) and later Fort George (for George III). They anglicized several Dutch street names but it was not for a decade or more that the British began to really make their mark on what was now called New York by designing new streets and building houses that reflected English rather than Dutch styles.

The fort used to stand on a hill, and the site was much nearer the water than it is today. After the British left, the fort was dismantled in 1790, and much of what was taken down

41

was used to create infill for the new Battery Park. The Brits parting shot when they sailed away in 1783 was to grease the flag pole near here that carried their Union Jack, making it difficult for waiting American forces to put up the Stars & Stripes in its place. However, on "Evacuation Day," plucky war veteran John Van Arsdale is said to have made it up the pole and did what needed to be done.

Follow the map into ❷❺ **The Battery**, named after the artillery batteries that once stood by the fort. If you were transported back to 1650, you would be walking into the water as nearly everything beyond this point is reclaimed land.

Walk to the north side to stop at ❷❻ **the Netherlands Memorial Flagpole**. This was a gift from the Netherlands in 1926 and commemorated the "purchase" of Manhattan from the Lenape people by the Dutch West India Company. It also tells us that on April 22, 1625, the Amsterdam Chapter of the Company approved the foundation of Fort Amsterdam and several farms.

Near here is a monument ❷❼ remembering a mini-British invasion that is often overlooked. **The Salvation Army** began on the streets

of East London in the 1860s, led by William and Catherine Booth. General William Booth was convinced by another Army officer named George S. Railton to expand into the United States. On March 10, 1880, Railton and seven female members of the Salvation Army arrived by boat and unfurled the Army's banner for the first time in America. Today there are several Salvation Army centers in New York, and many involved in them are unaware they owe their existence in some measure to a small group of Brits.

A little farther along is a sculpture ❷❽ of **Giovanni da Verrazzano** (c. 1485-1528), the Italian explorer and navigator who, in 1524, became the first European to enter New York Bay. He described it as "a very agreeable site located between two hills between which flowed to the sea a very great river." His report later helped Henry Hudson who arrived in September 1609 while working for the Dutch East India Company (they were not happy with him—wanting him instead to find the fabled Northwest Passage).

Now walk over to visit ❷❾ **Castle Clinton**. Tension between the United States and Britain continued well into the 19th century, and this fortification was built between 1808-1811 in anticipation of a British invasion. It was constructed on an artificial island, linked by a bridge, so if you had stood here when it was built, you would (again) be surrounded by water.

The building was later used for a variety of purposes, including as a venue for operas (the famous Swedish soprano Jenny Lind sang here). However, it is best known for being the first immigration registration center for the city. Operating between 1855 and 1892, over eight million people passed through here. The better-known Ellis Island became the new immigration center in 1892. It is incredible to think how many lives were changed by passing through this tiny building and that in the 1650s, the population of New Amsterdam was only around one thousand people. Castle Clinton is currently used as a departure point for visitors to Ellis Island and the Statue of Liberty, and hosts a small history exhibit.

You can now explore the Battery Garden at your leisure. When finished, you can cross to reach the subway station you started from.

2

CIVIC CENTER, CHINATOWN & LITTLE ITALY WALK

START AND FINISH: David N. Dinkins Municipal Building
SUBWAY STATIONS: Brooklyn Bridge/City Hall **4**, **5**, **6**, Chambers St **J**, **Z**

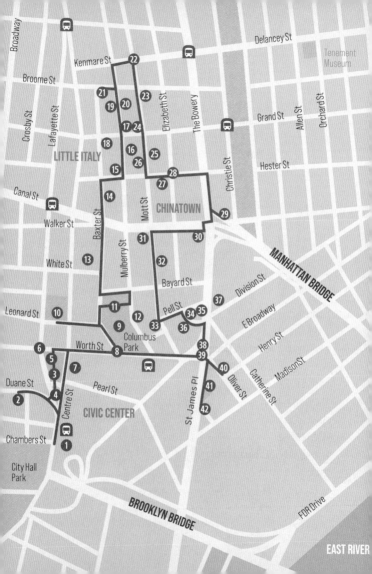

CIVIC CENTER, CHINATOWN & LITTLE ITALY

Distance: 3 Miles

1. David N. Dinkins Municipal Building
2. African Burial Ground National Monument
3. Thomas Paine Park
4. *Triumph of the Human Spirit*
5. Statue of Abraham de Peyster
6. Worth Street Station
7. The New York State Supreme Court Building
8. Five Points
9. Columbus Park
10. Collect Pond Park
11. Statue of Dr. Sun Yat-sen
12. Mulberry Bend
13. Manhattan Detention Complex
14. Church of the Most Precious Blood
15. Da Gennaro
16. Angelo's
17. Alleva Dairy
18. Location of a Laboratory of Nikola Tesla
19. Grotta Azzurra
20. Mulberry Street Bar
21. *Big City of Dreams* mural
22. Site of Prohibition Era Alcohol Market
23. 172 Mott Street
24. Di Palo's
25. Meitz Building
26. 135-37 Mott Street
27. Oversea Chinese Mission
28. Elizabeth Street
29. Mahayana Buddhist Temple
30. HSBC Bank Building
31. Chinese Merchants Association
32. Chinese Community Center
33. Transfiguration Roman Catholic Church and School
34. Hip Sing Charitable Funds Inc.
35. 13 Pell Street
36. Nom Wah Tea Parlor
37. Confucius Statue
38. Kimlau Square
39. Statue of Lin Zexu
40. Mariners' Temple Baptist Church
41. Site of the Cemetery of Congregation Shearith Israel
42. James Street

Exit the subway to begin at the David N. Dinkins Municipal Building, right in the middle of the Civic Center where New York City Hall and several important public agencies and courthouses are located.

Follow the map (north), looking to your right ❶ for the imposing **David N. Dinkins Municipal Building**. One of the biggest public buildings in the world, it has been home to many New York City public offices since 1913. It combines a variety of architectural styles, from Imperial Rome to the French Renaissance.

Its size is a testament to the ambition and growing importance of New York's municipal authority in the early 20th century, and the 25-foot gilded Civic Fame statue on top is the second largest in the city, right behind the Statue of Liberty. The model for the statue was Audrey Munson (1891-1996), now largely forgotten but in her youth a film actress, America's first "super model" who posed for the sculptors of a dozen Manhattan public statues. Originally called the Municipal Building, it was renamed in 2015 after David Norman Dinkins (1927-2020), the city's first African-American mayor (1990-93).

Continue north up Centre Street and bear left by Foley Square to turn left along Duane Street to reach ❷ **the African Burial Ground National Monument**. Construction for a new civic building in the 1990s uncovered a burial ground, the earliest and largest known African-American cemetery in the United States. It was first used in the early 1700s (after Trinity Church decreed no more African Americans could be buried in its graveyard). Covering over six acres, around 15,000 enslaved and free African Americans were buried here up until it closed in 1794.

Retrace your steps to Federal Plaza. Across Foley Square is ❸ **Thomas Paine Park**, named for the English radical thinker. Paine (1737-1809) was a true Enlightenment thinker, and after moving to America, he published radical pamphlets and books such as *Common Sense* (1776) that galvanized the American Revolutionaries of that era and helped change the history of the world.

There are two notable landmarks here.

The first is ❹ *Triumph of the Human Spirit*, dating from 2000 and sculpted by African American artist Lorenzo Pace. It was inspired by and commemorated African American slaves who were transported to New York and were buried nearby.

Enter the park to see ❺ **the statue of Abraham de Peyster** (1657-1728). Of Dutch heritage, he was born in New Amsterdam and, after the city was taken over by the British, served as its twentieth mayor in the 1690s and later as Governor of New York. The statue dates from the late 19th century and was originally located in Bowling Green Park.

What you won't see is a sculpture called the *Tilted Arc* by Richard Serra. The 120-foot-long, 12-foot high rusted-metal work stood nearby between 1981-89, but was so unpopular

it was removed—a very rare occurrence with public artwork. Serra went to court to argue the removal violated his rights under the First and Fifth Amendments. The metal sculpture remains in storage and Serra has said it will not go back on public display unless it is at its original location here.

Turn right onto Worth Street, named for William J. Worth, a Major General in the 19th century best known for his part in the American-Mexican War of the 1840s. He was later involved in a plot concocted by Cuban Freemasons to overthrow Spanish colonial rule on their island.

Underneath your feet ❻ lie the ghostly remains of one of the city's abandoned subway stations—the **Worth Street Station**. It was built for the IRT (Interborough Rapid Transit Company) and opened in 1904. Part of the city's original subway line, it remained in use until 1962. Down below are two platforms and four tracks, and it is a favored destination for subterranean urban explorers.

Over to the right ❼ is **The New York State Supreme Court building** that opened in 1927 and resembles a Greek temple. Lots of very serious things take place here, but of much more casual interest is the fact a scene in *The Godfather* (1972) was filmed here (Emilio Barzini is shot by a fake cop on the steps).

Dozens of other films and television shows have featured the building, including *Carlito's Way*, *Goodfellas*, *Kojak*, *Wall Street* and *Suits*. One of the oddest events to take place here in modern times was a demonstration by eighteen members of the Klu Klux Klan (including a child) on the steps of the courthouse on October 24, 1999, standing for over an hour in silence while thousands of angry New Yorkers (full disclosure, and the author) noisily protested about the Klan's presence.

The frieze above the entrance contains a mistake. It reads: "The true administration of justice is the firmest pillar of good government," taken from a letter written by George Washington in 1789—however, in 2009, it was discovered the quote should have read "The due administration . . ." (not "true"). Awkward . . .

Continue down Worth Street to stop ❽ at the corner of Baxter Street. This was once the intersection of three roads (Anthony Street (now Worth Street), Orange Street (now Baxter Street), and Cross Street (since disappeared). The intersection's shape gave rise to the area's name—the notorious **Five Points**.

Before this, a near 50-acre body of freshwater dominated this area. The Munsee—part of the Lenape tribe—lived by the water. When the Dutch arrived, followed by the British, it became known as the Collect Pond. It was the primary source of freshwater for the city and sounds pretty idyllic with people fishing here and skating on the ice in winter.

That would change as the city expanded northwards. By the early 1800s, the Collect Pond had become a putrid, stinking mess, largely the result of the tanneries, breweries, slaughterhouses, and other industries that used the water and emptied their waste products into it. A plan was hatched to drain the pond and fill it in so housing could be built on the site. This was complete by 1811, but it remained swampy, and only the poorest people would live there in tenement slums.

For around 70 years the Five Points district was notorious not only in New York but around the world. One visitor was Charles Dickens in whose footsteps you are following. "What place is this, to which the squalid street conducts us? A kind of square of leprous houses, some of which are attainable only by crazy wooden stairs without" (from *American Notes for General Circulation* (1842)).

Five Points was dominated by vicious gangs, brothels, gambling dens, animal-fighting yards and immortalized in the 1927 book, *The Gangs of New York* (Herbert Asbury 1889–1963), which in turn inspired the 2002 film of the same name by Martin Scorsese. This is also where immigrants would come to live, attracted by the cheap cost of living. The lucky ones made it out of the Five Points. You will learn more about the waves of immigrants who came here and gangs as you continue the walk.

Turn left and walk along the west side of ❾ **Columbus Park**, named for Christopher Columbus (1451-1506). Today the area is popular with members of the local Chinese community, with Chinatown dominating much of the district to the north and east of here. If you come on a weekend, you will see locals playing mahjong, catching up with friends and family, and practicing tai chi.

Turn left along Hogan Place to reach ⑩ **Collect Pond Park**. The park opened in 1960 and stands on part of the site of the old Collect Pond. The name is derived from the Dutch word "kolch," meaning small body of water. After the British took over New Amsterdam in 1664, the name was corrupted so it became "collect." In recent years archaeologists found part of the foundations of The Tombs—the notorious city prison built in 1838 on Centre Street nearby.

The old Collect Pond was 60 feet deep and fed by an underground spring. When the authorities decided to fill it, they leveled local hills and used the resulting debris. The sadly misnamed Paradise Square was built, but poor drainage plagued the area, causing problems for building foundations. Those who could moved away, leaving Paradise Square sinking. By the 1830s, the area was known instead as the Five Points, and during the remaining years of the 19th century,

became the center of the worst cholera outbreaks in the city.

Retrace your steps to Columbus Park, entering the park and walking over to the other (east) side. In the center ⓫ stop to see **the statue of Dr. Sun Yat-sen** (1866-1925). One of the most renowned figures in Chinese history, Sun was one of the key leaders of the revolution that led in 1911 to the ending of 2,000 years of imperial rule and the overthrow of the Quing Dynasty. He would become the first president of the new Chinese Republic and was known for his strong support of democratic ideals. Look for the inscription "All Under Heaven Are Equal"—a Confucian motto in Sun's own calligraphy beside his stamp.

Cross over to the east side to reach Mulberry Street, named for the mulberry trees that grew here long ago. This is the approximate site of Mulberry Bend, named for the slight kink in the route of Mulberry Street. This was regarded as the worst part of the Five Points, dominated by gangs, prostitution rings, and the scene of multiple murders. At various times gangs such as the Roach Guards, Dead Rabbits, the Whyos, The Five Points and Italian Mafia were based in Mulberry Bend.

What happened to the old slum tenements? In 1890 pioneering Danish-American photojournalist Jacob Riis (1849-1914) published *How the Other Half Lives: Studies among the Tenements of New York.* His photographs of the slums of ⓬ **Mulberry Bend** and the Five Points shocked many Americans and led to a slum clearance program that changed this part of the city forever. Riis described Mulberry Bend as "the foul core of New York's slums." Riis arguably changed this city (or indeed any other) more than any other photographer in history.

When Riis was wandering these streets, nearly 340,000 people were living in a square mile of the Lower East Side, making it the most densely packed urban area on earth, with ten to fifteen people living in the single rooms of rat-infested, dangerous tenement buildings. Numbers 49-50 on Mulberry Street are examples of the sort of tenement buildings that once dominated this area before the slum clearance took place.

Follow the map across to the northwest side of the park, to reach Baxter Street. In the 1870s, you would need to be careful walking along there due to the presence of the Baxter Street Dudes—a gang of kids, many of who worked as street newspaper sellers. Bizarrely, the Baxter Street Dudes ended up running a theater, the Grand Duke's Theater (at 21 Baxter Street),

writing and performing their own plays to audiences of around 300 people.

While street gangs first emerged in the city in the 1780s, more violent groups became prevalent from the 1820s. This was partly because of new immigrant groups arriving from Ireland, Italy, Poland, and Eastern Europe, often creating racially motivated friction with "nativist" gangs that resented newcomers arriving in America and competing for power and resources.

Continue up Baxter Street, stopping outside ⓑ **the Manhattan Detention Complex**. Dating from 1983, it is the fourth city jail in the old Five Points area known as The Tombs. The first, built in 1838, was designed in Egyptian-revival style that gave the appearance of an ancient tomb. It did not impress Charles Dickens who wrote of it: "What is this dismal fronted pile of bastard Egyptian, like an enchanter's palace in a melodrama?"

Each building had a bad reputation for corruption and the conditions prisoners had to endure. The building previous to the current one was the scene of a prison riot in 1970, in which a number of prison guards were held hostage. That version of The Tombs was closed in 1974.

When the current building was opened in the 1980s, local members of the Chinese community protested in the streets about the continued presence of such a grim institution so close to them. The Tombs has, unsurprisingly given its bad reputation, appeared in numerous films, television shows and books, and gets a mention in Beat legend William Burroughs' book *Junkie*.

Carry on up Baxter Street, home to a few bail bond shops whose clients are residing nearby. This is also the first glimpse of the many restaurants of Chinatown.

Street scenes

The origins of Chinatown go back to the mid 19th century when thousands of immigrant workers came to America to work on the new railways and take part in the California Gold Rush.

A man named Ah Ken is said to have been the first Chinese man to settle in the area in the 1850s, opening a boarding house for other Chinese men on nearby Mott Street. By 1900 over 7,000 Chinese men lived in the area (and only 142 Chinese women). Hostility against Chinese immigrants led to laws being passed that made it hard for other Chinese people to come to America.

This would continue until the Immigration and Nationality Act of 1965 allowed immigrants from Asia to settle more easily in America, and the population of Chinatown grew rapidly. The Chinese community here contains around 100,000 people, making it the highest concentration of Chinese people in the West.

Continue on, passing Chinese fish markets, pharmacies, banks, and gift shops. Cross Walker Street—named for an army officer and politician Benjamin Walker (1753–1818) who took part in the American Revolution. It also features in a now-obscure mystery novel from

1865 called *"Leaves from the note-book of a New York detective: the private record of J.B."* Written by a medical doctor and part-time author John Babbington Williams (1827-79), the book contains a story titled "The Walker Street Tragedy."

Cross Canal Street, named for the canal built in the early 19th century to help complete the drainage of the noxious Collect Pond into the Hudson River. The canal was only partially successful, becoming an open sewer itself, and was built over by the construction of Canal Street by 1820.

Soon on the right ⓮ stop outside **the Church of the Most Precious Blood**—the first evidence on the walk of the Italian community in this area, famous for being known as Little Italy. Completed in 1904, this beautiful and atmospheric Catholic church was built to serve the waves of Italian immigrants who had begun arriving in

large numbers in this part of New York seeking better lives. When the church was completed, the Italian population of Little Italy was just about to reach its peak of 10,000. It became so crowded, many sought to move away as soon as they could.

The church's history describes this time: "Opportunities were challenging for immigrants in their new land. Families were crammed into overcrowded, dismal and often unsanitary tenements. Italian immigrants, shunned by established New Yorkers, were not permitted to worship in the sanctuaries of established church structures, but were relegated to make-shift areas in basements." Many members of the congregation came from Naples and the Campania area of Italy, and brought with them a devotion to Saint Januarius, also known as San Gennaro, who became a martyr in Roman times. He is the patron saint of Naples and his feast day is celebrated on September 19. The church was given a relic of the Saint's blood by Franciscan friars.

The San Gennaro Feast in mid-September is one of the most popular events in Little Italy and has taken place since 1926. It involves a public procession featuring a statue of San Gennaro, carried from this church and along Mulberry Street, and the legend states that the dried blood of the saint contained back in Naples liquefies on the feast day. If it does not (as it did not in 2020) it is a bad omen . . .

Turn right onto Hester Street, named for Hester Leisler, daughter of a British lieutenant governor of the British province of New York in the late 17th century. Hester Street was also an important place for Jewish immigrants from Russia, the Balkans, and other parts of Eastern Europe in the late 19th century, many fleeing persecutions and impossible living conditions. Around two million Jews settled on the Lower East Side, living in cheap tenements and founding synagogues, schools, Yiddish theatres, newspapers, social clubs, political groups, and businesses of every imaginable kind.

Follow the map and turn left onto Mulberry Street, the heart of Little Italy. Today it is dominated by "red sauce" restaurants, competing for visitors. The number of people with Italian heritage living here has been in a long steady decline over the last few decades.

No trip to Little Italy can avoid stories about the Mob. **Da Gennaro restaurant**  on the corner (129 Mulberry) was once Umberto's Clam House. This is where on April 7, 1972, the mobster "Crazy Joe" Gallo of the Colombo crime family was shot dead while celebrating his 43rd birthday. The identity of the killer is disputed; however, hitman Frank Sheeran—immortalized by Robert De Niro in Martin Scorsese's film *The Irishman* (2019)—claimed he was the gunman, and the hit appears in a scene in the film. Gallo also inspired Bob Dylan's song "Joey."

Continue up Mulberry Street, passing the current site of Umberto's Clam House on the right (number 132). **Angelo's** of Mulberry Street is one of the oldest restaurants in Little Italy, first serving traditional Neapolitan food in 1902. Recently renamed Casa Di Angelo, famous guests over the decades have included Ronald Reagan and Kobe Bryant. Next door is Caffé Palermo, which has been featured in *The Sopranos*.

Cross Grand Street, stopping by the **Alleva Dairy**, which claims to be the oldest cheese shop in America, opening in 1892. It was founded by Pina Alleva, who arrived as an immigrant on the Lower East Side from

Benevento, Italy. Try some of the freshly made mozzarella or ricotta cheese.

Today Chinatown is a much larger place than Little Italy, but in the recent past, the changing demographics of the area caused some tensions. In 1974 *The New York Times* reported, "according to some Italian-American community leaders, an enormous influx of Chinese immigrants into the area threatens to engulf the old Italian community and destroy it."

"The Chinese are buying up our homes and they are forcing our people out," said Vincent Vitale, a Mulberry Street funeral director and lifelong resident of the neighborhood. "Families who have lived here for three, four generations have to move away." In the 21st century, these tensions have largely disappeared because the old Italian community has faded away, the only significant presence being the restaurants and shops you see today. Rent increases, and the small size of the apartments has caused most Italian-American families to move, although many return for events such as the famous Feast of San Gennaro.

Farther along Grand Street, ⓲ No. 175 was **the location of a laboratory used by inventor and genius Nikola Tesla** (1856–1943) in 1889. His involvement in the so-called "War of the Currents" saw his former boss Thomas Edison pitted against engineer George Westinghouse over the future of electricity generation transmission (A.C. or D.C.). This epic battle has recently inspired several books, television programs and films, including *The Current War* (2017).

Continue up Mulberry Street. On the left ⓳ at No. 177 is **Grotta Azzurra**, whose origins go back to 1908. In the early 1900s, the world-famous singer Enrico Caruso was a regular here, and the basement contains a small museum dedicated to the singer. The restaurant also counted Frank Sinatra and other members of the Rat Pack as regulars.

Opposite is ⑳ **the Mulberry Street Bar** at No. 176, another local institution, existing under different names right back to 1908. Another favorite hang-out of Sinatra, it has been used for scenes in several films and television programs, including *The Godfather Part III*, *9 1/2 Weeks*, *The Sopranos*, and *Donnie Brasco* (the characters played by Johnny Depp and Al Pacino meet in the bar). Café Roma next door has been run by the same family since 1891. Try one of their superb pastries.

When you reach Broome Street turn left and ㉑ walk a short way to see the huge and colorful *Big City of Dreams* mural, dating from 2015, the work of Tristan Eaton. Eaton was designing toys for Fisher Price when he was just 18, and his murals adorn walls all around the world, including in France, Australia, Denmark, Sweden, and Mexico.

Retrace your steps. Broome Street marks the southern boundary of NoLita—a contrived name made up in the 1990s for the area "North of Little Italy."

One of the finest scenes in *The Godfather Part II* was inspired by the Feast of San Gennaro procession that leads down Mulberry Street. In the scene, the young Vito Corleone (played by Robert De Niro) crosses the rooftops as the procession continues down below. It ends with his assassination of Black Hand gangster Don Fanucci. The actual scene was filmed on a set nearby on East 6th Street between Avenue A and B.

Turn right along Kenmare Street, named for a small town in Ireland. Why? Because that is where the mother of Tim Sullivan used to

live before poverty forced her to emigrate to New York in the mid-19th century. Her son also grew up poor; however, he made it out of the Five Points slum and became a successful businessman and powerful city politician known as "Big Tim" or "Big Feller." When the street was founded in 1911, Big Tim made sure it was named in memory of his immigrant mother's hometown.

Turn right onto Mott Street. Its name dates from the late 18th century, and possibly named for Joseph Mott, a local innkeeper and butcher.

At the start of the 1920s, during Prohibition, the intersection of Kenmare and Mott Streets was ㉒ the site of an illicit outdoor **Prohibition Era alcohol market** where sellers and buyers—often speakeasy owners—could do business,

Just over Broome Street at ㉓ No. **172 Mott Street**, there is another crime connection. Giosuè Gallucci (1864–1917) was born in Naples. By 1898 he was in New York, arrested for murdering a woman. He was acquitted and at the time was described as a young grocer and express-man with a store at 172 Mott Street. He would go on to establish an

extensive criminal empire in Little Italy and East Harlem. Known as the King of Little Italy, he had links with the Camorra, but ran afoul of other gangs. After surviving numerous assassination attempts that had killed ten of his bodyguards, he died after being shot (along with his son) outside a café on East 109th Street. In a sign of how much influence crime figures had over the lives of local residents, ten thousand people lined the streets to watch his funeral cortege pass by. It has been suggested he was the inspiration for the character of Don Fanucci in Mario Puzo's novel *The Godfather* (1969) and the film *The Godfather Part II* (1974).

Continue down Mott Street. On the corner ㉔ of Grand Street is **Di Palo's food shop**, another Italian-American institution with a classic Little Italy backstory. It all began with Savino DiPalo, a cheesemaker and farmer from Puglia in Southern Italy, who settled in Little Italy in 1903. He later opened his own diary shop—or *latteria*—on Mott Street. His daughter Concetta opened up her own shop—C. DiPalo—with her husband in 1925 at 206 Grand Street. It later moved to this location and today is still owned by the DiPalo family.

Scenes in *The Godfather* film were filmed nearby and in 2019, owner Lou Di Palo recalled (quoted in *The New York Times*) that his mother was making mozzarella when "this unkempt guy came in, and she knows he's from the film crew, so she tells him there's a lot of detail that's wrong and he should change it. I say to her, 'Do you know who that was, Ma?' It was Francis Ford Coppola; he became a fan and a customer."

It is also a favorite of another famous Italian-American director, Martin Scorsese, who in 2004 was quoted in *New York Magazine* as saying "I still like to go to DiPalo's Food Shop on Mott Street . . . Mr. DiPalo was good friends with my parents. Last time I was there, he told me some student who had just moved to the area came in and asked him, 'What made you open an Italian cheese shop in a Chinese neighborhood?' That sums up for me what  happened to Little Italy." Scorsese is a local boy done good, raised on nearby Elizabeth Street (between Houston and Prince).

Walk on down Mott Street, perhaps thinking of Ella Fitzgerald singing, "And tell me what street/compares with Mott Street in July;/ sweet push carts gently gliding by." From Roger and Hart's song "Manhattan." When it was composed in 1925, there were still carts on the street here.

Crossing Grand Street, you now pass locations that feature in a pivotal moment in *The Godfather* film. On the left, stop outside No. 128, with the ㉕ "**Meitz Building**" sign above the first floor. This was the location of the Corleone family's front business, Genco Pura Olive Oil. In the film, Don Corleone, played by Marlon Brando, is driven to the outside of Genco Oil. He gets out, then crosses the road to a fruit seller—in the film ㉖ located just outside **135-37 Mott Street**—and is gunned down outside. The scene is supposed to be on Mulberry Street, but Mott Street must have appeared to the film's director to feel more authentic. The set for the interior of Genco Oil is thought to have been built in a nearby warehouse.

When filming began in New York in 1971, this part of Mott Street was still dominated by the Italian-American community, and its decline—and the spreading out of Chinatown—means *The Godfather* not only covers past events but is itself a history piece.

Moving on, you soon reach Hester Street again. Turn right to see the famous "Welcome to Little Italy" sign.

Walk (left) down Hester Street. On the corner of Elizabeth Street is ❷ the **Oversea Chinese Mission**, the largest Chinese church in New York. By contrast with the Catholic churches once thronged with Italian-American and Irish worshippers, this is a thriving place with 1,500 attending each Sunday. It conducts services in Mandarin, Cantonese, and English and provides adult classes, language lessons, daycare and after-school programs. Founded in 1961, just as Chinatown was beginning to grow rapidly due to new arrivals, it also sends missions around the world.

You pass ㉘ **Elizabeth Street**, laid before the 1750s. Nicholas Bayard owned a farm nearby, and the street was named for his wife. Could she ever have imagined her name would also be used in a book title centuries later? *Elizabeth Street* (2009), by Laurie Fabiano, is set in the early 1900s and "brings to light a period in history when Italian immigrant neighborhoods lived in fear of Black Hand extortion and violence—a reality that defies the romanticized depiction of the Mafia." Over 8,000 Italian immigrants, many from Sicily, lived on Elizabeth Street.

Martin Scorsese's parents both had Sicilian heritage, and were born and lived on Elizabeth Street. Martin, then a child struggling with asthma, later lived here (with his grandparents at No. 241). He was often confined by illness to his bedroom and spent hours looking out of his window and observing the street-dramas of the largely Sicilian community outside. This profoundly influenced him and how he made films. He later recalled, "from that window you could see everything."

Continue along Hester Street. Not to be outdone by Elizabeth Street, Hester Street lent its name to a film. *Hester Street* (1975) was based on Jewish writer Abraham Cahan's novel *Yekl: A Tale of the New York Ghetto* (1896). One of the stars was Carol Kane and she received an Oscar nomination for her part. It follows the lives of Eastern European Jewish immigrants who arrive on the Lower East Side in 1896 and live on Hester Street. Today there is very little remaining evidence of the Jewish community on the streets you will walk through.

You soon reach The Bowery and turn right. One of the city's most famous streets and its oldest, its name is a corruption of the Dutch "Bouwerij" meaning farm. When this was New Amsterdam, there were once farms located by the old road that had been founded by the Dutch West India Company. Today you may struggle to imagine this place as a rural lane, this section of The Bowery lined with jewelry shops and Chinese businesses.

Former American President Theodore Roosevelt in his book *History as Literature* (1913) includes a chapter comparing Dante's *Inferno* to The Bowery, describing the latter as "one of the great highways of humanity, a highway of seething life, of varied interest, of fun, of work, of sordid and terrible tragedy; and it is haunted by demons as evil as any that stalk through the pages of *The Inferno*." Hard to imagine a US president today having the time or background to write a detailed work on such a serious topic.

Follow the map to stop outside ❷❾ the **Mahayana Buddhist Temple**. It owes its foundation to Annie Jin Ying, born in 1915 in Wuxi, China. Turmoil in China caused her to move with her family to Taiwan in 1949 and then New York in 1955. When she arrived, there was no Chinese Buddhist temple, so the Yings founded one and (in 1962) the first official Chinese Buddhist Association, Eastern States Buddhist Temple. Ying is credited as the first person to bring Chinese Mahayana Buddhism to the city.

Now cross over to Canal Street, looking for the ❸❶ distinctive **HSBC Bank building** on the corner. A local landmark, this was originally the home of the Citizens Savings Bank from the 1860s, and they commissioned this unusual, Beaux-Arts style domed building that was completed in 1924. In 1910 the bank's customers included immigrants from 25 countries such as Russia, Poland, Ireland, and Germany, a sign of how this part of the Lower East Side was once dominated by new arrivals from Europe.

Walk on, passing Elizabeth Street again. This has an additional name—Danny Chen Way. It commemorates local boy Danny Chen (1992-2011), who joined the US Army and committed suicide in Afghanistan after suffering bullying and racial harassment from his fellow soldiers. Several soldiers were later court-martialed, and this sign was dedicated in 2014 on Memorial Day. It serves as a reminder of the prejudice faced by many people of Asian heritage in America, something that has existed ever since the Chinese first arrived in the 19th century, and which in recent years has attracted media headlines after unprovoked attacks against Asian Americans in New York.

Press on, turning onto Mott Street again. It was on Mott Street and surrounding streets that the original Chinatown began, and on all sides is evidence of the strength of the community. One is visible on the corner ③—the **Chinese Merchants Association**, with the pagoda on top.

One reason that so many strong community organizations formed in Chinatown was the Chinese Exclusion Act of 1882. It prevented new arrivals from China and denied those already here many rights other New Yorkers

Street scenes

took for granted. In the face of such hostility, the community had to look after itself or fail. As you have seen on many streets today, what happened next is obvious.

If you think American-China relations are difficult today, the Chinese Exclusion Act, and later extensions, caused friction with the ruling Quing dynasty in China. This led to The Chinese Boycott of 1905 in which the Quing dynasty ordered the boycott of American goods. In the early 21st century, the boycotting of goods and services by either country remains a favored tactic to achieve diplomatic results.

Next up on the left is ❷ the **Chinese Community Center**, the district's "town hall." It is home to the Chinese Consolidated Benevolent Association (CCBA), established in 1883. This umbrella organization covers 60 other bodies that represent everything from religious groups to trade organizations. The Center is also home to the New York Chinese School.

The Chinatown community is complex, almost impossible for an outsider to fully grasp. It is certainly not homogenous, and tensions have arisen over the decades as new arrivals have upset the equilibrium because they have different traditions, languages and cultures. For example, in 1994, *The New York Times* reported how, "For more than a hundred years, Chinatown has absorbed the different waves of Chinese immigrants, from the Taishanese earlier this century to the ethnic Chinese from Vietnam in the 1980s. But now, there are growing strains between the established Cantonese community and the latest group of immigrants, the Fujianese, who have poured in from mainland China in the last four years."

Continue to ㉝ where you stop by the "Church of Immigrants"— the **Transfiguration Roman Catholic Church and school**. Since 1853, it has served Irish, then Italian, and now largely Chinese-Catholic worshippers. Look for the memorial to members of the church who died in 1917-1919 while fighting in World War I. It tells you a lot about who lived in this area at that time, and is dominated by Italian surnames— Marcello, Torraca, Forlini . . . Today, regular services are held in English, Cantonese and Mandarin.

Retrace your steps slightly and head down Pell Street, part of the original few streets that made up the 19th century Chinatown. In the 1890s, around 2,500 Chinese lived in densely packed buildings in this area. The criminal activities of a minority of Italian-Americans are well known throughout the world because of *The Godfather*,

The Sopranos, Goodfellas, et al., but Chinatown has its own issues with crime, although it tends to be more hidden from the media and those outside of the community.

Pell Street is associated with the Hip Sing Association (HSA). Its origins go back to the Hip Sing Tong, originating in San Francisco at the time of the Gold Rush. Branches of the Hip Sing Tong spread to other Chinatowns across America, including New York in the early 1900s. The Hip Sing Tong became involved in criminal activities and the infamous series of Tong Wars with other local gangs that lasted into the 1930s.

Many "Tongs"—ostensibly fraternal organizations—were founded in the early 20th century to protect their members from anti-Chinese prejudice and, without support from the city's police force, to settle disputes within the community. Some became associated with criminal activities, including the Hip Sing Tong. Later in the 20th century, the Hip Sing Tong pulled away from direct criminal activity but was believed to use violent gangs, such as the Flying Dragons, to help when needed. Today the HSA is based at No. 15 on Pell Street ❸❹ (there is a sign for **Hip Sing Charitable Funds Inc.**).

One day in August 1994, Chinatown came to a stop for the funeral procession of Benny Ong, who had died at 87. The powerful head of the Hip Sing Tong, he lived on Pell Street and *The New York Times* reported, "A parade of more than 120 black limousines extended like a long exclamation mark on his role as the Godfather of New York City's most enduring ethnic neighborhood."

No. 13 ❸❺ has been described as the first opium den to open in Chinatown, dating to 1868 and said to have been founded by Wah Kee, an early resident of this district. Over subsequent years many wealthy and outwardly respectable New Yorkers came slumming to Chinatown to discreetly enjoy the substances on offer. The last traditional opium den is thought to have closed in 1957 (located at 295 Broome Street).

Opposite, at 12 Pell Street, is the site of the Pelham Café, a ragtown piano saloon owned in the early 1900s by a notorious Russian Jewish mobster named Mike Salter. He employed a tough, teenage boy raised on the Bowery as a singing waiter. The waiter, also a Russian Jewish immigrant, was called Izzy Berlin

(1888-1989). Salter is said to have forced Berlin to write his first song, "Marie from Sunny Italy," in 1907. From these humble beginnings in Chinatown, Izzy Berlin would adopt the name Irving and go on to write standards such as "White Christmas" and "God Bless America."

Now head down Doyers Street, a tiny thoroughfare that vies for the title of being historically one of the most violent and notorious streets in New York. It became known as "Murder Alley" (or the "Bloody Angle") in the press after a Tong war broke out at the site of the former Chinese Opera House in August 1905. Previously regarded as neutral territory, members of the Hip Sing Tong entered the theater and began shooting, killing four members of the On Leong Gang.

Pass a famous local institution ❸❻ the **Nom Wah Tea Parlor**. Founded in the 1920s as a bakery and tea parlor, it has retained its vintage appearance, and you should definitely try the dim sum. It has appeared in many films and television programs, including *Premium Rush*, *Reversal of Fortune*, *Law and Order*, and *All Good Things*. Doyers Street has also appeared in films such as *John Wick Chapter 3: Parabellum*.

At the bottom, cross over to reach Division Street, so-named as it marked the boundary between farms owned in the 18th century by James Delancey and the Henry Rutgers family.

Look over to ❸❼ the **Confucius statue** that stands outside the Confucius Plaza Apartments dating from the mid-1970s. Not far to the north of here once stood an infamous Bowery bar called the Morgue where a violent gang named The Whyos offered customers a menu of services—most types of punishment, mutilation and murder, together with prices. The Whyos were the most organized crime gang of their time, dominating the Five Points and Mulberry Bend. One of their leaders was Dandy Johnny Dolan, a fashionable killer who embedded axe blades into his boots.

Walk along Chatham Square to reach ❸❽ **Kimlau Square**, named for Chinese-American bomber pilot Benjamin Ralph Kimlau, who died in action over the Pacific in World War II. There is also a monument in the form of a gateway to Americans of Chinese descent who lost their lives in defense of democracy and freedom. It has historical significance as the memorial to Kimlau dates from the early 1960s and was connected to an effort to repeal laws restricting Chinese immigration by pointing out the contribution Chinese-Americans had made to the United States. This aim was achieved with the passing of the Immigration and Nationality Act in 1965.

You will also find a statue of ❸❾ **Lin Zexu** (1785-1850), a Qing dynasty official from Fuzhou in Fujian Province, China, best known for his role in the Opium War of 1839-42. He opposed the British import of opium into China because of the devastating impact it had on the Chinese population, but his efforts to try and stop the British led to a war that China lost. The impact of this humiliation on China still reverberates in UK-China relations to this day.

The statue has a wider significance as Lin Zexu is a Fujianese hero, and was erected in 1997 by new immigrants from Fujian province in China. The statue

looks out over where many Fujianese arrivals opened businesses, showing once again how Chinatown is constantly evolving. There is even a neighborhood nearby known as Little Fuzhou because it became home to immigrants from Fuzhou in Fujian Province of China.

Cross back over Chatham Square, named for William Pitt, Earl of Chatham (1708-1778), who served as British Prime Minister. The name is an echo of a time when the British controlled New York, although after they left most street names that glorified British figures were swiftly changed.

Now follow the map down Oliver Street to reach ❹ the **Mariners' Temple Baptist Church**. A chapel was founded here in 1795 as a mission for European seamen—hence the name—arriving in ships along the East River. The building you see today was inaugurated in 1845.

The site was gifted by Henry Rutgers (1745-1830), the philanthropist and Revolutionary War hero who was descended from Dutch settlers. This is the oldest site for continued Baptist worship in the city.

Retrace your steps, turning left onto St. James Place where the first opening on the left **④** is the site of **the cemetery of Congregation Shearith Israel**, founded by Spanish and Portuguese Sephardic Jews in 1654. The location of their original cemetery is now lost, but this was their second and in use from 1683-1833. Until 1825, it was the only Jewish congregation in New York, and those buried here included over 20 Jews who fought in the Revolutionary War.

Just past here on the same side and on the left is **④ James Street**—once home to the James Street Gang led by Italian-American mobster Johnny "The Fox" Torrio. His infamous protégé was Al Capone, who would later move to Chicago in 1921 to work for Torrio again and begin his own meteoric rise as a mob boss. Capone was also a member of the local Five Points Gang, another feared gang in which future mob legends such as Lucky Luciano learned their trade.

You can now start to retrace your earlier route along Worth Street, passing the Five Points site and turning left down Centre Street.

Soon you will reach the Brooklyn Bridge/City Hall subway station again, where the walk ends.

3

TRIBECA WALK

START AND FINISH: Finn Square
SUBWAY STATION: Franklin St ①

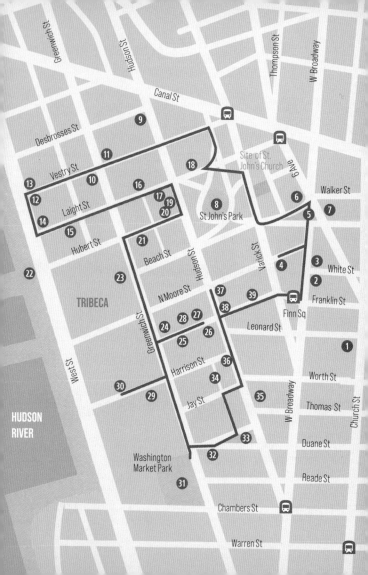

TRIBECA

Distance: 2 Miles

1. 56 Leonard Street
2. One White Street
3. Gideon Tucker Building
4. Hook and Ladder Company No. 8 Fire Station
5. Tribeca Park
6. Thread Building
7. 32 Avenue of the Americas
8. St John's Park
9. 195 Hudson Street
10. 434 Greenwich Street
11. 443 Greenwich Street
12. 67 Vestry Street
13. 70 Vestry Street
14. 92 Laight Street
15. The Sugar Warehouse Condominium
16. 54-58 Laight Street
17. The American Express Stables
18. The Grabler Building
19. American Express Building
20. American Express Building
21. 17 Hubert Street
22. Former location of an Immigration Pier
23. Global Headquarters for Citigroup
24. 375 Greenwich Street
25. 187 Franklin Street
26. Former Building of Engine Company No. 27
27. 180 Franklin Street
28. 176 Franklin Street
29. Nine Federal-style Houses
30. The Frieze refers to Pier 23
31. Washington Market Park
32. 188-190 Duane Street
33. Duane Park
34. Sky Bridge
35. Former Western Union Building
36. 81 Hudson Street
37. Bubby's
38. 110 Hudson Street
39. Urban Archaeology

As you exit the station, the view one block to the south is dominated by ❶ the extraordinary "Jenga" building—otherwise known as **56 Leonard Street**. Designed by Swiss architectural firm Herzog & de Meuron and completed in 2017, this is one of the most striking buildings in Manhattan and the tallest in Tribeca. Some apartments here sell for around $50 million. Herzog & de Meuron is in demand around the world, and past work includes the Beijing National Stadium in China and Tate Modern in London.

Not long ago Tribeca did not exist. The area existed, of course, but as an unremarkable and run-down part of the Lower West Side. However, around 1974 the current name was born, originally written as TriBeCa—an abbreviation of Triangle Below Canal Street.

Since the 1970s, Tribeca has become ever more fashionable, and its boundaries have expanded to Canal Street, Murray Street, Broadway, and the Hudson River. As was the case with SoHo, it was artists who led the charge here, forming the TriBeCa Artists' Co-op and overcoming zoning restrictions that otherwise prohibited artists from living in commercial buildings. In recent years, Tribeca—largely because of the efforts of Robert De Niro (more on him later)—has become hyper-gentrified. It is now a favorite spot of many of the city's most wealthy residents, including celebrities who appreciate its relative quietness compared to other areas.

Walk up West Broadway, originally Chapel Street, named for St. John's Chapel (more on that later too).

You pass Nos. 217-219 on the right, which contain luxurious apartments as well as an indoor basketball court. Take the first right onto White Street. On the corner ❷ is **One White Street**. On April 1, 1973,

John Lennon and Yoko Ono signed a "Declaration of Nutopia," with the address of the Nutopian Embassy given as One White Street. The April Fool's day declaration included the lines: "NUTOPIA has no land, no boundaries, no passports, only people. NUTOPIA has no laws other than cosmic." The couple claimed diplomatic immunity (as they were ambassadors of Nutopia). This was all linked to Lennon's attempts to avoid being kicked out of the country by the Nixon administration, Nixon was convinced the former Beatle was radicalizing young people, and fueling the anti-war movement.

Look for the old ghost signs for Goodall Rubber Co. up above on the building next door.

Opposite is ❸ a two-and-a-half story oddity dating from 1809 and built for **Gideon Tucker**, who ignored the popular Federal style of the era and instead opted for an older, Dutch style. Tucker was a prominent politician and businessman, and after his death in 1845, the building was used for various purposes, including a bar. If you had stood here in the early 1800s, the rest of the properties on White Street would have resembled the Gideon Tucker building. As the 19th century

went on, all the buildings like this were demolished and replaced by much taller non-residential structures.

White Street has many cool connections. Farther along at No. 77 (not visited today) was the legendary Mudd Club, the underground equivalent to Studio 54 in the late 70s and early 80s. Talking Heads, Allen Ginsberg, Lou Reed, Debbie Harry, William Burroughs and Jean-Michel Basquiat (including with his band) were regulars. It was one of two venues mentioned in the Talking Head's 1979 song "Life During Wartime" ("This ain't no Mudd Club or CBGB" . . .).

Continue up West Broadway and turn immediately left onto North Moore Street. On the left ❹ is the iconic "Ghostbusters Building"— the **Hook and Ladder Company No. 8 fire station**. It is featured in both the 1984 and 1989 *Ghostbusters* films. The filming of the first *Ghostbusters* film here caused traffic to grind to a halt. It so happened that world-famous sci-fi writer Isaac Asimov was stuck in that traffic jam. Incensed, he got out of the car and stormed into the film set to complain to actor Dan Aykroyd. Aykroyd was a huge Asimov fan, so being told off by his idol left him crushed.

In the film, the character Spengler (played by Harold Ramis) says of the firehouse, "I think this building should be condemned . . . The neighborhood is like a demilitarized zone." These days, Tribeca has some of the highest real-estate prices in Manhattan.

The firehouse used to be twice its current size. In the early 20th century, nearby Varick Street was widened, leading to the firehouse being cut in half. Hook and Ladder Company No. 8 was one of the many fire companies that responded to the terrorist attacks of September 11, 2001, and lost fireman Lt. Vincent G. Halloran that tragic day.

Retrace your steps and continue up West Broadway, soon reaching triangular ❺ **Tribeca Park**. If you had stood here in the early 1700s, you might have had to swim as this area was part of the Lispenard Meadows (or Swamp). This muddy swamp was acquired by local landowner Anthony Rutgers in the 1730s and drained.

On the other (north) side of the park is ❻ the elegant **Thread Building**. Completed in 1895, it was designed in a Renaissance Revival style by architect William B. Tubby (1858-1944). He was responsible for many buildings in New York and in Brooklyn in particular. It was built for the Wool Exchange, a long-forgotten venture for wool traders who also spent their leisure time in the luxurious Wool Club inside. When the exchange failed, the building was taken over in the early 1900s by the American Thread Company, which stayed here until 1965. Apartments in the Thread Building and nearby converted warehouses and commercial buildings regularly sell for between $2 to $8 million, and some go for much more.

The Thread Building was one of the earliest to be converted for residential purposes in the late 1970s and has attracted high-profile tenants, including Naomi Campbell, Isabella Rossellini and Cindy Lauper.

In 2018 one lucky owner purchased an apartment for $8.9 million and then discovered during a renovation a previously hidden wall mural by artist Keith Haring (1958-1990). Haring produced the work in the late 1970s when this was a student gallery. Such a piece is probably worth over $1 million but impossible to remove from the apartment. The owner clearly had the best bragging rights at any Tribeca dinner party.

On the right (east side) of the park is ❼ the stunning Art Deco former AT&T Building at **32 Avenue of the Americas**. It was completed in 1932 and designed by Ralph Walker (1889-1973), one of the city's most influential architects in the mid-20th century. He was responsible for other buildings covered in this book (the Stella Tower in Soho, the Verizon building in Chelsea, and 60 Hudson Street seen later in this walk). The Art Deco designs inside the lobby are very impressive. The Tribeca Film Festival and Tribeca Film Institute have offices here, both founded largely through the efforts of Robert De Niro.

From Tribeca Park, head left (west) down Beach Street, then right up Varick Street. The latter is named for Mayor of New York Richard Varick who served between 1789 to 1801.

On your left is ❽ **St. John's Park**. This also stands on the site of the former Lispenard Meadows. Land in this area was gifted to Trinity Church in 1705 by Queen Anne of England. By the late 1700s Trinity was hoping to cash in on the steady move up Manhattan by wealthy New Yorkers. A map of the 1790s shows that Hudson Square had already been laid out, making this one of the oldest residential squares in New York. In those days the shoreline was at Washington Street, three blocks to the west of here. Over subsequent years an almost equivalent amount of land has been reclaimed from the Hudson River.

St. John's Chapel was built on Varick Street in 1807, and Hudson Square was later renamed St. John's Park. This became a fashionable residential district, imitating the elegant squares then being constructed in London's growing West End.

On the left overlooking the park is a pedestrian bridge, which you now take.

On the other side you come down onto Laight Street.

On the south side is the strange no-man's land of St. John's Park that today is not accessible by the public because it is surrounded by the busy approach road to the Holland Tunnel.

It is such a contrast to how the park would have appeared in the mid-19th century, full of tall trees, with fine row houses on all sides.

What happened to this once-fashionable area? A big reason for its decline was the opening of the Erie Canal in the mid-1820s. The canal connected the interior of the country and the Great Lakes with the Hudson River (at Albany). From there, transport could continue along the Hudson River to the port of New York and the Atlantic. The cost of transport along the new route dropped dramatically and New York received a major economic stimulus that particularly benefitted the west side of Manhattan facing the Hudson River.

Piers facing the Hudson River were full of merchant ships, while the area inland from the shoreline became dominated by warehouses, factories, abattoirs and transportation firms. This deterred middle class and wealthy New Yorkers from living here, and the death knell for St. John's Park came when it was acquired in 1866 by Cornelius Vanderbilt's Hudson River Railway Company. This then became the very unfashionable site of St. John's Park Freight Depot. St. John's Chapel lost its congregation and was demolished in 1918.

Laight Street was named in honor of William Laight, a wealthy merchant and patriot during the Revolutionary era and also a vestryman at Trinity. The National Archives contains a letter written by Laight to statesman John Jay dated October 3, 1775. Why of interest? Well, the two men both had streets in the district named after them (you will pass Jay Street later).

Head east along Laight Street and then left around the bend up Vestry Street. It is named for either the vestry of St. John's Chapel or Trinity church.

As you go round the bend, to the right over the fence is the Holland Tunnel road and then Canal Street on the other side. Hard to imagine today, but there was an actual canal dug in the early 19th century in order to drain polluted water from the Collect Pond (near today's City Hall) into the Hudson River. The Collect Pond was emptied in 1811, and Canal Street constructed over the route by 1820.

Vestry Street is full of the sort of commercial buildings that would once have employed thousands of people, but as industry began to leave New York, they have often been converted into residential premises. To see a great example of this, turn right onto Hudson Street to see ❾ **No. 195** (second building on the left). This was the home of Jay Z and Beyoncé, bought for a mere $6.8 million in 2004. It covers 8,000 square feet and has another 3,000 square feet in terraces.

Jay Z mentions the area in his hit, "Empire State Of Mind," "Yeah, I'm out that Brooklyn, now I'm down in Tribeca/Right next to DeNiro, but I'll be hood forever." In 2008 the couple were married on the roof where they held a star-studded party to celebrate. The details of the event remained a closely guarded secret, and even afterwards, Jay Z denied a marriage had taken place.

Retrace your steps and continue along Vestry Street. Much of the credit for Tribeca becoming a sought-after location for celebrities goes to Robert De Niro, dubbed by some

as the area's unofficial mayor. Perhaps no other district in Manhattan in living memory has become so associated with a single person. He grew up not far from here, and his role in revitalizing the area through investment in a film center, the festival, restaurants and other ventures was recognized in 1997 when he was awarded the Jacqueline Kennedy Onassis Medal by the Municipal Art Society. At the ceremony he quipped, "I just want to thank the Municipal Art Society for holding this downtown, because I really don't like to go above 14th Street."

Soon you reach the corner of Greenwich Street. Try and imagine how, in the 18th century, this thoroughfare marked the western edge of Manhattan, with the Hudson River on the other side. As more land was reclaimed, Greenwich Street has ended up about a tenth of a mile inland.

Stop to admire ❿ **No. 434** on the southwest corner of Vestry and Greenwich Streets. It contains the ghost signage for "Warehouses" on the frontage.

Most of what you see around you dates from the late 19th and early 20th centuries, when this was the center of the textile industry, with many large warehouses used to store goods coming in from the piers along the Hudson River and the train depot. As with neighboring Soho, as industry left, artists moved in, and all these buildings transitioned from manufacturing and storage to residential.

The artists in Soho were followed by galleries, restaurants, hotels and upmarket residential conversions. Tribeca followed a similar pattern, except it remained more faithful to its original character, lower-key than Soho and relatively quiet, as you can probably see today.

A quiet, central location in Manhattan with lots of good restaurants, galleries, and other nearby amenities attracts celebrities who can pay more than $20 million for the best apartments.

Walk right (north) a short way up Greenwich Street to ⑪ **No. 443** on the right. It has been described as "paparazzi-proof" and one of Tribeca's grandest recent celebrity-magnet conversions. It contains amenities that protect residents' privacy, who are often film or pop stars or CEOs of major companies. These include a 71-foot indoor pool and Turkish steam bath. Built in 1882, this was once a book-bindery factory. What workers in the factory would have thought about future occupants paying over $50 million for an apartment will never be known. In the early 21st century, this is perhaps the coolest celebrity building in Manhattan and, indeed, the whole world. Celebrities linked with this address include Harry Styles, Meg Ryan, Ryan Reynolds, The Weeknd, Justin Timberlake and Jessica Biel.

Now retrace your steps and continue westward along Vestry Street, crossing over Washington Street. At the end are two interesting buildings. On the left is ⑫ the former Great Atlantic and Pacific Tea Company (A&P) Warehouse at No. **67 Vestry Street.**

This is another typical, yet also extraordinary, Tribeca story. The original building was designed by Frederick Dinkelberg, best known for his work on the Flatiron Building. Completed in 1897, it was used

as a warehouse for tea products, and after A&P moved away, artists moved in during the 1970s. Well-known figures such as Andy Warhol, Marisol, Wim Wenders and Robert Wilson have lived here. Recently it has been the subject of controversy over plans to redevelop the site. Hopefully, it will still be there when you visit.

Opposite on the north side is ⓑ **70 Vestry Street**, a recently completed residential building that looks like a boring office block that could have been built in any city in the world. However, in Tribeca, nothing is as it seems. Celebrities who have owned apartments here include Tom Brady and Gisele Bündchen (they reportedly sold their apartment in 2020 for $36 million) and British F1 motor racing world champion Lewis Hamilton. The building also appears in the 2021 Netflix reality series about fashion designer and model agency CEO Julia Haart, *My Unorthodox Life*.

At the end of Vestry Street, turn left (south) to continue along West Street. Long ago, the piers on the Hudson would have been thronged with ships, sailors, passengers, dockers, and railway workers. Dry goods would have been brought back and forth from the warehouses, factory buildings, and Hudson railway depot you have already passed. In the 1880s, opposite Vestry and Laight Streets, you would have found the Jersey City Ferry, the Mary Powell steamship that went to West Point, the Albany & Troy Line (Pier 39), and the Old Dominion S.S. that traveled to Norfolk and Richmond (Pier 37).

If you need a break, you might want to cross over to the Hudson River Greenway and sit on one of the benches to admire the view of

New Jersey. When ready, turn left onto Laight Street. On the corner and left side of **Laight Street** is ⑭ a former 19th century cast iron and masonry warehouse at No. 92, and you guessed it, converted into luxurious apartments and branded River Lofts. One sold in 2019 for $19 million. Meryl Streep, Chris Martin, and Gwyneth Paltrow are reported to have lived on the street.

Turn round to look at ⑮ No. 79 on the right, **The Sugar Warehouse Condominium**. There is a sign reading "The United States Sugar Buildings." This enormous building was constructed by the Grocers Steam Sugar Refining Company in 1853 and, standing ten stories high, was at the time one of the tallest buildings in Manhattan. It was later sold to the United States Sugar Refining Company.

A sugar refinery stood nearby, processing sugar that was brought from around the world

and unloaded at nearby piers. It was one of the earliest commercial buildings to be built in what is now Tribeca, and New Yorkers at the time must have gazed at it and wondered how dramatically their city was changing. Around 2000 a developer bought the whole building for $15 million, and today individual apartments can sell for about $7 million.

Continue along Laight Street. Like Vestry Street, it is normally very quiet, and you can begin to understand why celebrities are attracted to the area. This area also has links with the British monarchy. As mentioned before, Queen Anne granted land to Trinity Church, and Queen's Farm that once stood here was named after her. Later, after the British had been kicked out, the name changed to the more politically correct Church Farm.

The next stop is on the left, just after Greenwich Street, ⑯ at Nos. **54-58 Laight Street**. This is a former warehouse built in the 1870s for a wealthy ship chandler named Henry J. Meyer. It replaced older residential houses constructed in the area when it was still fashionable. The Civil War and the arrival of the freight terminal helped drive wealthy residents away, so this whole area was redeveloped for warehouses like this. The architectural style is unusual, described as Rundbogenstil—a German interpretation of the Romanesque Revival.

Almost opposite on the right-hand side of Laight Street is ⓱ **The American Express Stables** (55 Laight Street). It runs all the way down Collister Street for one block to Hubert Street. Today a giant in the world of financial services, American Express began in 1850 as an express mail business. Two of its founders were Henry Wells and William Fargo, who would soon move on to their own firm—Wells Fargo. The first building here was constructed in the 1860s, and expanded a number of times after that. Look for the American Express terra cotta bulldog on the facade. The horses left when American Express moved on in 1918.

Continue to Hudson Street. On the corner at 161 Hudson Street is a building that was once home to Wetlands Preserve club, which operated from 1989-2001. Described as the CBGB equivalent for the psychedelic-jam band scene, it had a strong eco-activist edge, and had a reputation for overt pot-smoking and all night music jams. Bands such as the Spin Doctors, Dave Matthews Band, and Disco Biscuits were regulars here and *The Village Voice* called it 'a secret society, a temporary autonomous zone, a late-night slackers sanctuary." Gentrification of the area helped kill off the club.

Turn right. Look over to the north side of St. John's Park where you can see ⓲ **The Grabler building** (44 Laight Street), which also displays ghost signage. This grand Renaissance Revival style building dates from 1896 and was leased to the Bowling Green Warehouse Company and Independent Warehouse, Inc. It was later taken over by the Grabler Manufacturing Co., which produced pipe fittings (the building sign was a clue).

As you walk down Hudson Street, the second building on the right—❶ a narrow three-story red brick design—was also part of the **American Express building** you just passed.

Now turn right onto Hubert Street. It is named for another vestryman of Trinity Church named Hubert Van Wagenen, his name suggesting a Dutch heritage. On the right you pass ❷ the other side of the **American Express building**, indicated by another bulldog.

As you pass ❸ **No. 17** on the left, look for a group of ghost signs on a building dating from 1889. It was used for storing carpets and then in the early 20th century as a coffee roasting facility and for advertising.

At the very end of Hubert Street ❹ and West Street is the **former location of an immigration pier** used between 1847 and 1855. For thousands of people, this part of the city was their first taste of life in the United States. However, local people protested about poor immigrants clogging up their streets, so the city had to look for other solutions. It would be several decades until the famous immigration center on Ellis Island was opened.

Turn left onto Greenwich Street, with more ghost signs visible on your left ("For the Trade," "Coffee Roasting"). If you could travel back in time, the smell of tea, coffee, spices and other foodstuffs would probably be astonishing to modern senses.

Continue south down Greenwich Street, looking over to the right to see ❺ the vast **global headquarters for Citigroup**, dating from 1988. The other side of the complex faces out onto the Hudson. This modern building stands in sharp contrast to neighboring 19th century warehouses and is a reminder of how financial services firms have thrived in recent decades while industry has largely disappeared.

The area occupied by the bank and right down to the World Trade Center was once home to the Washington Market, which first started in around 1812 and dominated the land up to the Hudson until it closed in 1962 (relocating to Hunts Point in the Bronx). If you had taken this tour in the late 1960s, this area was then known as Washington Market, not Tribeca.

In 1872, *The New York Times* described the market as follows: "filthy as it is, cramped, cabined and confined, the epicure grasps the luxuries of an entire continent and the fruits of the islands in the tropic seas. Of such enterprise and such a trade New York ought to be, and indeed is, proud, though it cannot be concealed that the auspices under which it has grown up have not been encouraging, and the conveniences and facilities extended to it have been remarkably scanty." In the late 19th century, it boasted 500 vendors, and it must have been pretty chaotic as thousands of wagons traveled back and forth to bring products to sell.

Today, the view on the west is dominated by ugly residential apartment blocks. Walk for a few minutes to reach Franklin Street on the

left, named for Benjamin Franklin (1706-1790). Look up at No. **375 Greenwich Street** for the "B Fischer & Co" sign. This refers to Benedickt Fischer (1841-1903), a German immigrant who arrived as a teenager in America in 1855 and became a wealthy entrepreneur, involved in various businesses, including dealing in spices, tea, and coffee. This impressive eight-story building, from 1905, is one of two in Tribeca that bears the name of his family business. It was later home to the Martinson Coffee Company.

Today No. 375 has a very different resident—the Tribeca Film Center, founded by Robert De Niro and film producer Jane Rosenthal. She has worked closely with De Niro for decades and recently helped produce *The Irishman* (2019), starring De Niro. De Niro and Rosenthal also started Tribeca Enterprises in 2003, and it serves as a hub for several creative ventures such as Tribeca Productions, Tribeca Studios, and the Tribeca Film Institute. The impact of the September 11 attacks also inspired De Niro and Rosenthal to begin the now world-famous Tribeca Film Festival in order to help revitalize the area.

The *New York Times* in 2015 described how "Tribeca has evolved rapidly in recent years, and the architect of much of that change has been De Niro. His ongoing business ventures in the area have transformed Tribeca from a crumbling industrial precinct into a magnet for celebrities and well-to-do families, and he is now considered the neighborhood's unofficial ambassador." Tribeca has become a brand name for businesses around the world that want to project a cool, sophisticated urban image.

De Niro knew the area well when it was still up and coming, and he recalled to *The New York Times*, "I was down there looking for a space to set up a training gym for *Raging Bull*," he said. "I found this great loft space, but I liked it so much that I wound up living there. I did my training at a regular gym on 14th Street instead . . . It was basically the idea of having a big loft with very few broken-up rooms."

Continue down Franklin Street, and on the left (also part of the old Fischer building) you pass the Tribeca Grill. Opened in 1990, it is co-owned by De Niro and influential New York restaurateur Drew Nieporent. They have also partnered with Nobu Matsuhisa to create the Nobu restaurant business.

Look on the right for ㉕ the unique design of **No. 187**. Designed by Jeremy Edmiston, it converted an existing family home to allow more privacy and light. The resulting "flaming" metal exterior is one of the most unusual structures in the city and was unveiled in 2017.

Walk a little farther down, stopping at No. 173 (on the right) ㉖. This is the **former building of Engine Company No. 27**, completed in 1882. Being a firefighter then was even more dangerous than to-day. In March 1904, a fire on nearby Duane Street left every man in Engine Company 27 disabled. The *Evening World* reported, "The men fell unconscious in the burning building, and while they lay on the inside twenty other firemen, who attempted to go to their rescue also fell insensible." Only one man, Thomas McGirr survived, the reporting continuing, "Engine Company No. 27 has been wiped out three times. McGirr is the only original

member of the company, all of his old comrades having met death in the past three years."

Opposite at **No. 180** look ㉗ for the sign for Roethlisberger & Co, "Established 1856" which sold cheese. It is a reminder of what used to bring people to this area before De Niro and the film community arrived.

Next door (on the right) at ㉘ **No. 176** is an interesting three-story building from 1907 that has been home to many different tenants over the years. One in the early 1900s was the Boosters' Club—a trade body of fruit and wholesale merchants who sought to "boost" or protect their commercial interests against competitors. In those days this area was the wholesale-food center of New York.

Booster clubs were found all over the United States but faded away by the 1920s. Later the Franklin Inn operated here, raided by Prohibition agents in 1926 and 1932 for illicit sales of liquor. No. 176 was later used for storage and commercial purposes, and then—in a sign of how Tribeca was gentrified—became home to an art gallery in the late 1970s and (in 1982) the River Run Café. The River Run was one of the first upmarket eateries to open in Tribeca, although few from those pioneering days have lasted as long as the Tribeca Grill.

Now retrace your steps along the cobblestones of Franklin Street to reach Greenwich Street again. It is hard to believe it today, but long ago when this street was laid out, you would have been near the edge of the Hudson River. The landfill and expansion that took place from the 1800s completely altered the shoreline. Now turn left onto Greenwich Street, and follow the map to reach ㉙ Harrison Street.

This is famous for its **nine Federal-style houses** built from the 1790s to 1820s. This area was still fashionable and remained so until the 1860s. Some of the houses were moved here during redevelopment of a stretch of Washington Street in the 1970s when the original World Trade Center and housing project at Independence Plaza were being constructed.

No. 27 is from 1796 and designed by John McComb, Jr. (1763-1853), the leading architect of the 1790s to 1820s. He also designed Castle Clinton (the main immigration center before Ellis Island) and Gracie Mansion. These buildings would not look out of place in Georgian London and McComb was heavily influenced by British architects such as Scottish-born Robert Adam. Make sure you see the three houses hidden around the corner.

Walk down Harrison Street towards the Borough of Manhattan Community College. Look for a ㉚ strange frieze above the middle of the street that looks like something out of

the Soviet Union. This was once part of the West Side (or Miller) Highway constructed between 1930 to 1950. The famous/infamous Robert Moses was involved in the planning of the highway and it was named after Julius Miller, Manhattan Borough President. It was later demolished (completed by 1989) and many friezes like this were lost. However, Dan McCarthy bought this one and persuaded the authorities to install it here. **The frieze refers to Pier 23**, which up until the 1960s would have been a bustling place packed with ocean liners, passengers and with sailors from all around the world coming and going.

The College is enormous, with around 27,000 students. Notable people who have studied here include singer and actress Queen Latifah, rapper Cardi B, actress Gabourey Sidibe and rock star Kid Chaos (The Cult, Guns N'Roses). Grammy-award winner Cardi B worked in the Amish Market in Tribeca (on Park Place). She was fired from there, and became a stripper across the road at the New York Dolls club when she was 19.

On September 11, 2001, the college's gymnasium was used to triage survivors of the attacks on the World Trade Center.

Continue south down Greenwich Street, passing Jay Street on the left (as mentioned earlier, named for Statesman and letter-writer John Jay) to reach ❸ **Washington Market Park**, named after the famous market. It opened in 1983 and, once again, it was largely the work of community activists that prevented this site from becoming a parking lot, and instead ensured it became one of the very few public parks in

Tribeca. Also nearby is the Tribeca Performing Arts Center, another cultural hub in the area.

Now head left up Duane Street, named after James Duane (1733-1797), vestryman of Trinity Church and Mayor of New York in the 1780s —the first after the British evacuation. Walk along the street full of gorgeous historic buildings (look for ❸❷ the "tea" ghost signage outside **Nos. 188-190** on the right). In the 19th century a number of buildings along here were used for a wide variety of purposes, including the manufacture of safety matches, baking powder, and it was also home to egg and butter merchants. Next door (No. 184) is home to the excellent Laughing Man Café, co-owned by actor Hugh Jackman. If you think New Yorkers take their coffee seriously, it is nothing compared to Australians.

Soon you reach ❸❸ **Duane Park**, a small triangle of land bought by the city from Trinity Church in 1795 (for $5).

Head left from the park up Staple Street to see (just north of the intersection with Jay Street) the ❸❹ **sky bridge**. Built in 1907, it was used to bring patients from a stable used for horse-drawn ambulances to a hospital on Hudson Street. More recently, it was owned by fashion designer Zoran Ladicorbic. For

decades, he used it to commute from his apartment on Hudson Street to his office on Jay Street, called "the most unique commute in the city" by one realtor.

In an interview with *The New York Times*, De Niro was asked if a hidden part of the area captured the essence of Tribeca. He replied, "There is a very narrow street between Harrison Street and Duane Street which has a little bridge across it—a bridge that goes between the buildings—and cobblestones on the street, and there's a little park down the end. It's really classic Lower Manhattan, and you'd hardly

know it was there." Now you do. Recently a condominium here connected by the bridge has been offered for more than $30 million.

Turn right along Jay Street. You reach Hudson Street with the vast ❸❺ 24-story 60 Hudson Street, formerly the **Western Union Building**, on the other side. This art deco gem was completed in 1930 and, like the former AT&T building seen earlier, was designed by Ralph Walker. Cross over to look at the beautiful entrance doors.

In the Western Union days, this was known as the "Telegraph Capital of America," and was an important communications hub. Western Union left long ago but, in a sign of the times, it became a colocation center and one of the most critical communications hubs for internet traffic in the world.

Turn left, continuing north up Hudson Street. On the south-west corner of Hudson and Harrison Streets is **No. 81** ❸❻, a small three-story building constructed by Captain Henry Mason Day, Jr. This ambitious and energetic man was awarded the French Legion of Honor during World War I, and ran his family's fruit and nut import business from here after it was built in 1919. But he wanted more than nuts, and later travelled the world working in the oil business, co-owned a stock exchange firm, and got into many scrapes, one of which resulted in him being imprisoned.

Continue north for a couple of blocks, and stop on the right at **37** **Bubby's** (120 Hudson Street). This celebrity hang-out is a good place for a stop as you near the end of the walk. It also features in a scene in the film *The Devil Wears Prada* (2006). (Nate, played by Adrian Grenier, gets a job as a cook, and Andy (Anne Hathaway) celebrates her job here).

Retrace your steps down Hudson Street, turning left onto Franklin Street. No. **110 Hudson Street** **38** on the corner with Franklin was built for the

Borden's Condensed Milk Company in 1904. De Niro was reported to have bought an apartment on the tenth floor and convinced Harvey Keitel to move into the building.

Continue down Franklin Street, where musician Taylor Swift and film director Peter Jackson have also been reported to own properties. **Urban Archaeology** ❸❾ is on the left (No. 158). De Niro is a fan, in a *New York Times* interview stating, "I remember when Urban Archaeology opened, years ago . . . a pioneering store, definitely, but it was also the perfect kind of store to open in Tribeca as the neighborhood was becoming more residential. I bought stuff from them for my Tribeca loft, and I still go there from time to time—not necessarily to buy anything, but just to look around."

At the end is Franklin Street subway station and the end of this walk.

4 SOHO WALK

START: Intersection of W. Houston and Varick Streets

SUBWAY: Houston St ①

FINISH: 195 Spring Street

SUBWAY: Spring St ⓒ, ⓔ, ⓕ

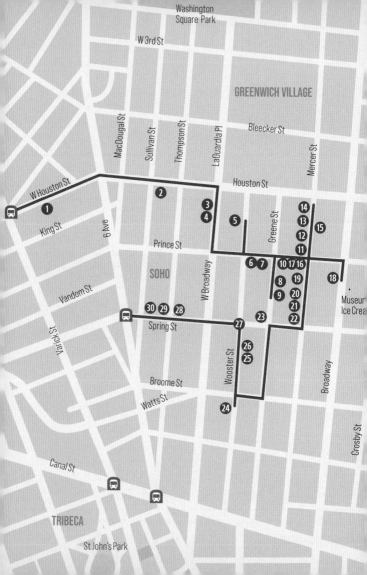

SOHO

Distance: 1.8 Miles

This walk starts at Houston Street station at the intersection of West Houston and Varick Streets. Surprisingly, given how well known this district is today, the name SoHo is modern. It was first used in a report written in 1962 by urban planner Chester Rapkin to describe the area South of Houston Street and down to Canal Street. The east and west boundaries vary according to who you talk to, but for this walk, it is assumed they are Crosby Street (east) and Sixth Avenue (west).

When the Dutch West India Company controlled Manhattan in the second half of the 17th century, many formerly enslaved Black people were allowed to settle in this area. It was then open land, about two miles north of New Amsterdam's northern boundary along Wall Street. The first Black settlement on Manhattan later gave way to farms, most of the land here part of a landholding owned by politician and slave trader Nicholas Bayard (c. 1644–c. 1709). After the Revolutionary War, the Bayard family struggled financially and sold off large tracts of their land, which led to the development of new residential streets. By the 1790s, many of the streets you will walk along today were already laid out.

In around 1810, the fetid and polluted Collect Pond was filled in and drained by a canal (giving Canal Street its name). Much of the soil and rock used to fill in the Pond came from levelling a local rocky outcrop named Bayard's Hill. Spring Street (seen later) would become the first road developed here, attracting wealthy Manhattanites who now felt comfortable moving north. By 1825, three- and four-story Federal-style row houses began to appear on the streets of SoHo.

By the 1850s, the section of Broadway on the east side of SoHo was, briefly, the city's entertainment center, boasting vaudeville theaters, casinos, bars, hotels, and pleasure gardens. There was also a darker side, with many brothels springing up on side streets.

Walk eastwards along West Houston Street, passing ❶ the **Film Forum** on the right. This is one of the best independent cinemas in the country and since 1970 has shown the kind of films any self-respecting local hipster loves to see.

After a few minutes ❷, stop on the right at the historic church of **St. Anthony of Padua** on Sullivan Street. Its origins go back to 1859 as part of the first parish in America established specifically for Italian immigrants. Why was it necessary? The Catholic Church was worried immigrants would, over time, loosen their ties with the faith they were born into, and the founding of the church helped keep the flock together.

Franciscan Friars have long been involved in running this church. Inside is a stained-glass window depicting St. Anthony. Anthony (1195-1231) was a Franciscan friar who was born in Portugal and died in Padua, Italy. He is the patron saint of lost things.

A young man of Padua making his confession to St. Anthony, admitted he had once kicked his mother so hard she had fallen over and hurt herself. St. Anthony muttered, "the foot that strikes father or mother deserved to be cut off." The pious young man took the priest

literally and went home to chop off his own foot. Anthony, no doubt a little embarrassed, quickly performed a miracle by re-attaching it. Stranger things have happened in Manhattan.

The Italian Renaissance-style building dates from the late 1880s. A nearby park (by Sixth Avenue and Prince Street) is named after Father Richard Fagan, a friar at the church who died in 1938 while helping colleagues after a fire broke out. He jumped out of a window to escape the flames and died of his injuries. He was only 27 years old.

You will pass several streets named after figures from Manhattan's past on this walk. Many of these date from the late 18th century, when original street names from the era of British rule were substituted with patriotic names of figures from the Revolutionary War. Sullivan Street was named by 1799 for a Revolutionary War general named John Sullivan, although I prefer the original name—Locust Street—probably named for the locust trees that stood on the Bayard Farm in this area. (Locust Valley in Long Island, less than 30 miles from here, is also named after the locust tree).

Walk on along West Houston Street, passing the intersection with Thompson Street, named for Irish-born Revolutionary War general William Thompson (1736-1781), and originally called Prospect Street.

Turn right down **West Broadway**, stopping outside ❸ **No. 468** on the right to see the first of the fine former industrial buildings that make SoHo such a distinctive area architecturally.

Dating from 1886, this was originally the Marvin Safe Company building. Different floors were used for manufacturing safes, sales-rooms for customers, and for painting products. Two hundred and fifty people worked here for Marvin, so try and imagine how busy this area would have been in the late 19th century when there were hundreds of similar-sized businesses all around the district. Interestingly, given the move to electric cars in the 21st century, the bottom floor was leased to the C & C Electric Motor Company, producing as early as 1888 units for "general manufacturing and mechanical purposes."

Why did commercial businesses come to dominate what is now SoHo? A major reason was a shift in shipping trade from the east to the west side of Manhattan, due to the opening of the Erie Canal (completed 1825) and development of Cornelius Vanderbilt's west side Hudson River Railway Company and St. John's Freight Terminal in the 1860s. Good transport links attract businesses, from warehouses for dry goods to manufacturers. At the same time, from the mid-19th cen-tury, a revolution took place in the construction of commercial build-ings with the introduction of cast-iron frames. Widespread use of such frames can be credited to the pioneering architect and inventor James Bogardus (1800-74). Cast-iron framed structures were cheaper to build and could more easily be decorated to reflect evolving architectural styles. As wealthier residents who had first come to the area's newly developed streets began to move northwards, many of their houses were gradually pulled down and replaced with the cast-iron industrial buildings you see today.

Continue down West Broadway, today full of upscale shops, galleries, and beauty care businesses. How times have changed. Years ago, the number of brothels along this stretch gave rise to a nickname "Rotten Row."

Stop on the right at ❹ **No. 462—the George Bergès Gallery**. Recently Bergès added Hunter Biden, son of President Joe Biden, to his roster of artists. Prices for self-taught Biden's art are said to range from $75,000 to $500,000. In 2021 Bergès told the press, "I always tell [Biden] when people ask how long it took to make a particular painting, you tell them 51 years . . . Your whole life." The gallery attracts regular visitors such as Spike Lee and Susan Sarandon.

As the 20th century progressed, Manhattan underwent deindustrialization, a trend that accelerated after World War II. This led to this area's decline, and by the 1950s, most industries had left. The once smart cast-iron buildings were becoming dilapidated, and used for storage or sweatshops. There were frequent fires, and the run-down nature of the area led to a subsequent nickname—Hell's Hundred Acres.

However, as the area hit rock bottom, seeds were sown for its future gentrification. Artists, often struggling financially, were attracted by the empty loft spaces and low rents. They began arriving in the late 1950s, stubbornly overcoming practical and legal problems such as zoning laws that prohibited many buildings from being used for residential purposes. Often artists had no running water or electricity and were required to post signs outside reading "A.I.R"—artist in residence—to alert the fire department to their presence. Robert De Niro lived in the area in the early days of his career, recalling in 1997, "They were aware of lofts, of industrial . . . whatever ya wanna call it; culture, blah blah . . . way before they became fashionable. SoHo was a lot different [then]. It was just a total industrial area that nobody thought of as a place to live. Warehouses, factories, stuff like that."

The impact of these pioneering artists on SoHo's deserted streets was profound. As more artists flocked here, they were followed by galleries, other creative businesses, and those just attracted to the area's growing reputation as a cheap, Bohemian enclave. By the 1970s, SoHo was transformed but not yet gentrified. That would follow, obvious today as you pass dozens of upscale hotels and clothing boutiques. The gentrification of SoHo would become a case study that would be repeated in many other parts of the city during the next few decades.

Turn left onto Prince Street, named for a prince, although no one is sure which one. Take the first left onto Wooster Street. At **No. 141** is ❺ **The New York Earth Room**, a unique interior earth sculpture created in 1977 by the artist Walter De Maria (1935-2013). Maria played in the pre-Velvet Under-

ground band The Primitives with John Cale and Lou Reed (check out their song "The Ostrich") before becoming an internationally renowned artist. Visit www.diaart.org/ for current opening times.

Return to Prince Street, looking out for ❻ the ghost signs outside the charming two-story buildings between **No. 120 to 124 Prince Street** advertising stationery, office supplies, "Manifold Books," "Lithographing," and other items from the past. In the last few decades SoHo has become uber-fashionable, as will be evident by the shops and art sellers lining Prince Street. David Bowie, when he lived on nearby Lafayette Street, was a regular at Olive's sandwich shop when it was based at No. 120 Prince Street.

Head left down Prince Street, stopping outside ❼ **No. 112,** a handsome, tall cast-iron structure dating from 1889 and designed for a fur importer. It was designed in a Neo-Greek style that was very popular at the time. If you walk around the side of this building (onto Greene Street), look for a *trompe-l'œil* (French for "deceive the eye") mural created by the internationally renowned artist Richard Haas (b. 1936) in 1975. Now considerably faded and partly covered by graffiti, it was meant to imitate the iron façade of No. 112.

The upper floors of this building were used by artists in the 1970s, the classic SoHo loft origin story. Maya Lin (b. 1959), best known for designing the Vietnam Veterans Memorial in Washington D.C, used to live here. She was reported to have sold her apartment for over $4 million in 2014.

Continue down Greene Street and stop outside **No. 110**. On the sidewalk ❽ is a 90-foot-long reminder of SoHo's recent past when it was still becoming gentrified. The work is by Belgian artist Françoise Schein and titled **"Subway Map Floating on a New York Sidewalk."** It was installed in 1985, stainless steel concrete with lights and reflecting the artist's view of the subway system, "like a flux inside a living body." Schein had only recently graduated when she came up with this piece and faced opposition from certain quarters before it was eventually installed. It would win her an award, and she has gone on to have her art pieces installed in cities around the world.

No. 112 (at the time of writing a Stella McCartney shop) ❾ was once home to **Greene St. Recording**. The recording studio opened in the 1970s and is best known for being favored by pioneering hip hop acts such as Run D.M.C, Public Enemy, L.L. Cool J, Afrika Bambaataa, and De La Soul. It closed in 2001. Look at No. 110 next door with the sign "CHARLES BROADWAY ROVSS" above the entrance. You will learn a little more about this later on in the walk.

Retrace your steps to Prince Street and turn right. The next

stop is on the right **⑩** outside **No. 102**, the site of **Molly's apartment** in the hit movie *Ghost* (1990). Molly, played by Demi Moore, practiced her pottery here with her ghostly partner Sam (Patrick Swayze). The standout performance was Whoopi Goldberg's portrayal of psychic con artist Oda Mae Brown. In the film, she stands on the sidewalk shouting up for Molly to come down and speak to her. Who knows—Sam may still be up there . . . The film may be more than three decades old, but the musical version of *Ghost* today plays in theaters around the world.

Walk on, stopping next outside **⑪** the luxurious **Mercer Hotel** on the left-hand corner of Mercer Street. It describes itself as "the first hotel to offer an authentic taste of loft living." *Tatler* has described it as "the over-hyped, column-filling, impossible to-get-a-room-in Mercer." Poverty-stricken artists living illegally in decrepit SoHo buildings in the 1960s could never have imagined the humble loft would become so coveted.

The hotel opened in 1997 and quickly became a favorite with film stars and celebrities.

Russell Crowe's privacy evaporated at 4:20 a.m. one morning in 2005 when he threw a telephone that injured desk clerk Nestor Estrada. Crowe, then at the height of his fame, was arrested. His actions drew the attention of the worldwide media. He had also made arguably the most expensive telephone call in history as it was reported he settled a lawsuit over the attack for $11 million. At the time, Crowe said, "I really didn't mean to hit the guy. I just wanted to get the f***ing phones to work." This superb Romanesque Revival SoHo landmark dates from 1888 and was built by John Jacob Astor II, a member of the famous Manhattan Astor dynasty.

Turn left (north) down Mercer Street. It is named (you guessed it) for a Revolutionary War hero, General Hugh Mercer (1726-77), who died from injuries received during the Battle of Princeton. Before 1799, it was Clermont Street.

Mercer, born in Aberdeenshire, Scotland, led an extraordinary life. He trained as a physician before joining the rebel army of Bonnie Prince Charlie in 1745. He survived

the slaughter of the Battle of Culloden when the British army of King George II triumphed and—now a fugitive—escaped to America. He had many more adventures, becoming a good friend of George Washington before gaining revenge over King George III in the Revolutionary War.

Continue up Mercer Street to **No. 149** on the left. This ⓬ exceptional three-story house dates from 1826 and was built by **Robert Schuyler** in a late-Federal style. Schuyler was a member of a prominent city family who had first arrived in Manhattan in the mid-1600s.

117

In the early 1800s, this part of the city represented the northern limit of respectable society, and many merchants and their families lived in the vicinity.

There was more available space to build in those days and fewer people to compete with for real estate, so three (and a half) stories made sense. As demand for space grew as the 19th century went on, buildings got taller (obvious as you look around). Before the introduction of the elevator in the 1850s, New York's buildings were generally limited to six stories.

By the mid-19th century, wealthy residents had largely moved away, one reason being the area's reputation as a red-light district. For much of the 1850-60s, this house was a brothel, run by Mrs. Van Ness, and then later Madame Bell. It appeared in numerous media reports, usually concerning patrons who were robbed during their clandestine visits.

Continue along on the left to **No. 155**, at the time of writing ⓭, a branch of Dolce & Gabbana. The second story contains the sign for **"Firemen's Hall."** This had its origins in the early days of volunteer fire fighting companies in the city. They were then largely social and fraternal groups—for example, one was called the Knights of the Round Table. This building was constructed in the 1850s, and in 1919 a strapping 6 foot 2 fireman named

Joseph Pohler made the surprising move into films, starring as Tarzan in *The Revenge of Tarzan* (1920). The fireman, only the second actor to portray the famous character adopted the screen name Gene Pollar, and this was the beginning of the Tarzan film industry (Edgar Rice Burroughs' first Tarzan story appeared in 1912).

By 1966 Pohler was the oldest person alive to have played Tarzan. A publicity event that year featuring a reunion of Tarzan actors forgot to invite him, and he complained the organizers thought he was already dead.

Walk a little farther **14** to **Nos. 165-7** on the left, a fine cast-iron structure from the 1870s. This was previously the site of a riding school and livery stables. This building was home to furriers, and Mercer and Greene Streets were at the center of the fur trade. The garment and furrier businesses moved north around 1918, and buildings were used for many other purposes. In the 1930s, this building was used by mobsters for bootlegged alcohol, and in October 1939, a major F.B.I. surveillance operation resulted in the arrest of mobster Joseph "Black Lefty" Lapadura and others in his gang. It was described at the time as the largest bootleg ring since Prohibition.

Retrace your steps up Mercer Street. The street is one of many around here that have changed dramatically over the decades. Whereas once prostitutes and mobsters worked here, now celebrities spend millions on apartments. Rock star Jon Bon Jovi sold a penthouse at **No. 158** (on the left) **15** for $34 million in 2015. Other notable recent residents in this tall building, dating from 1895, include Arianna Huffington

(of *Huffington Post* fame) and hotelier André Balazs, owner of the Mercer Hotel and the famous Chateau Marmont in L.A.

Walk back to Prince Street. Opposite the Mercer Hotel is ⓰ the **Fanelli Café** at No. 94 Prince Street. It was founded in 1847, making it the second oldest continually operating establishment of its kind in New York. Originally a grocery store, it later became a bar and speakeasy. It was bought by ex-boxer Mike Fanelli in 1922, and his family sold it in 1982. Long before it became a spot favored by tourists, the café was one of the few places where artists and residents of pre-gentrification SoHo could socialize. In the 1960s, Mike was about to eject a sleeping patron until someone pointed out "da bum" was Bob Dylan. The clientele included artists such as Chuck Close, and boxer Rocky Graziano.

Next door at No. 96 is the former site of ⓱ the **Paula Cooper Gallery**. Founded in 1968, it was the first art gallery to open in SoHo and helped pioneer the change from a relative backwater into what you see today.

Appropriately for its era, the first show was a benefit for the Student Mobilization Committee to End the War in Vietnam. The gallery moved to nearby Wooster Street in 1973 and, like many galleries, has since relocated to Chelsea as real estate prices in SoHo soared. A *New*

York Times article from 2021 described Cooper, then 83 and still running a gallery, as a "female legend." (You can see Cooper's current gallery in Chelsea on the Chelsea walk in this book). As art galleries have moved, high-end clothing boutiques have often taken their place, attracting so many shoppers it can be a challenge to navigate these streets, particularly on the weekend.

Carry on to Broadway, turning right to see ⑱ the **Little Singer Building** (second one along) at **Nos. 561-3**. Dating from 1904, it was designed in an Art Nouveau style by Ernest Flagg (1857-1947) and is an elegant 12-story delight. Look for the complex wrought-iron tracery and railings. It was once occupied by the Singer sewing machine company, at the time one of the most influential companies in the world. It was called "Little" because Flagg would later design the Singer Tower (149 Broadway), the tallest building in the world when it opened in 1908. When demolished in 1968, it was, and still is, the largest skyscraper to be peacefully demolished.

If you are feeling a little hot, you may wish to take a detour now to the **Museum of Ice Cream** opposite (558 Broadway).

One block to the east of here is Crosby Street, regarded by some as the eastern edge of SoHo. Although not visited on this walk, fans of the film *Ghost* might want to pay homage to Sam on Crosby Street (between Prince and Spring Streets) as it was here he was murdered when out with Molly.

Retrace your steps along Prince Street and turn left (south) down Mercer Street. There are too many historic cast-iron buildings along the route of this walk to cover individual examples in any detail. The official SoHo-Cast Iron District covers nearly 500 historic structures, most built towards the end of the 19th century.

Look to the right ❶⑨ at **Nos. 123-125** for a tall building bearing the sign "Charles Broadway Rouss" (you will recall similar signage on Greene Street). Charles Baltzell Rouss (1836-1902) was an eccentric Virginian who fought for the Confederate Army before arriving in New York in 1866. He was described in 1892 as "an ardent, aggressive Southerner . . . He came without money or influence, and with $11,000 of ante-bellum debts hanging over him . . . " Despite time in a debtor's prison, he founded a successful business selling everything from clothing, household furnishings, to hats, and oversaw branches worldwide. He liked Broadway so much he changed his name to refer to it. When he went blind, he offered a prize of $100,000 to anyone

who could cure him. Being a busy person, he hired a blind man to be experimented upon on Rouss's behalf.

Two buildings down on the same side is ❷ **Nos. 117-119**, dating from the early 1890s. As mentioned earlier, Mercer Street was once a key location for milliners and furriers. The Metropolitan Fur Company was based here, advertising capes and jackets in 1894 with the rather aggressive promise "WE WILL MEET ALL COMPETITION / A TRIAL WILL CONVINCE YOU." Within a few years, most businesses like this would move north to what would become known as the "Garment District." This building would be used by a variety of companies in the following years, from picture framers to gaslighting firms.

A mysterious death took place here on January 2, 1898. A woman named Ellen Ryan came here with her married landlord Martin Farrell, who also looked after the boilers. The building was then empty (it was a Sunday), and Ellen died, Farrell claiming it was due to her falling down an elevator shaft. However, the police were not convinced, and he was charged with homicide.

Continue down Mercer Street, one of the most attractive in the district. Like many streets, it has been gentrified in the last few decades. Sculptor Richard Nonas (1936-2021) was part of the early wave of artists who moved to SoHo in the 1960s. He would later recall, "It was almost like being in the country in the middle of the city . . . It was only toward the '80s . . . that I knew anybody who made enough money to hire an architect or a plumber."

Stop outside ❷ **No. 105 Mercer Street**. This dates from 1820 and is similar to the former residence and brothel you saw earlier on Mercer Street (at No. 149). This was initially occupied by Mary Boddy,

described at the time as a seamstress but who may have been a dressmaker, the latter profession better paid.

As this area declined, No. 105 is believed to have become a brothel. A 19-year-old woman who lived here in 1853 committed suicide after buying (according to a newspaper report) "an ounce of laudanum and a shilling's worth of vitriol." She may have been a young prostitute looking for a way out.

This amazing building weathered the changes that took place in SoHo, used by various businesses from the 1870s, including furriers, before becoming dilapidated. A young jewelry designer moved in during the 1960s, and by 1980 a group of artists had taken over this historic building. It has retained its Federal-style elements, such as the red brickwork and archway over the main door. There is also a roof deck. A seamstress could not afford to live here today—it was recently on the market for around $4.5 million.

You next reach Spring Street, most likely named for a spring found on the Bayard farm. On the corner of Mercer Street is ㉒ **No. 107**, a Federal Style brick house that is the oldest in SoHo and dates back to c. 1806-08.

Turn right onto Spring Street and walk to ㉓ **No. 129** on the right, another Federal style relic from the early 1800s that is today dwarfed by its newer neighbors. This dates from 1817, and in the mid 19th century was used for meetings by many interesting groups, including veteran soldier associations and African American Republicans (who met here in 1872 to discuss their support of President Ulysses S. Grant). If the shop is open, you can enter to see the remains of an 18th century well in the basement.

The building is said to be haunted by the ghost of Gulielma Elmore Sands, who, at age 21, disappeared in December 1799 and was found dead early the following January inside the Spring Street well. The tragedy became known as the "Manhattan Well Murder." The principal suspect was her boyfriend Levi Weeks, but he was lucky enough to secure the legal services of Alexander Hamilton and Aaron Burr and was acquitted. In 1804 Burr would kill Hamilton in their famous duel. The Spring Street Ghost has annoyed many people working here over the years (so it is said).

Now head left down Greene Street, named in the late 1790s, most likely for Nathanael Greene (1742-1786), another Revolutionary War figure. Regarded as the second-best general after Washington, Greene made a key contribution to the defeat of the British. After leaving the army, he became a plantation and slave owner, dying at age 43.

Continue down to reach Broome Street, where you turn right. It is named for politician and merchant John Broome (1738-1810). After the defeat of the British in the Revolutionary War, Broome helped New Yorkers continue to indulge in their love of tea by importing huge amounts from China, which pioneered the new Republic's trade relations with the Far East.

Take a moment to appreciate your surroundings. If it were not for the efforts of a stubborn group of people that included figures such as Jane Jacobs (1916-2006), you might not see much at all except The

Lower Manhattan Expressway (LOMEX). From 1929 to 1969, planners such as controversial public official Robert Moses wanted to build a highway cutting across Manhattan approximately between Delancey and Broome Streets. Moses and others believed the area now called SoHo and parts of Greenwich Village were too dilapidated to remain as they were, and the LOMEX would help revitalize depressed areas.

Jacobs, a journalist, writer, and activist, wrote what would become an influential work named *The Death and Life of Great American Cities* (1961). She and other campaigners helped defeat Moses and the supporters of the LOMEX, and you should be thankful to them as you walk today. She sent a copy of her book to her nemesis Moses, and he returned it, adding a caustic reply. He was not a good loser.

Continue along Broome Street, stopping by the entrance to Wooster Street, thought to be named for Revolutionary War General David Wooster (1711-1777).

No. 53 on the southwest side of the intersection of **Wooster Street** ㉔ has a fascinating history. The building dates from the mid-1820s when this was still a respectable middle-class street. However, by the 1850s and 60s, this was a brothel. In 1858, The *New York Times* reported Captain Turbull "made a descent on No. 53 Wooster Street, and had all the inmates locked up and committed to answer." It later became a factory. In the 1870s, Wooster Street alone had around 27 brothels, with another 52 on Greene Street.

In 1971 the building's roof was used by dancers in Trisha Brown's famous dance work entitled "Roof Piece." Dancers dressed in orange stood on top of a number of local buildings. The first would make a semaphore-style movement, and others would try and copy it before passing the message on to others. Brown died in 2017, but the Trisha Brown Dance Company continues and describes how its founder's "earliest works took impetus from the cityscape of downtown SoHo, where she was a pioneering settler."

It was pressure groups such as the Artist Tenant Association and SoHo Artist Association that led to the authorities rezoning the district in 1971. For the first time, artists could legally live where they worked. This helped change Wooster Street forever, attracting more artists, actors, and others in the creative world.

Now head north up Wooster Street. On the right is ㉕ **No. 76**, a symbol of underground SoHo that has largely faded. In 2015, *Whitewall*, an art publication, described how this address "used to be the hideaway of Warhol, a place where Jean-Michel Basquiat, Keith Haring, and Julian Schnabel would hang. The ground floor acted as

Grace Jones' restaurant at one point, and at another served as a temporary exhibition site for Yoko Ono's tribute to the art of John Lennon." The magazine noted "the once bohemian neighborhood has long since turned into a saturated grid of big-name and big-chain storefronts and shop . . . The group of artists, influencers, and creatives that once defined an era are long gone."

Next door ㉖ is **No. 80**, which also has an important place in SoHo's cultural history. It was bought by a group of artists in 1967 and became the first artists' co-op in SoHo. A key figure here was George Maciunas, a founder of the influential Fluxus art movement. Artists based here included Jonas Mekas, Trisha Brown, and Robert Watts. Works were also shown here by many artists, including Yoko Ono, Hermann Nitsch, Nam June Paik, and Andy Warhol. The importance of this site is reflected in it being the subject of a book, *Illegal Living—80 Wooster Street and the Evolution of SoHo* (Roslyn Bernstein & Shael Shapiro).

Keep going to reach Spring Street again. If you stand by the traffic light on the right-hand corner, you are exactly ㉗ where Michael Caine (playing Elliot) runs up Wooster and turns right onto Spring Street in a scene from Woody Allen's film *Hannah and Her Sisters* (1986).

Turn left onto Spring Street, where old buildings are now home to fashionable boutiques. There has been considerable friction between locals and their representative organizations and the City Planning Commission about rezoning plans that could create more high-end apartments in SoHo. At one public meeting in 2021, a local shouted, "SoHo doesn't need more luxury housing! Build 100 percent affordable housing." Similar tensions are found in many other parts of the city and are likely to continue for years to come. One important local organization is The SoHo Alliance, founded in 1981, which succeeded the

SoHo Artists Association that began in 1968. The Association helped legalize loft living in the area, which also began its gentrification. It was at one of their meetings that the name "SoHo" was adopted for wider use.

Keep going, passing West Broadway. As SoHo became popular with the rich and famous, actress Meg Ryan moved in at 420 West Broadway in the early 2000s, owning two apartments there. Other celebrities who have lived in this area include actors Claire Danes and Willem Dafoe.

Reach the corner of Thompson Street. On the right-hand corner is Famous **Ben's Pizza** of Soho **㉘**. Apart from making excellent pizza, it featured in a scene involving Agent J (Will Smith) in the film *Men In Black 2* (2002).

Across the street is **㉙** a paddleboard court with its own film connection. In *Big* (1988), the character played by Tom Hanks plays here. It is part of the **Vesuvio Playground**, named after the Vesuvio Italian bakery on Prince Street. Why name a park after a bakery? Bakery owner Anthony Dapolito (1920-2003) was born on Houston street and for over 50 years served on the local community board. He worked with Jane Jacobs and others to fight Robert Moses's redevelopment plans. He also helped establish

local parks, including this one named in his memory.

Continue along Spring Street, passing No. 195 on the right-hand corner (with Sullivan Street). This was once ㉚ the **Mezzogiorno Restaurant**. It was here that Molly (Demi Moore) and Oda Mae Brown (Whoopi Goldberg) met to discuss Sam (Patrick Swayze) in *Ghost* (1990). Sam looks on as they talk about him, and he gets Oda Mae to refer to "Ditto." This startles Molly as it was Sam's phrase.

You can now finish the walk here. The Spring Street subway station is nearby, or follow the map up Sixth Avenue then left onto West Houston Street to return to the start.

5

THE BOWERY WALK

START: Sara D. Roosevelt Park
SUBWAY: Grand St  B, D
FINISH: Astor Place
SUBWAY: Astor Pl 6, 8 St-NYU R, W

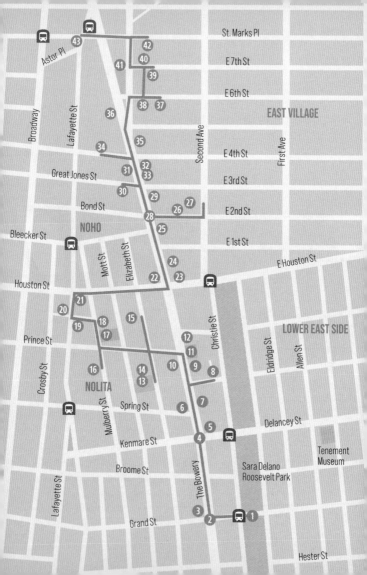

THE BOWERY

Distance: 2.3 Miles

The station is next to the ❶ **Sara Delano Roosevelt Park**, named for President Franklin Delano Roosevelt's mother. She wasn't happy about it, and in 1934 she formally objected to the plan, proposing it be named after Charles B. Stover, the city's Parks Commissioner. The Board of Aldermen overruled her, in what may be the only time a prominent New Yorker did not want to be immortalized by having a place named after them. The park was built after walk-up apartment buildings were demolished to make room for it, over what was previously an African-American burial ground.

Head for Chrystie Street, originally called First Street. When the Commissioners' Plan of 1811 proposed a grid system for the expanding city north of Houston Street, it was thought that the name First Street would be confused with the new numbered street names, and so it was renamed after Colonel John Chrystie (1788–1813). A controversial character, he fought in the War of 1812, but was blamed by fellow officers for a defeat in battle and accused of cowardice.

If you had stood on this spot on Chrystie Street on June 28, 1776, you would be part of a crowd of 20,000 New Yorkers watching the hanging of Irish-born soldier Thomas Hickey for sedition and mutiny, and he may also have been part of a plot to assassinate George Washington. Two hundred and thirty-six years later, Hickey has re-appeared as a character in *Assassins Creed III,* a video game.

Follow the map up **Grand Street**, surrounded on all sides by Asian-American businesses, and turn right onto **The Bowery**. This ❷ **intersection** is at the heart of what has become to be known as Little Saigon, due to the number of Vietnamese immigrants who have settled here.

On the left (north-west corner of Bowery and Grand Street) ❸ is an impressive building at **No. 130**. Despite looking like something from Ancient Rome, it was constructed in the mid-1890s for The **Bowery Savings Bank** (look for the sign). The bank was founded in 1834, and the building was designed by the famous architect Stanford White (1853-1906). The use of classical style was considered innovative at the time, and subsequently became the trend for banks across America. Photos from the time show The Third Avenue Elevated Railway—or 'El'—running right outside the entrance of the bank and up The Bowery.

In 2019, Capital One Bank, which had taken over The Bowery Savings Bank, came across old records of the Saving Bank's customers. This treasure trove of information says a lot about the local residents in the late 19th and early 20th centuries, when waves of immigrants settled on the Lower East Side, including Irish, Italians, Chinese, and Eastern Europeans.

Continue up Bowery, the oldest street in New York. In the 17th century, The Dutch West India Company encouraged settlers to found farms—in Dutch "bouweries." A number were linked by an existing Native Ameri-

can trail that became known as Bouwerie Lane. You soon notice the Asian-American influence visibly fades away, and the next stretch contains a number of nondescript buildings. This is just a faint reminder of when the Bowery was an infamous slum, the original Skid Row. In the 1930s, this thoroughfare was the last resort for thousands of homeless and vulnerable people, reduced to sleeping on the street or in the Bowery's flophouses that forced people into tiny cubicles with no ceiling. Watch Lionel Rogosin's excellent film *On the Bowery* (1956) for a look back to that time.

On the left you will pass Broome Street, named for John Broome (1738-1810), a New York merchant who served as Lt. Governor of the state. He was also an officer in the Second New York City Regiment of militia during the American Revolution and pioneered the importation of tea from China.

Ahead, cross over ❹ **Delancey Street** and Kenmare Streets. Delancey Street was once known as a major shopping district for the Jewish community on the Lower East Side. *Crossing Delancey* is a play that was made into a successful film (1988), both written by Susan Sandler. Described as the ultimate Jewish rom-com, it captures an era when the Jewish community in this area was prominent. The film was directed by Joan Micklin Silver, who also directed *Hester Street* (1975), an often neglected gem about Eastern European Jewish immigrants on nearby Hester Street in the 1890s.

Delancey Street is named for Étienne de Lancy (1663-1741), a member of an aristocratic French Huguenot family, who fled religious persecution in his homeland and arrived in New York in 1686. A successful merchant, he changed his first name to Stephen and he, and his family, became prominent figures in the life of British New York. Their mansion would later become the famous Fraunces Tavern on Pearl Street. The family owned 339 acres from here to the East River. The grid pattern of streets they established on their holding was largely retained on the Lower East Side, although Delancey Square, visible on a map of 1776, was never constructed. The family lost their New York estate when they backed the British side during the Revolutionary War.

Now turn right down Delancey Street and stop outside ❺ **No. 6** on the north side, a building dating from 1928. For years it was a shoe store, hence the sign for "Tree Mark Shoes." Today, it is the well-known music venue **The Bowery Ballroom**. Just a few of the world-famous artists who have played here include Lady Gaga, Patti Smith, Metallica, Radiohead and Lou Reed. Part of the foundation of the old cinema that stood here before 1928 can be seen inside.

Retrace your steps to continue up Bowery. Opposite is Kenmare Street with its own interesting history. The controversial Tammany Hall politician and theater owner "Big" Tim Sullivan (1862-1913) named it after the Irish village his mother had been forced to leave because of the Irish Famine in 1849. Less than 2,400 people live in Kenmare today, but back then it was part of the 100,000 acre Lansdowne Estate, owned by Lord Lansdowne and located in County Kerry on the southwest tip of Ireland. In the late 1840s, many residents of the

estate were dying due to the Irish Famine. Instead of supplying food or money, Lord Lansdowne got rid of his problem by funding the emigration of his starving tenants to America, forcing them to start again in the slums of the Lower East Side. Tim Sullivan never forgot his mother's difficult start in life.

Continue on, passing Spring Street whose name refers to a spring found near here on a farm. On the left-hand (northwest) corner at **190 Bowery** is ❻ a six-story Renaissance Revival-style building covered in graffiti. It was originally the home of The Germania Bank of the City of New York when it was completed in 1899.

The bank was founded elsewhere on Bowery in 1869 to provide banking services to the 250,000 German immigrants that had settled on the Lower East Side and in the East Village, giving rise to the name Little

Germany or *Kleindeutschland*. This was not unusual—many immigrant groups struggled (and still do) to be accepted by established banks or other businesses, so they often set up their own support networks.

The Germania Bank changed its name during World War I because of anti-German sentiment and later disappeared, like most old banks, in a wave of mergers and rebranding.

In 1966 photographer Jay Maisel (b. 1931) bought the 72-room building and stayed for 49 years, living with his family and working out of a studio there. During that time most people thought "The Bank" had been abandoned. In the late 1960s Maisel rented studio space to artists Adolph Gottlieb and Roy Lichtenstein. Keith Haring used to draw "chalk babies" outside and Maisel later said, "I *never* washed off any of Keith's stuff."

Maisel's photographs captured how this area changed over the decades from Skid Row into the gentrified place you see today. He also took shots of famous people such as Marilyn Monroe, Billie Holiday and the jazz legends of the 1950s and 60s. His image of Miles Davis appears on the cover of *Kind of Blue* (1959). He may well be the richest photographer ever to live in New York – he bought the building

Street scenes

for \$102,000 and sold it in 2014 for \$55 million. A documentary about Maisel's life, *Jay Myself* (2018), is a fascinating look into the life of the artist and what he collected in this building.

Continue up Bowery. On the right at **No. 207** ⑦ is the site of "Big" Tim Sullivan's Clubhouse, where he secured local voter support by offering Christmas dinners to 5,000 people who lined up around the block. Today it is much quieter, and you will notice small art galleries—a different vibe to the start of the walk.

Next, turn right onto Rivington Street, and then left down narrow ⑧ **Freeman Alley**. If you like street art, this is a fantastic diversion and one of the most famous graffiti spots in New York. In the 1980s, this spot was known for heroin dealing and gang violence.

Return to Bowery and stop outside ⑨, the landmark building of the **Bowery Mission** on the right. This is home to the oldest Christian rescue mission in the city and has provided shelter and food for thousands of people since it was founded in 1879. The building was originally owned by a firm of undertakers and coffin makers and dates from 1876. The Mission has been here since 1909, and has weathered huge changes in the Bowery over that time.

Look for the stained glass—there is a chapel within, and you may be able to get inside and see it. The Mission is a reminder of darker days, when Skid Row was dominated by a transient, impoverished population that included many immigrants. For many, places like this were the only support they could expect to receive. President Taft visited the Mission one night in 1909, entering through Freeman Alley and giving a rousing speech to people in the chapel.

Opposite ⑩ at No. **222 Bowery** is another building associated with great artists and cultural icons. In the 1920s, the city's first YMCA branch had more than 700 members, all young men, of which 400 were Italian and 100 were Irish.

Beat legend William S. Burroughs (1914-1997) lived here on and off from 1974 in a window-

less apartment (hence it was called The Bunker). His cultural influence was, and remains, immense—influencing everyone from David Bowie to Allen Ginsberg and beyond. Anyone whose face is featured on the cover of the Sgt. Pepper album has to be cool, and visitors here included Andy Warhol, Mick Jagger, Lou Reed, Patti Smith, Susan Sontag and Allen Ginsberg. Read *With William Burroughs: A Report From the Bunker* (1981) by Victor Bockris to find out more.

Mark Rothko (1903–1970) also lived and painted in a second-floor studio here between 1957-1962. When he moved in, he was not yet a world-famous artist, and the surrounding area was known for violence and drugs. In 2012, one of his paintings from this era, *Orange, Red, Yellow* (1961), sold at auction for $86,882,500. This is also where he created his iconic Seagram murals and paint flung around by Rothko has been preserved on some of the floorboards inside his former studio.

Rihanna shot a music video here, and other artists who have lived here—one of the coolest addresses in Manhattan history—include French painter Fernand Léger and poet John Giorno.

If this area has given you the taste for seeing some modern art, head over to ⑪ the **New Museum** (just up from the Bowery Mission) at 235 Bowery. With a cost of $50 million to build, it opened here in 2007 and—given its proximity to the Bowery Mission—has attracted criticism for the way extreme wealth and poverty now sit side by side on the Bowery. Just up from the museum at ⑫ 245 Bowery was the **Sunshine Hotel**, one of the last operating flophouses in the area. The Bowery has always inspired creative people, and this flophouse was no exception as filmmaker Michael Dominic made a riveting and award-winning documentary about the struggles of those who lived here—*Sunshine Hotel* (2001).

Now for a little detour away from the Bowery (don't worry, you will rejoin it later). Turn left down Prince Street. There has been much speculation about which prince this is named after (no, not a British one). One explanation is that it was named for Samuel Prince (b. 1728), a wealthy cabinet maker who owned land in the area.

Turn left for a short detour down Elizabeth Street to visit ⑬ the **Elizabeth Street Garden**, one of several delightful community gardens founded on vacant plots in this part of

the city. It occupies the site where a 19th-century school once stood. The variety of sculptures lend this garden an eccentric air, but do not take it for granted. Developers have their eye on this site.

Next door at **No. 209** ⑭ is a former fire station built in the 1880s for **Hook and Ladder Company No. 9**. This company responded to the tragic Triangle Shirtwaist factory fire of 1911 that killed 146 garment workers, mostly women and girls. The first sliding pole used by New York firefighters was installed here. Try to imagine horses pulling the fire truck out from the ground floor. It later became a bakery—look for the old sign for La Rosa & Son Bread Co.

Retrace your steps up Elizabeth Street. Nicholas Bayard (1642–1709) was another Huguenot refugee who arrived in New Amsterdam and made a fortune. The nephew of Peter Stuyvesant, he owned a large farm in this area, the main building standing on a site on the west of Bowery by Broome Street.

The Bayard family was part of prominent New York society for many decades, and much of their money, and influence, was derived from slave-produced commodities. They owned slaves and Nicholas's grandson—also named Nicholas—gives us an insight into the past in his will of 1765. In it he recorded gifts of human beings to his children: "*I also leave [his son Stephen] my negro wench, "Molly," and my negro man, "Quimono". I leave to my daughter Elizabeth 30 Lots of ground being part of my farm lying in the Bowery . . . I also leave her my negro girl 'Celia'.*" Perhaps one day streets will be named after Molly, Quimono or Celia rather than the grandson Nicholas Bayard's wife Elizabeth.

Return to Prince Street. Take a small detour up Elizabeth Street. Both parents of Martin Scorsese (b. 1942) were born on the street, each one the child of Italian immigrants (his maternal grandparents were from Ciminna, his paternal grandparents were from Polizzi Generosa, both in Sicily). As a child, Martin lived with family at his grandparents (No. 241) before moving to ⑮ No. **253 Elizabeth Street**. Often confined to his bedroom due to asthma, he watched the activities of the neighborhood from his third-floor window, which would greatly influence his later films. Back then, Italian religious festivals regularly took place in the nearby streets, linked to the same festivals in Italy. Today, Elizabeth Street is gentrified and there is little evidence of the way of life Scorsese knew, except for the occasional festival, such as the Feast of San Gennaro each September. Now celebrities such as Billy Joel and Gabriel Byrne own multi-million dollar properties on the street.

Mulberry Street, 1900

Continue along Prince Street, turning left onto Mulberry Street. Stop ⑯ outside **No. 247** on the right—the site of the former **Ravenite Social Club**. This unassuming building has an almost unbelievable history. Its origins go back to 1926, when it was founded as the Alto Knights Social Club and became a social hub of the Italian-American community in Little Italy.

Gangster Lucky Luciano was just one of the mob figures who came here, and later it came under the control of the Gambino crime family, one of New York's infamous Five Families. The FBI's surveillance of the Social Club resulted in vital recordings that led to them raiding the club in December 1990. This helped secure the conviction of "The Dapper Don" John Gotti (1940-2002), then head of the Gambino family.

Retrace your steps to walk north up Mulberry Street, named for the mulberry trees that are thought to have grown here in the 18th century. On the right is ⑰ **St. Patrick's Old Cathedral**. As with the Ravenite Social Club, if a building could speak this one would certainly have tales to tell. When it was consecrated in 1815, the Catholic Cathedral was far outside the residential streets of Manhattan, and would have been surrounded by farmland and meadows. Much of the funding for construction came from Irish immigrants.

The arrival of these Irish immigrants, mainly Catholic, into the Lower East Side created tensions with locals, mostly Protestants who regarded themselves as true Americans under threat from a Papal conspiracy. Street battles and riots involving Irish and "Nativists" explains why there is a defensive wall around Old St. Patrick's. Built in 1834, the wall was a necessary barrier when the cathedral was threatened with destruction by angry mobs on a number of occasions.

In 1836 The Ancient Order of Hibernians (AOH)—a Catholic fraternal organization—was founded on the Lower East Side and its headquarters were once located on Prince Street. The AOH became an important part of the Irish immigrant community and helped it withstand years of hostility. In the 1850s, the AOH organized blockades around the walls of the cathedral to protect it against attacks.

In the 21st century, the Manhattan County Board of the AOH holds meetings in the Parish House of the former cathedral. The AOH is heavily involved in the famous St. Patrick's Day parade, which used to end at the old cathedral until 1830.

The status of old St. Patrick's changed when the current St. Patrick's Cathedral was built (dedicated in 1879). It is now only a parish church, but a very special one. It has been featured in many films, including (inevitably) Coppola's *The Godfather* (baptism scene), *The Godfather Part III* and Scorsese's *Mean Streets* and *Who's that Knocking at my Door?* Martin Scorsese was an altar boy until he kept turning up late for early mass, and attended St. Patrick's School and Youth Center nearby. The teenage Robert de Niro also regularly attended mass here.

In 1826 three immigrants staged an opera at the then cathedral, today credited as marking the arrival of Italian opera in America. One immigrant, Lorenzo Da Ponte (1749-1838), had written the libretti for three Mozart operas.

Living in this area is expensive, and dying can be tough on the wallet too. In 2020 it was reported that the church was putting its last remaining empty crypt on the market for $7 million. You can also visit the catacombs here.

Continue up Mulberry Street, passing ⑱ the small parish building that is used by **The Knights of Columbus**, founded in 1882 to help Irish immigrants (look for their coat of arms).

Turn left onto narrow Jersey Street. At the bottom you reach Lafayette Street. On your immediate left ⑲ at No. **285 Lafayette Street** is a lovely ten-story building dating from 1912. David Bowie (1947-2016) lived here with his wife Iman until his death. The Bowie apartment was sold for $17 million in 2021.

Almost opposite at ⑳ **No. 292** Lafayette Street is the site of superstar artist **Keith Haring's The Pop Shop**. It was opened by Haring (1958-1990) in 1986, and closed in 2005.

Turn right up Lafayette Street, named for the French General Marquis de Lafayette (1757-1834). He was welcomed as a popular hero when he returned to visit New York in the 1820s, just before this street was opened. As a young man he played a key part in the American Revolutionary War, and then returned to France where he also took part in the French Revolution.

On your right is the ㉑ **Puck Building**. It is owned by Kushner Companies, founded by real-estate developer Charles Kushner. He was convicted for witness tampering and tax evasion in 2005 and pardoned by President Trump in 2020. By coincidence his son, Jared, is Trump's son-in-law and became the most famous Kushner family member during the Trump presidency, almost single-handedly securing peace in the Middle East (not).

The Puck Building, built in two stages in the 1880s and 90s, is an example of the obscure German Rundbogenstil style (round-arch style). Its name reflects that it was once the home of Puck—a groundbreaking satirical magazine published between 1871-1918. Originally a German-language publication, it became very popular—probably equivalent to *Saturday Night Live* today.

Media tycoon William Randolph Hearst took over the magazine

in 1916, and, unsurprisingly, he did not waste much time getting payback for the way Puck had ridiculed him in the past. The magazine closed two years later. Look for the two gilded figures of Puck—a mischievous fairy and jester in Shakespeare's *A Midsummer Night's Dream.*

The Puck building has appeared in many films and television shows, including *When Harry Met Sally* (1989), in the scene where they attend a wedding and later a New Year's Eve party. If you decide you'd like to live here, an apartment here will cost you over $25 million.

Turn right onto East Houston Street, named for William Houstoun (1755-1813). He was a son-in-law of local landowner Nicholas Bayard and represented Georgia at the Continental Congress and later the Constitutional Convention as the United States of America was forged in the 1780s. Houston Street also appears in two modern city districts—North of Houston Street (NoHo) and South of Houston Street (SoHo). Tourist warning—it is pronounced "How-stun."

Walk for a few blocks, and just after Elizabeth Street on the left ㉒ is the famous **Houston Bowery Wall**. It became part of the city's graffiti subculture in the 1980s, and is where Keith Haring created his first large outdoor mural in 1982. This was the site of a mural by Banksy in 2018 and other famous street artists have worked here. Recently, Haring's works have sold for over $6 million; Banksy's work sells for up to $25 million.

Continue on to reach ㉓ the **Liz Christy Community Garden** on the left. This was the first community garden in New York, so, like the graffiti wall, was literally groundbreaking.

It began with "Green Guerillas," gardening activists including local resident Liz Christy, who took over an abandoned plot and started growing things there. It is a great place to stop and appreciate how guerrilla gardeners around the world can turn neglected urban spaces into somewhere special, often fighting opposition from landlords, developers and civic authorities.

Just behind the garden, as you walk up Bowery, is the site ㉔ of a far darker place. On the right is No. 295 Bowery, long ago the site of a debauched dance hall run by Irish immigrant John McGurk. In 1899 a woman killed herself on the premises by drinking carbolic acid, soon followed by perhaps a dozen others who died or attempted suicide (the exact figures are debated). It became known as **McGurk's Suicide Hall** and the owner reveled in the extra business he won when the city's press had a field day printing salacious stories about the goings-on in Bowery dive bars. In later years the building was home to a flop house,

and in the 1960s it became a female artist co-op whose residents included feminist writer Kate Millett (1934-2017). In 2005, the 19th-century structure was demolished and replaced by the glass and steel Avalon building.

Walk up Bowery, immortalized in many songs and films, as in Bob Dylan's "115th Dream": "I walked by a Guernsey cow/Who directed me down/To the Bowery slums/Where people carried signs around Sayin', "Ban the bums." Between 1946 and 1958 there were 48 films in *The Bowery Boys* series, the American public loving stories of tough, funny kids from the original "Skid Row."

Walk on. Just up on the right is ㉕ the site of legendary music club **CBGB** (Country, Blue-Grass & Blues). Founded in 1973, it is best known for the golden years in the mid-70s when iconic artists such as Patti Smith, The Ramones, Blondie, Talking Heads and Television all performed. If Punk and alternative music had a spiritual home it was CBGB's and when it closed in 2006 part of New York's soul died with it.

Follow the map down East 2nd Street to visit—if you are lucky—two beautiful open-air sites. The first is ㉖ **Albert's Garden**, a community garden founded in the 1970s.

If you are visiting on the fourth Sunday of the month from April to October you may also be able to visit the ㉗ **New York Marble Cemetery** (entrance around the corner on Second Avenue, check the website for additional opening times, marblecemetary.org). The oldest non-sectarian cemetery in the city, it was founded in 1831 in response to a city-wide ban on burials below Grand and Canal streets. Outbreaks of yellow fever and other diseases made the authorities wary of burials in residential areas, so the founders of this cemetery offered 156 underground marble vaults that only the wealthy could afford. Records show there were 145 various causes of death, from Consumption (or TB) at number 1, to yellow fever at number 145. The intriguing "Defective Organization" makes it to number 110. The last burial took place in 1937.

Street scenes

Return to Bowery and see the ㉘ additional name on the street sign for East 2nd Street. **Joey Ramone Place** is named for the lead singer of the Ramones, who died in 2001 and is known as the voice of punk rock in America. Born Jeffrey Ross Hyman in Forest Hills, Queens, in 1951, he named himself "Ramone" from Paul McCartney's occasional stage name Paul Ramon.

Continue up Bowery, and on the right you will pass ㉙ **The Bowery Hotel** at **No. 335**. Opened in 2007, this is perhaps the greatest single example of how skid row has become hipster heaven (at least for some). If you need to stay somewhere before the Met Gala, this is a good option. The hotel is a favorite of celebrities from Tom Brady, Kristen Stewart, Jennifer Lopez, Sting, Keith Richards, Taylor Swift to Paul McCartney. In February 2022 the press reported Aquaman star Jason Momoa used his superhero strength to carry a drunk man out of the hotel bar, accompanied by cheers from other patrons.

Continue up Bowery. On the left ㉚ at No. **57 Great Jones Street** is where Brooklyn-born artist Jean-Michel Basquiat (1960-1988) lived and worked from 1983. The former stable was owned by his friend and mentor Andy Warhol (there is a plaque). Starting as a graffiti artist, Basquiat sold his first painting to Debbie Harry for $200 when he was only 21. He would go on to collaborate with Warhol and establish an international reputation. However, his life ended here on August 12, 1988 from a heroin overdose. His body was discovered by his girlfriend Kelle Inman. In 2017 one of his paintings sold for $110 million.

Opposite at No. **350 Bowery** (at the corner of Great Jones Street) is where ㉛ Hungarian composer Béla Bartók (1881-1945) lived in the 1940s. He had fled Europe to escape fascism but his years in America were not happy ones. He struggled to gain recognition in his adopted country and died of leukemia. Only ten people attended his funeral.

Back on Bowery on the right-hand side is ㉜ local institution **Phebe's Tavern and Grill** (No. 361), which opened in 1968 and might be a good place for a stop. Two doors down at **No. 357** is ㉝ the former **Germania Fire Insurance building** dating from the 1870s and just one of dozens of institutions founded to serve the residents of "Little

Germany" that settled in the thousands in this area during the 19th century.

On the left, turn down East 4th Street to visit ❸❹ the **Merchant's House Museum**. This exceptional building dates from 1832, and for nearly one hundred years was owned by the Tredwell family. Today it is the best-preserved 19th century family home in the city, notable for its Greek revival style interior and late-Federal façade. Visit the museum website to see current opening times (merchantshouse.org).

Return to Bowery, which officially ends here and the street becomes Cooper Square. On the other side of the street is ❸❺ a modern residential block that stands on the site of the **Five Spot Jazz Club** (5 Cooper Square). Operating here between 1956 to 1962, it became famous for hosting the greatest jazz artists of the era, including Billie Holiday, Thelonious Monk, Charles Mingus, and John Coltrane. Writers such as James Baldwin, Gregory Corso, Jack Kerouac and Allen Ginsberg came here. Leonard Bernstein visited in 1959 to see Ornette Coleman's free improvisation set and told people it was "the greatest thing that has ever happened in jazz."

Up ahead on the left look for ❸❻ the sign for the **Village Voice**. This was the old office

for the famous pioneering alternative newspaper for a few years from 1991. *The Village Voice* was founded in 1955 by Norman Mailer and others, and helped galvanise the growing countercultural movement in the city. It set a template for underground newspapers later founded around the world.

This part of the Bowery (today 32 Cooper Square) was once home to Columbia Hall, a gay nightspot and male brothel in the 1890s that was owned by a gangster connected to the infamous Five Points Gang. Also known as Paresis Hall, it was used by Cercle Hermaphroditos—described today as the first transgender advocacy group in the country and formed "to unite for defense against the world's bitter persecution."

Now cross onto East 6th Street to visit ㊲ the **Ukrainian Museum**. This area is part of the East Village and known as Little Ukraine. The origins of the Ukrainian community here go back to the last quarter of the 19th century, and by the mid-20th century around 60,000 Ukrainians lived in nearby streets.

The museum was founded in 1976 by the Ukrainian National Women's League of America and contains a vast collection that celebrates Ukrainian history and culture, including folk art and a photographic archive that captures Ukrainian immigration over the decades.

Retrace your steps, looking for the ghost sign above ㉟ Nos. **212/14** (originally **Wm. Rosenbaum & Bro.**, plumbing suppliers). This two-story commercial building dates from 1924 and brothers William and Charles Rosenbaum came to New York from the former Austro-Hungarian Empire in 1888. Turn right up Taras Shevchenko Place. It is named for one of the greatest figures in Ukrainian literature who lived from 1814 to 1861. At the end on the right is ㊳ **St. George Ukrainian Catholic Church**. The origins of the church go back to 1905.

Ahead of you is ㊵ the famous **McSorley's Old Ale House** that claims it was established in 1854 by John McSorley, an Irish immigrant who made a new life in New York. Imagine a fantasy night here with all the famous figures

who drank here. Abraham Lincoln talking politics with John F. Kennedy and John Lennon, while Woody Guthrie sings a song with Frank Sinatra and poet e.e. cummings sits in a corner composing "i was sitting in mcsorley's" (1923)—"outside it was New York and beautifully snowing/Inside snug and evil."

It is said Elvis came here for several drinks after playing a show in 1964 and gave a performance to a no doubt startled group of male customers.

Women were barred until a landmark court case led to a new city ordinance in 1970 that banned discrimination against women. That same year, Barbara Shaum, who ran a leather goods store two doors down, was invited by the manager of McSorley's to be the first woman to enter the bar. Ms. Shaum returned in 2015 at age 85 to be served another fine ale.

Follow the map to reach Third Avenue, with ㊶ **Cooper Triangle and the Cooper Union Foundation building** beside it. They are named for Peter Cooper (1791-1883), one of the greatest men of his age who made a fortune from industry. His many inventions include America's first steam locomotive and powdered gelatin, and he founded Cooper Union for the Advancement of Science and Art. By the standards of the day, he was an enlightened philanthropist, against slavery, concerned about the rights of Native American Indians and committed to creating educational opportunities for ordinary people. Cooper ran for president in his mid-80s and one can only speculate about what he might have achieved had he won.

The Cooper Union Foundation building opened in 1859 and included the world's first elevator shaft as Cooper—always looking ahead—believed the elevator was soon to be introduced. It is perhaps best known for being where Abraham Lincoln made a famous political speech about slavery and other issues. The Cooper Union Address, on February 27, 1860, helped transform his fortunes and propelled him to the presidency. The current academic building with its cutting edge design dates from 2009 and stands opposite at 41 Cooper Square.

Now turn right down St. Marks Place to ㊷ **No. 12** on the right, and look up to see the sign reading *Deutsche-Amerikanische Schützen Gesellschaft.* When this area was still *Kleindeutschland*, or Little Germany, this building (dating from 1889) was home to the German American Shooting Society. The Society was founded in 1857 by immigrants from Northern Germany and still exists under the name **The New York Schuetzen Corps.** (today based in New Jersey). The ground floor of No. 11 opposite appears in a scene in *Men in Black 2* (2002).

Retrace your steps and head over to Astor Place. It is named for John Jacob Astor (1763-1848), who was born in Walldorf, Germany. Then known as Johann Jakob Astor, he arrived in America when he was about 20 and made his first fortune as a fur trader. The country's first multi-millionaire, he and his descendants would make the Astor family one of the most famous in the world. John Jacob Astor helped transform this area into one in which the wealthier residents of the city invested in mansions and town houses, and they also patronized the grand **Astor Opera House** (located on the site of ㊸ No. 21 Astor Place nearby).

On May 10, 1849, the infamous **Astor Place Riot** broke out by the Opera House. Today the reason seems bizarre—tens of thousands of people caught up in a rivalry between two actors playing Macbeth. However, one was English—William Charles Macready—and the other was American—Edwin Forrest. The rivalry triggered popular unrest in a period when anti-British sentiments existed in many communities. Around 10,000 people came here to demonstrate (Macready was performing in Macbeth at the Opera House) and violence broke out.

The walk ends here at Astor Place subway station.

6 WEST VILLAGE WALK

START AND FINISH: "The Cage,"
West 4th Street Court
SUBWAY STATION: W4 St/Wash Sq Ⓐ, Ⓑ,
Ⓒ Ⓓ Ⓔ Ⓕ Ⓜ

WEST VILLAGE

Distance: 3.4 Miles

This walk concentrates on the West Village, and also part of Greenwich Village. Exit the subway onto Sixth Avenue (also known as Avenue of the Americas).

The first thing to stop at is ❶ **"The Cage,"** the legendary West 4th Street Courts. It doesn't look like anything special, but is renowned for the physical style of street basketball—or streetball—played here. It also hosts a popular streetball tournament.

On the other side of Sixth Avenue, opposite The Cage, is ❷ the **IFC Center**, an art-house movie theater. Constructed in 1807, it was originally a Dutch church, and in the 1930s became The Waverly Theater. The Waverly was part of the bohemian, artistic scene that the Village has long been known for.

It even gets a namecheck in the song "Frank Mills" from the

musical *Hair*, that premiered off-Broadway in 1967 and centers around a hippy "tribe" in New York. This is also where the first midnight, interactive showings of *The Rocky Horror Picture Show* began in 1976, and so much fun was had that similar events began to take place at other theaters in New York, and then around the world.

On the north side of The Cage, cut through ❸ **Golden Swan Garden**. A ground-level foundation

stone dates it to 1937, and includes the names of two legendary city figures—Mayor Fiorello La Guardia, and Commissioner Robert Moses. The Garden is not much to look at, but it is named after an old Irish dive bar called the Golden Swan that stood nearby. In the early 1900s this tavern was the haunt of artists, writers, anarchists, prostitutes, gangsters and bohemians and became so notorious it was known as the Hell Hole. Eugene O'Neill drank there and his experiences directly influenced the characters of his play *The Iceman Cometh* that center around Harry Hope's saloon.

From the Garden, turn onto West 4th Street to see ❹ the **Washington Square Diner**. Bohemian favorite The Mad Hatter Tearoom stood here in the early 20th century, and from 1945 to 1970 this was the Pony Stable Inn. The "Pony" was a lesbian bar and an important site in LBGTQ history. Beat poet Gregory Corso worked here in the early 1950s, and was visited by Jack Kerouac and Allen Ginsberg, among others.

Retrace your steps and cross over Sixth Avenue, looking for ❺ the sign for **Cuba** up high. In 1945 Mayor La Guardia sponsored the re-naming of Sixth Avenue as the Avenue of the Americas in order

to express Pan-American unity. In 1959 medallions bearing the coat of arms of Western Hemisphere nations were added to 300 lampposts along the Avenue. Most were removed in the 1990s, however, Cuba has survived—surprising given the difficult relations between the US and Cuba during the Castro era. The coat of arms you see for Cuba was adopted in 1906, and the key represents Cuba's position between the two Americas.

Head down the other side of West 4th Street, stopping first at ❻ **No. 161** on the right. In December 1961 Bob Dylan moved here—his first rented apartment—with his girlfriend Suze Rotolo. Until then, he had been couch surfing and staying in a local hotel since arriving in New York, so it was the beginning of some stability in his life. Suze was a major influence on Dylan during their three-year relationship, and she was politically active. A number of his songs were written about Suze but their relationship faltered after Dylan shot to fame.

In February 1963, CBS staff photographer Don Hunstein spent time with Dylan and Rotolo taking publicity photos. You can see online photos of the couple standing on the snowy sidewalk near these steps.

Continue on to Jones Street on your left. This ❼ is where Dylan and Rotolo linked arms in the freezing cold and walked down Jones Street towards West 4th Street while Hunstein took photographs. The couple had just gotten back together again after a seven month break, so perhaps they were clinging to each other for reasons other than the temperature. One shot was selected for what would become the iconic **cover of *The Freewheelin' Bob Dylan*** (1963). This was Dylan's second studio album, and the one that propelled him from the Village folk scene into an international star and, many years later, the Nobel Prize for Literature.

Keep walking along West 4th Street to reach Sheridan Square on the right. Dylan's famous song "Positively 4th Street" (1965) is thought to have been inspired by this street, and is a bitter critique of his old Village folk friends that had turned on him.

Nos. 1 and 2 ❽, today occupied by the Axis Theater Company, was the **site of the Café Society** nightclub that ran for a decade from 1938. It was the first racially integrated club in the country. Billie Holiday sang "Strange Fruit" there for the first time. John Hammond, the record producer who helped the careers of Holiday, Dylan, Aretha Franklin, and countless others, had a role here in picking acts. In around 1961, Bob Dylan was just one of many folk singers who stayed with Miki Isaacson on the fourth floor, and was also when he first met Suze Rotolo, who lived with her mother and sister on the third floor.

The Square ❾ (really a triangle) was named in 1896 after General Philip **Sheridan** (1831-1888), a leading military commander

during the Civil War. Years before, the land here had been a trading post of the Sapokanikan Indians before being paved over in 1830. A grumpy-looking Bob Dylan was photographed sitting on a bench in the park on January 22, 1965, by Fred W. McDarrah.

Walk round to ⑩ Ten Sheridan Square, also known as **The Shenandoah**. This fine 14-story building dates from 1929 and was designed by Emery Roth (1871-1948), a Hungarian and Jew whose family fled poverty to start a new life in the United States in the 1880s. Roth worked on some of New York's most outstanding apartment and hotel buildings of the early 20th century, including The San Remo, Ritz Tower, Warwick Hotel, and The Beresford. Get close up at street level to admire the intricate architectural details and sculptures. Shenandoah comes from an Algonquian Indian word for stream or great plain.

Bear left around the edge of the Square and Chase Bank onto Grove Street, stopping at ⓫ the Starbucks at 72 Grove Street. This building dates from 1842. In the 1930s this was **Jack Delaney's Restaurant**, popular with writers and artists in the Village. In 1939 the young Jack Kerouac was brought here by his father, "little knowing how much time I was destined to spend around that square, in Greenwich Village, in darker years, but tenderer years to come."

Greenwich Village was first farmed by the Dutch, including tobacco. It developed into a country hamlet, recorded in 1713 as "Grin'wich," and parts were settled by African Americans (known as "Little Africa" long ago). As marshland was drained, residential streets were laid out. The Village's population grew as many fled here to escape cholera and yellow fever downtown in the 1790s-1820s. The development of Washington Square, and the arrival of New York University in the mid-19th century heralded more change.

Next door to the Starbucks is 70 Grove Street, an odd-looking building. This is because it was brutally cut in half when construction work took place from 1913 to extend Seventh Avenue south to Varick Street. Several

other buildings were demolished as the road was widened. Hard to imagine today, but this street was named in 1829 after the poplar trees once found here.

Retrace your steps down West 4th Street (with Chase bank on your right) and then turn right onto Barrow Street, named for Thomas Barrow, an artist and vestryman of Trinity Church from 1790 to 1820.

The  Barrow Street Ale House is on the left at **No. 15**. Dating from 1897, this building was originally a horse stable—look for the original horse pendant up high. The most memorable tenant was **Café Bohemia**, based here between 1955-60.

The first Miles Davis Quintet played here, and the cover photo of the Davis album *'Round About Midnight* (1957) was taken at the club. Other jazz legends who recorded live albums here include Charles Mingus (check out the album *Mingus at The Bohemia* (1955)) and Art Blakey (*Art Blakey & the Jazz Messengers at the Café Bohemia* (1955)).

From the 1940s, the Village became a favorite haunt of the Beats and Jack Kerouac, who came here regularly to pay homage to his jazz idols.

No. 17 next door dates from 1834. Horses used to walk through the large entrance you see today in order to access stables to the rear. There were also two neighboring houses like this, originally owned by the Cox brothers. They were carters, whose profession centered around horse-drawn transport. In 1897 it was owned by an Irish blacksmith named Michael Hallanan. He made a fortune from patenting a rubber pad used on horseshoes, and became known as the "Greenwich Village Blacksmith."

Continue down Barrow Street, looking for the ⓭ plaque outside No. 16 on the right which commemorates former resident and baseball legend **Hank Greenberg** (1911-1986). His family were Jewish immigrants from Romania who settled in the Village. Greenberg had to battle anti-Semitism throughout his career, perhaps explaining why he was one of the few players to support Jackie Robinson when the latter became the first African-American to join the major leagues. At the height of his career, Greenberg left behind a $55,000 a year salary to sign up for the army during World War II. He served 47 months in the army—more than any other baseball player at the time.

Carry on down Barrow Street, stopping at ⓮ **Greenwich House** at No. 22 on the left. It was established in 1902 to help immigrants new to the city, and was known as a "Settlement House." Art and education were a key focus, and notable figures such as Jackson Pollock and Eleanor Roosevelt were supporters of Greenwich House. Today it runs a theater, pottery classes, and a nursery school among other activities, and is still helping the local community. The young Robert De Niro went to the nursery school attached to Greenwich House.

Walk on, crossing over Seventh Avenue and Bleecker Street to continue down Barrow Street, which is lined with stunning early 19th century houses. One example ⓯ is **No. 39** on the left, which dates

from 1828. This used to be called **Reason Street** in honor of the book *The Age of Reason* (1794) by one-time Village resident and Englishman Thomas Paine (he lived at what is today 309 Bleecker Street, and died—penniless—at 59 Grove Street on June 8, 1809). Paine's writings were enormously important to the American Revolution, but as an atheist, he was not approved of in many quarters including local landowner Trinity Church. They dropped Reason Street for Barrow Street. Personally, I think it should be renamed Reason Street in honor of Paine's often overlooked contribution to the birth of the United States.

Paine could never have imagined in his final days of poverty that houses along here and nearby streets could be valued at $12 million and more. Many were built in the early and mid-1800s by developers cashing in on the panic felt by wealthy resi-

dents downtown who wanted to get away from densely populated streets afflicted by cholera and yellow fever.

Near the end of **Barrow Street** on the right ⑯ is **No. 56**, dating from 1889. It is shorter than many of the other buildings, explained by the fact it was originally a horse livery stable, and not a townhouse.

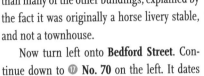

Now turn left onto **Bedford Street**. Continue down to ⑰ **No. 70** on the left. It dates from 1807 and was constructed for sailmaker and court officer John P. Roome (there is a plaque).

Almost opposite, at **No. 69**, is ⑱ where the fabled Beat writer William Burroughs (1914-1997) lived from 1943, a decade before writing his best known works *Junkie* and *Naked Lunch*. During this period he was close to Lucien Carr and Dave Kammerer (the latter lived at 48 Morton Street nearby), and they often visited Chumley's together (seen shortly). Carr is less well-known today, but he is most notable for having introduced Burroughs to Kerouac and Ginsberg, the three key figures at the heart of the Beat movement.

It was during this period in the 1940s that the core of the Beat Generation formed, with Burroughs exploring the city's underbelly with new friends such as Carr, Allen Ginsberg and Jack Kerouac. However, tragedy struck in 1944 when Carr, fighting off a sexual assault from Kammerer, stabbed Kammerer to death in Riverside Park. Carr went to Burroughs and Kerouac for help, and their involvement dragged them into what became a sensational murder case that led to Carr being convicted of second-degree manslaughter.

Walk back up Bedford Street looking out for ⑲ **Nos. 75 ½ and 77** on the left. The first is the narrowest house in the city—just 9 ½ feet wide. Poet Edna St. Vincent Millay lived here in the early 1920s. Next door at No. 77 is the Isaacs-Hendricks house, built in 1799 and the oldest building in Greenwich Village. It used to be a farmhouse owned by Harmon Hendricks. In 1989 it was purchased by **Jacqueline Thion de la Chaume, wife of actor Yul Brynner.**

When researching this book, I had a conversation with two elderly gentlemen outside here. They were despairing of the rising real estate prices and how speculators were "flipping" houses on the street to make a buck. Then one told me he had lived in the area for several decades and owned a 16-bedroom house (he had combined three apartments together) and the other gentleman walked back to

his six-bedroom house around the corner. It struck me as a very "Village" conversation.

Turn left onto **Commerce Street**, heading down to ⑳ **The Cherry Lane Theater** at **No. 38.** This was founded in 1923 and is the oldest continuously running off-Broadway theater. The building dates from 1817, originally a farm silo, and another reminder that the Village was actually once a real rural village. The theater has always had a reputation for the avant-garde. One notable event took place on March 2, 1952 and was called *An Evening of Bohemian Theatre.* Performances included

Pablo Picasso's play *Desire Caught by the Tail,* and plays by T.S. Eliot and Gertrude Stein. The theater was also the location for the premiere of plays by figures such as Samuel Beckett and Sam Shepard.

Retrace your steps to Bedford Street and turn left. It is most likely named after Bedford Street in London, itself named after the Duke of Bedford. Bedford is a town about 50 miles north of London and Andrew Russell (b. 1962), the 15th and current Duke of Bedford, studied at Harvard.

Shorty on the right at **No. 86** is the **site of** ㉑ **Chumley's.** This was originally a blacksmiths, then in the 1920s Leland Stanford Chumley opened a bar and restaurant that was completely anonymous from the outside (the entrance was through a courtyard on Barrow Street). It became a legendary haunt during Prohibition, and frequented by countless Village types including John Steinbeck, Eugene O'Neill, Edna St. Vincent Millay, e.e. cummings, Norman Mailer, all the Beats and William Faulkner. With all this socializing, it is hard to imagine when all

the plays, poems and books were actually written. The term "86 it"—or make a swift exit—is said to have come from patrons rushing out to avoid the raids by Prohibition officers.

A little farther up on the left at **No. 95** ㉒ look for the sign for "J.Gobel & Co.—Est. 1865." This was used as a horse stable by the firm.

Continue on to reach Grove Street. At the intersection, look up ㉓ to your right to see the much-photographed No. **90 Bedford Street**. Why? This was used for the exterior shot of the apartments where Monica, Rachel, Joey and Chandler lived in the hit-series *Friends*.

Cross over, passing No. **17 Grove Street** ㉔, to see an unusual and rare clapboard-style house on the corner. It was built for a window-sash maker named William Hyde and dates from 1822. It was valued at $100 in the 1820s and listed for sale for $12 million in 2019. The third story was added in 1870. There is, it is rumored, a secret tunnel underground that connects this property with Chumley's.

Turn left onto Grove Street, where after the third house on the left you see ㉕ the discreet gate leading to **Grove Court**. If I were forced to live in the Village, this would be one of my top picks. If you peek through here you can see houses dating from the early 1850s and Grove Court was first laid out in 1848. In the early 1900s, Grove Court was dominated by Irish working-class families and known as Pig's Alley. There was even a local gang called the Pig's Alley Gorillas. This was the setting for "The Last Leaf" (1907)—a short story by O. Henry about a young female artist dying of pneumonia and watching the leaves on a nearby ivy creeper (don't worry, she survives).

Retrace your steps and continue along Bedford Street to ㉖ the Twin Peaks building on the right at **No. 102**. This was originally a row house of 1830 that was radically redesigned in 1925. Its highly unusual Swiss Chalet style appearance seems to embody the quirky, Bohemian reputation the Village had at the time. Silent film star Mabel Normand (1893-1930), who starred alongside Charlie Chaplin and "Fatty"

Arbuckle in many films, smashed a bottle of champagne against a gable in the opening ceremony. Some have suggested Walt Disney lived here but there is no evidence to support this.

Continue up to reach **Christopher Street**, named for Charles Christopher Amos who owned the land around here (hence Charles Street nearby). To your right ㉗ at **No. 121** is **The Lucille Lortel Theatre**, an off-Broadway Playhouse that has been running since 1955. It was known as the Theatre De Lys until 1981.

In the early 1960s, Bob Dylan came here to see Bertolt Brecht's *The Threepenny Opera*, with his girlfriend, Suze Rotolo, working on the production. The production had a big impact on Dylan, particularly the song "Pirate Jenny," which Dylan would credit with inspiring his own songwriting. He would later recall in his memoir, *Chronicles Volume 1*, "I'd think about this later in my dumpy apartment. I hadn't done anything yet, wasn't any kind of songwriter but I'd become rightly impressed by the physical and ideological possibilities within the confines of the lyric and melody."

The building began as a cinema in 1926 and was later bought by a wealthy financier for his wife, Lucille Lortel (1900-1999). The daughter of Jewish immigrants from Poland, Lortel became a stage actress and appeared in some early silent films. She later became a theatrical producer and director and owned this theater.

Now turn left onto Christopher Street, then right up Hudson Street. On the left at Nos. **509-511 Hudson Street** is ㉘ a fine building from around 1820 when the Village was being transformed from a rural hamlet into a new fashionable suburb. As a rule of thumb, if you see a brick building that is two or two-and-half stories high, it is old—often from the first half of the 19th century. New York's buildings got steadily taller as the need for space became greater, and construction techniques and materials improved.

Continue up Hudson Street, passing ㉙ **No. 521**. In the mid-1940s, this was the childhood home of Robert De Niro. He moved here with his artist mother Virginia Admiral after she separated from his father, the painter Robert De Niro Sr. The future actor grew up in an artistic, bohemian environment, his parents mixing with figures such as Anaïs Nin, Henry Miller and Tennessee Williams.

Continue up Hudson Street. This stretch was home to many other notable people over the years. You pass Charles Street where photographer Diane Arbus lived for nine years at No. 131, then Perry Street where anti-corruption cop Frank Serpico lived at No. 116.

You pass on the left ③⓪ No. **555 Hudson**, home to Jane Jacobs (1916-2006). She lived here from 1947-1968, and during this time wrote her best known work *The Death and Life of Great American Cities* (1961). She is credited with helping change how many people saw their urban environment and led the fight against developers and officials such as Robert Moses who wanted to tear down great swaths of the city in the name of "improvement." She chose a nice place to live—a rowhouse dating from 1842.

Continue on to reach ③① the fabled **White Horse Tavern**. If you are interested in the Village's literary and musical connections, you simply must pay homage with a drink here. You will be following in the sometimes unsteady footsteps of Jane Jacobs, James Baldwin, Jack Kerouac, Dylan Thomas, Allen Ginsberg, Bob Dylan, Jim Morrison, Norman Mailer, and Hunter S. Thompson.

The tavern opened in 1880, and was a speakeasy during Prohibition and a haunt for sailors and longshoremen working on nearby docks and piers along the Hudson River. But it was the people who came here in the 1950s to 1960s that made it known throughout the world. Welsh poet Dylan Thomas started coming here in 1952. On November 4, 1953, he claimed to have drunk 18 straight whiskeys, before returning to the Chelsea Hotel and then back to the White Horse where, shortly after and desperately ill, he was injected with morphine by a quack doctor before going into a coma. He died on November 9. He was 39.

On the same side as the Tavern, turn left onto West 11th Street, then right up Greenwich Street. When you reach **Bank Street** turn left a short way to where ㉜ **John Lennon and Yoko Ono** lived in a modest apartment at **No. 105** between 1971-73. The couple rented the apartment from Joe Butler, a member of The Lovin' Spoonful, and Lennon released his album *Some Time in New York City* (1972) while living here. It was after a robbery here that the couple, fearful of their safety, moved to The Dakota. The sad irony is that The Dakota is where Lennon would be murdered as he walked out of the building one day in 1980.

The couple, under surveillance from the FBI, regularly went next door to No. 107 to use the phone at avant-garde composer John Cage's house. Lennon once said, "I should have been born in New York, I should have been born in the Village, that's where I belong." While living here, Lennon had visitors such as activists Abbie Hoffman and Jerry Rubin. As word spread that he lived here, fans began to turn up. One was Jesus. When Lennon asked his assistant to clarify, he was told it was "Jesus from Toronto," to which the former Beatle replied "We don't know that one."

Turn left onto Bank Street, named in the early 1800s for the Bank of New York and another bank that moved here to avoid quarantine rules being imposed in lower Manhattan because of yellow fever. On the left at ㉝ is **HB Studio**, a respected acting school founded in 1945 by Austrian Herbert Berghof, who came to the city in 1939 to escape Nazi oppression.

Alumni include Al Pacino, Sarah Jessica Parker, Christopher Reeve, Barbra Streisand, Steve McQueen, Whoopi Goldberg, Sigourney Weaver and Robert De Niro.

Continue along Bank Street to reach the intersection of Washington Street. On the northwest corner is ㉞ the **Westbeth Artists Housing complex**. This incredible site, originally comprised of 13 buildings, was constructed for Western Electric in 1868, and was later taken over by Bell Laboratories in the late 1890s. Demonstrations were held here of the first talking film, the binary computer, TV broadcasts and the condenser microphone. Today it is hard to imagine the hyper-gentrified Village being the site of the biggest industrial research complex in the country, but for many years that was the case. Scientists at Bell Labs were also involved in secret research for the Manhattan Project that produced the first atomic bombs.

Bell stayed here until 1966. The empty buildings were then turned into live-work spaces for hundreds of artists and opened in 1970. It later incorporated performance and rehearsal spaces, and became home to a number of cultural organizations. The photographer Bob Gruen was a Westbeth resident and good friends with John Lennon and Yoko Ono. In June 1975 Lennon came looking for Gruen's studio at Westbeth and got lost inside the complex. He was approached by numerous artists living there looking for Lennon's input and when he eventually found Gruen's apartment he remarked, "Man, you've got some weird neighbors." Gruen took some of the most iconic shots of Lennon, including the one in which he wears a t-shirt that says "New York City," taken on the terrace of Lennon's East 52nd Street apartment.

Notable residents include Diane Arbus (she committed suicide at Westbeth in 1971), actor Vin Diesel, artist Robert De Niro Sr., and jazz musician Gil Evans. If you look up to the second floor you can see part of the old High Line elevated railway, a larger section of which is now a major city attraction.

Now return back the way you came along Bank Street, crossing over Greenwich Street, to reach Hudson Street again. Bear left, with the Bleecker Playground on your right, then bear right to Bleecker Street. There is ㉟ a striking Art Deco building overlooking the playground.

This is **Abingdon Court** (the address is 75 Bank Street). In the early 1940s, the teenage Betty Bacall (1924-2014) moved here with her mother Natalie. In 1941 she attended a nearby acting school and dated classmate Kirk Douglas. In 1942 Betty was crowned "Miss Greenwich Village," and chosen to participate in the "Miss America" beauty contest. Her career moved very quickly—by 1944, at age 19, she was starring with Humphrey Bogart in *To Have and Have Not*.

Now called Lauren Bacall, she would marry Bogart, and star in other classics such as *The Big Sleep*, *Key Largo* and *How to Marry a Millionaire*. She also had a relationship with Frank Sinatra.

Proceed eastward along Bank Street. On the left at **No. 63** is ③, where English Sex Pistols bassist Sid Vicious died of a heroin overdose on February 2, 1979. He was on bail after being charged with the murder of his girlfriend Nancy Spungen at the Chelsea Hotel on October 2, 1978. The former Sex Pistol was 21 when he died, Spungen just 20.

Other notable people who have lived on Bank Street include rock star Mark Knopfler, Jon Dos Passos (best known for *The 42nd Parallel*), Ezra Pound, Patricia Highsmith, politician Bella Abzug, and John Cheever. Recently houses on Bank Street have been valued in excess of $20 million. If you want to know more, check out *Growing Up Bank Street: A Greenwich Village Memoir*, by Bank Street resident Donna Florio. Just a few hundred yards from here on West 12th Street is a townhouse reported to have been purchased in 2015 by Facebook's Mark Zuckerberg for over $22 million.

Now turn right onto Waverly Place. Full of lovely homes, this used to be the very-cool

Bank Street

sounding Art Place, but in 1833 it was named after Scottish writer Sir Walter Scott's once hugely popular series of historical novels (actually spelled *Waverley* and first published in 1814). Regarded as the first historical novels, *Waverley* achieved a success similar to the Harry Potter books of today. About a dozen towns in places from Ohio, Florida and Alabama are also named after the work. No one is sure why Americans dropped the "e" in Waverley, but it is certain that the hero of Scott's first novel was Edward Waverley, an Englishman. This is ironic given the authorities of New York did their best to change the names of pre-Revolutionary era streets with an English connection.

Waverly Place is so cool that the character Don Draper from the series *Mad Men* has an apartment here. He lived at 104 Waverly Place (as seen on a check in one episode). It is also where young wizards lived in the hit sitcom *Wizards of Waverly Place* (2007-2012) that starred Selena Gomez.

On the right (after crossing West 11th Street) you pass ❸❼ **St. John's in the Village Episcopal Church**, and the 99-seater off-Broadway **Rattlestick Theater** at 224 Waverly Place.

At the bottom you reach Perry Street, named for Oliver Perry (1785-1819), a naval commander. It is not visited on this walk, but *Sex and the City* fans might want to visit Carrie Bradshaw's apartment (the exteriors of No. 64 then No. 66 Perry Street were used in the show, but the interior was filmed on a set in Silvercup Studios in Long Island City, Queens). Other residents of Perry Street have included Norman Mailer and Henry Miller.

At the corner of Waverly Place and Perry Street is what must be the city's thinnest building, and just beside it ❸ at 178 Seventh Avenue is the **Village Vanguard**, a jazz venue that opened in 1935. All the great jazz artists have played here, as well as Woody Allen, Woody Guthrie, Lead Belly, and Barbra Streisand. Many live albums have been recorded here, including *Live at the Village Vanguard* by the John Coltrane Quartet in 1961.

Now continue down Seventh Avenue South and turn right on Charles Street. Walk along to **No. 53**, ❹ the home of the **Congregation Darech Amuno** (also known as The Greenwich Village Synagogue). The congregation was founded in 1838 and was located in various places before converting the brownstone here into a place of worship. Services began here in 1917. After World War II the congregation was joined by survivors of the Holocaust, including Nathan Steiman who was one of 1,200 Jews saved by Nazi Party member Oskar Schindler (immortalized

in Thomas Keneally's book *Schindler's Ark* (1982) and Spielberg's film *Schindler's List* (1993). For many years, the Andy Statman Trio and guests have played Klezmer and Bluegrass music here each Thursday.

Folk legend **Woody Guthrie** (1912-1967) ❺ lived at **No. 74** on **Charles Street** in the early 1940s. In 1954 he wrote a song called "Old Man Trump." It was not recorded by Guthrie and includes the lines:

"I suppose Old Man Trump knows Just how much Racial Hate He stirred up."

Old Man Trump was Fred Trump (1905-1999), father of President Donald Trump. Real estate man Trump Sr. was accused of discriminating against non-white tenants in his rental buildings, and Guthrie lived in a Trump apartment complex in 1950.

Now retrace your steps and turn right down **West 4th Street**. At ⑪ **No. 228** on the right, stop to admire the extravagant decorative art on the façade of this building that dates from around 1899. Look for the spread-eagles and bearded faces. This tenement was built to attract working-class residents in the Village.

Continue on to Christopher Street where you turn left onto **Stonewall Place**. Walk a little farther along until you shortly see on the left at **No. 53** ⑫ the **Stonewall Inn**. Today, this is the most famous gay bar in the world, all because of what happened here between June 28 to July 3, 1969, when the gay community fought back against police oppression. A police raid triggered the Stonewall riots, and the anniversary of the event would lead to the first gay pride marches in US cities in 1970.

The Stonewall riots would change the gay liberation movement forever, and there are related monuments in Christopher Park

opposite. Confusingly there is also a statue of General Sheridan, placed here rather than in nearby Sheridan Square. The Mafia used to own the Stonewall Inn, and musician Lou Reed lived above the inn in the early 1970s after leaving the Velvet Underground. He lived here with Rachel Humphreys, his partner who he met performing as a drag queen in the Village's 82 Club. The Inn occupies what were originally horse livery stables built in the mid-19th century.

Continue along what is now Christopher Street to stop outside ⓭ the **Northern Dispensary**, a sturdy-looking building from 1831. As the Village became transformed into a residential district in the early 19th century, many people such as tradesmen moved here without the means to afford medical care. It was called "Northern" because when it was built this was as far as residential Manhattan went. Local doctors proposed a free medical clinic to address the problem.

The original building was only two stories, but demand for services resulted in an extra story being added in 1855 (look for the different color of brick). The clinic finally closed in 1989 after controversy erupted over its approach to treating HIV patients.

Continue along **Christopher Street**, full of charming properties such as  **No. 18** on the right-hand side that dates from 1915.

Turn right onto narrow, winding Gay Street. Perhaps surprisingly, the name has no connections to the LGBTQ community, but was named for a Colonial-era family who owned land or lived here. Up until the early 20th century there were many African-Americans living here, including two artists named Hawkins and Collins who exhibited their work at their home at 11 Gay Street in 1903.

This charming thoroughfare has attracted video makers, and videos for Cyndi Lauper ("Girls Just Want to Have Fun") and Sheryl Crow ("A Change Would Do You Good") include scenes shot here.

While Gay Street seems very quiet today, it has many secrets. **No. 13** on the left-hand side was  **home to William Kunstler** (1919-1995), one of the most high-profile and controversial civil rights lawyers in American history. He defended the Chicago Seven in 1969-70, and other clients include Jack Ruby, the Black Panthers and the Weather Underground group. He was portrayed by British actor Sir Mark Rylance in the film *The Trial of the Chicago 7* (2020).

Gay Street

Pulp fiction writer **Walter Gibson** (1897-1985) lived at No. ㊻ **12 Gay Street**, and believed it was haunted (it is a stop on ghost tours today). It is said to have inspired his enormously successful series *The Shadow*. Orson Wells played the character in the radio adaptation in the 1930s.

The house was also home to Howdy Doody puppeteer Frank Paris, and in the 1920s to the Pirate's Den speakeasy. This was connected to Jimmy Walker, corrupt mayor of the city from 1926 to 1932, who housed mistress and actress Betty Compton here. In October 2021 the house was raided by the FBI because it was linked to multi-billionaire oligarch Oleg Deripaska, once the richest man in Russia.

At the end of Gay Street turn left, along Waverly Place, and then left up Sixth Avenue. Turn right onto **West 8th Street** and stop at ㊼ the **Electric Lady Studios** at **No. 52** on the right. Jimi Hendrix used to play at a club at this location, and in 1968 bought the building and converted it into a music studio. The opening party in 1970 was attended by Patti Smith, Ron Wood and Eric Clapton. After Hendrix's death, the studios carried on, and many great artists have recorded here including David Bowie, Stevie Wonder, The Rolling Stones, Led Zeppelin, Adele and Daft Punk.

Go back to Sixth Avenue and continue up, passing **Jefferson Market Garden** 48 on the left. This tranquil place is worth a stop. A Women's House of Detention was built on the site in 1932 before being pulled down in the 1970s. One inmate was radical feminist Valerie Solanas who, in June 1968, entered The Factory and shot Andy Warhol three times. He survived but the near-death experience affected him profoundly.

Just after the Garden is 49 **Jefferson Market Library**, a local landmark dating from the 1870s. It was originally a courthouse, in use until 1945. Since 1967 it has been used as a library.

Past the Library, turn left onto West 10th Street, then take the next right to stop at the gated entrance to 50 **Patchin Place**. In the early 20th century this short, residential street was home to many famous Village artists and writers, including e.e cummings, John Reed and Louise Bryant, where they worked on *Ten Days that Shook the World*, Djuna Barnes, and—for a short while in 1943—Marlon Brando.

Retrace your steps, continuing up Sixth Avenue, then right onto West 11th Street. At  **No. 72** on the right is the historic **Second Cemetery of the Spanish and Portuguese Synagogue**. It traces its origins to the first 23 Jews, mainly of Spanish and Portuguese heritage, who arrived in New Amsterdam in 1654.

Walk along **West 11th Street**. The Irish writer and bohemian  Oscar Wilde (1854-1900) stayed at **No. 48** on the right-hand side in 1882 after a triumphant one-year-long lecture tour of the country. During his short career, he achieved great fame for his plays such as *The Importance of Being Earnest* and the novel *The Picture of Dorian Grey*.

Continue on to  **No. 18** on the same side. One of the strangest events in Village history took place here on March 6, 1970, when members of the radical terrorist group the Weather Underground (or Weathermen) accidently blew up the building as they were making bombs in the basement. Three members of the group were killed, and Kathy Boudin and Cathy Wilkerson escaped and ran away. The house was owned by Wilkerson's parents who were away at the time. At the time of the bombing, actor Dustin Hoffman was living at No. 16 with his family.

Soon you reach Fifth Avenue where you turn right, passing on the right **West 10th Street**. Walk down a short way where on the left ❺❹ at **No. 14** you find the property where **Mark Twain** lived in 1900-1901. It is known as the "House of Death" because so many deaths and supernatural events have been recorded at the site, including sightings of Twain's ghost.

Retrace your steps to Fifth Avenue, flanked by tall apartment blocks that seem very impersonal compared to the much more modestly sized early 19th century houses you have seen so far in the Village.

Next, take a right down **West 8th Street** to ❺❺ **The Marlton Hotel** at **No. 5**. This striking building dates from 1900 and was home to many of the Village's bohemian characters over the decades. Most notably, Jack Kerouac wrote the novellas *The Subterraneans* and *Tristessa* here. Others who have lived here include actors Julie Andrews, Mickey Rourke, Maggie Smith, John Barrymore and Lillian Gish, and Beats Gregory Corso, and Neal Cassady. Valerie Solanas, who shot Warhol, was staying here at the time of the attack.

Washington Square

Return to Fifth Avenue and continue down to reach Washington Square Park, the spiritual home of Greenwich Village. Many of the people mentioned so far, from Bob Dylan to David Bowie and the Beasts, have spent time in this park so I suggest you do the same.

When finished, you can exit and walk down MacDougal Street and then right onto West 3rd Street to return to Sixth Avenue and the start of the walk.

7 CHELSEA WALK

START AND FINISH: Intersection of 23rd Street and Sixth Avenue

SUBWAY STATION: 23 St Ⓕ, Ⓜ

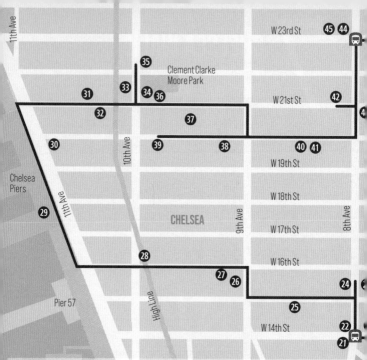

1. **Poster House**

2. **Site of Catholic Church of Saint Vincent De Paul**

3. **Traffic Cafeteria Site**

4. **Third Cemetery of the Spanish and Portuguese Synagogue**

5. **O'Neill Building**

6. **Adams Dry Goods**

7. **Former Episcopal Church of the Holy Communion**

8. **Kleinfeld Bridal**

9. **Chelsea Green**

10. **Engine 3, Ladder Company 12**

11. **Site of Siegel-Cooper**

12. **Iglesia Pentecostal Monte De Sion**

13. **The Rubin Museum of Art**

14. **The Donut Pub**

15. **219 West 14th Street - De Niro**

16. **Int'l Brotherhood of Teamsters**

17. **Former Roman Catholic Church of Our Lady of Guadalupe**

18. **La Nacional**

W 22nd St

W 20th St

7th Ave

6th Ave

W 15th St

CHELSEA

Distance: 3.6 Miles

From the subway, cross and continue westward along West 23rd Street. Chelsea in the early 21st century is known for its art galleries, historic residential streets, and being a neighborhood favored by the gay community. However, much of what you see today is relatively new—there was very little here before the mid-19th century. Sixth Avenue is the eastern boundary of Chelsea, the other edges being the Hudson River (west), West 14th Street (south), and 30th Street (north).

The modern era really began with a farm owned in the 18th century by Jacob Somerindyck and his wife. It was acquired in 1750 by Thomas Clarke, a British ex-army captain who renamed his landholding "Chelsea" after the district of London and specifically the Royal Hospital Chelsea established by King Charles II for military veterans.

The hospital is still going strong today. Charles II's brother was James, Duke of York, after whom New York was named.

The first stop is ❶ on the right at **No. 119**—the **Poster House**, the first museum in the country dedicated to the history of posters. The contribution of posters to art and popular culture is often overlooked, so is worth a visit. It is housed in a striking ten-story building dating from 1901. This area became an important theater

district after the Civil War, although this shifted north to Times Square in later years. By the time this building was constructed, this was a largely commercial area and this building was home to the National Cloak Company that provided tailoring services for the wealthier class of New York women.

Next door 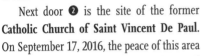 is the site of the former **Catholic Church of Saint Vincent De Paul**. On September 17, 2016, the peace of this area was disturbed at 8:31 p.m. by the explosion of a pressure-cooker bomb planted by Ahmad Khan Rahimi (b. 1988). Thirty-one people were injured. The shrapnel bomb was placed in a container in front of No. 133. Rahimi, working alone, was later imprisoned for life for this and other explosions in Manhattan and New Jersey, which caused mayhem in September 2016. The Church was one of a number of buildings damaged by the explosion.

This church has a French connection as it was founded by the Society of the Fathers of Mercy, a organization of French Catholics eager to provide somewhere for their congregation to worship (and prevent them from attending French Protestant churches in the city).

The parish was founded in 1841 and was surprisingly liberal for its day, with integrated services at which African-Americans were encouraged to participate. This church building dates from 1869, an era when this part of Chelsea was home to several French institutions and many French-speaking residents. On June 6, 1944, over a thousand French exiles and French soldiers attended a mass to pray for the success of the D-Day landing that had begun earlier that same day in Normandy.

In 1952 another French-German connected event took place here—the marriage of the French singers Edith Piaf and Jacques Pills. Marlene Dietrich served as the maid of honor. In 1959 Pills came in last place in the Eurovision Song Contest. The following year, his daughter Jacqueline Boyer was the winner. Sadly, the church was closed in recent years and at the time of writing, stands empty, a relic of the city's French heritage.

Carry on down West 23rd Street, stopping outside **No. 163** on the right-hand side. Look ❸ for the sign reading "Traffic Building." This is another relic, this time of the **Traffic Cafeteria** that was one of many low-cost automats and cafeterias used by ordinary New Yorkers in the past that have largely disappeared. The building dates from the late 1920s, an elegant construction with a sophisticated brick and terra cotta design. The Traffic Cafeteria was plagued by labor unrest and mob intimidation and closed by the early 1940s.

Carry on, turning left down Seventh Avenue and continuing down before turning left onto West 21st Street.

Walk down West 21st Street to reach, on the right, ❹ the historic **Third Cemetery of the Spanish and Portuguese Synagogue**. Its history goes back to the foundation of the Congregation Shearith Israel, the first Jewish congregation in the country. Twenty-three Jews arrived in New Amsterdam in 1654, and

Congregation Shearith Israel can trace itself back to these first arrivals. In later years the congregation moved its burial ground as New York expanded northwards. This was the third cemetery used from 1829 until burials were banned in Manhattan below 86th Street in 1851. Burials then moved to the Beth Olam Cemetery in Queens, still in use today. Shearith Israel was very influential in the early history of the city's Jewish community as it was the only Jewish congregation in New York City from 1654 until 1825.

Follow the map and make a right onto Sixth Avenue, stopping to look **❺** at the historic **O'Neill Building** on the right. If you look up high, you can see the name "Hugh O'Neill" at the top. This was originally Hugh O'Neill's Dry Goods Store, and the cast-iron building was completed by 1895.

In the late 19th century, hundreds of department and other retail stores were built to attract wealthier consumers, and the concentration

was so great it later became known as The Ladies' Mile Historic District. The Historic District covers over 400 buildings between (approximately) 15th to 24th Streets. Like most other department stores nearby, this building was no longer used for its original purpose by World War I, as tastes changed.

O'Neill, like many department entrepreneurs, was an immigrant to New York. He arrived at age 14, having been born in Belfast in 1843. The original building was only four stories, and in the 1890s, the fifth story with two great domes was added. The original corner domes later disappeared and what you see today is a recent restoration. Why such large windows? When it was built, there was no electricity, so lots of natural light was required, and O'Neill also wanted passers-by traveling on the elevated railway (or El) to see what he was selling.

Next door is ❻ an equally grand building occupied by a branch of Trader Joe's. It was built initially for the **Adams Dry Goods department store** and dates from 1899. The timing was not good as within a few years the best department stores headed towards Fifth Avenue. The site was later taken over by the famous confectionery firm founded by Milton S. Hershey. This became the center of Hershey's chewing gum manufacturing business, but this new offering was never successful, and the plant closed in 1924.

Opposite the O'Neill Building ❼ is a former pretty neo-Gothic church with a strange history. **The Episcopal Church of the Holy Communion** was founded in the 1850s and designed by architect Richard Upjohn, also responsible for the current Trinity Church on Wall Street. It was popular with wealthy residents of Sixth Avenue, but its congregation declined in the second half of the 20th century, and it closed. It has since been used for a variety of purposes, including the Limelight nightclub, notorious for the hard-partying that took place here.

Andy Warhol was the host of the opening party in 1983 and it gained a legendary reputation, attracting celebrities and artists such as RuPaul, Madonna, Tupac, and Boy George. Author Frank Owen, an expert on the city's club history, described it as "a place where drag queens were shoving Christmas lights up their butt, people were having sex all over the place, it was like the last days of the Roman Empire." It later became associated with crime and drug dealing. One club night promoter was Michael Alig, a key member of the "Club Kids" who were prominent in the city's nightclub scene in the late 1980s and early 90s. Alig was convicted for the manslaughter (and dismemberment) of the alleged drug dealer and fellow Club Kid Andre "Angel" Melendez.

Now follow the map right up West 20th Street, passing first ❽ **Kleinfeld Bridal**. This famous

wedding dress business dates back to 1941 and even stars in its own long-running television series *Say Yes to the Dress* (first series 2007). Walk past this to stop (at 140), the site ❾ of **Chelsea Green**. This popular local space opened in 2019, the first new park in Chelsea for four decades. It is not to be confused with the model and professional wrestler Chelsea Green (b. 1991). The site of the park was once occupied by Grammar School No. 55. It opened in 1865 as more people arrived to live in Chelsea.

Continue along, then left down Seventh Avenue and left again onto West 19th Street. Walk a little way down where on the right ❿ is the base for **Engine 3**, **Ladder Company 12** of the 7th Battalion of the Fire Department of the City of New York (FDNY). Firefighters have been here since 1965. There are plaques outside commemorating those from the station who lost their lives on September 11, 2001. They were not the only ones to make a sacrifice. When I was shown around, I asked how many who attended on that terrible day were still working and the answer was none. Many had been badly affected by inhaling toxic dust and were forced to retire early.

Continue along. In the 1870s, a violent Irish Catholic group named The 19th Street Gang, led for a while by "Little Mike," were known for mugging people on the street, but were said to have been lenient to those intended victims who convinced them of their Catholic faith.

Soon you reach Sixth Avenue again. On the other side at **No. 620** is ⓫ another vast former department store opened by the **Siegel-Cooper** business that began in Chicago. Its New York expansion resulted in its second department store here, which opened in 1896. At the time, it was not only the largest department store in the Ladies' Mile Shopping District but the whole world.

It was also innovative in using a steel-frame structure. The Beaux-Arts design is the work of De Lemos & Cordes. It was almost a mini-city in its own right, employing 3,000 people and offering a gym, infirmary, dentist, theater, and enormous restaurant.

Now walk down a couple of blocks to West 17th Street and turn right. At **No. 120** ⓬, on the left is the **Iglesia Pentecostal Monte De Sion**—a Spanish-speaking congregation. You will learn more about Chelsea's Spanish heritage shortly.

Farther up on the same side is ⓭ **The Rubin Museum of Art**, unique in its promotion of the ideas, cultures, and art of Himalayan regions. It originated out of the private

collection of Shelley and Donald Rubin. After the museum opened in 2004, it was visited by His Holiness the Dalai Lama who blessed the museum and thanked the couple for preserving Himalayan art. Donald Rubin founded MultiPlan, Inc., a multi-billion dollar technology firm focussing on healthcare.

Follow the map, and turn left onto Seventh Avenue.

Walk for a couple of blocks, turning right onto West 14th Street. On the right is ❶ **The Donut Pub** at No. 203—a great place for a stop if you need a sugar-boost. Open since 1964, it was founded by Buzzy Geduld, a true tough Brooklyn-born legend. In the 1960s, Buzzy was laid off twice from Wall Street jobs so he turned his hand to the donut business. He ended up going back into finance, selling his brokerage business to Merrill Lynch for $920 million. At the time of writing, he is CEO of Cougar Capital and still comes here every Saturday to check on his Donut Pub. He said in 2015, "donuts taught me how to run a business. Running a donut shop is no different than running a brokerage."

Stop outside ❶ **No. 219**, which was where the young Robert De Niro lived with his mother Virginia in a two-bedroom apartment after she split from his father, Robert De Niro, Sr. Both of the future actor's parents were artists, and he was brought up in a bohemian circle that hugely influenced his own career choices. Virginia lived here until 1964, using a studio within the apartment for her art. After she moved out, her son Robert lived here into the early 1970s.

Opposite at 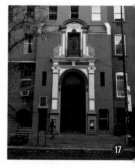 **No. 216** is a branch of the **International Brotherhood of Teamsters** (Local 237). It dates from 1952 and today has 24,000 members who are public employees in government agencies, libraries and schools. The young Robert De Niro no doubt looked across at this building without any idea he would one day portray real-life hitman Frank Sheeran, who claimed he killed Teamsters president Jimmy Hoffa. (De Niro played Sheeran in *The Irishman* (2019)).

Continue just past De Niro's old residence, and at **No. 229** is ⓲ the former **Roman Catholic Church of Our Lady of Guadalupe**, founded in 1902. It was the first church in the city to hold a mass in Latin and Spanish and part of an area (between Seventh and Eighth Avenues) that for decades was widely known as "Little Spain" on account of the Spanish, South American and Puerto Rican immigrants who settled here in the 19th and early 20th centuries. This became one of the city's first Hispanic communities, and if you want to know more, watch Arthur Balder's excellent documentary *Little Spain* (2011). Balder has said, "Almost no one knows that there was a 'Little Spain' in Manhattan, just like there's a 'Little Italy.' That's what's fascinating." Today, almost twenty percent of the

country's population is Hispanic, and the importance of this area to the community's history deserves to be better known. Beat legend Jack Kerouac used to attend mass in the church with poets Philip Lamantia and Howard Hart.

A little farther on at **No. 239** is ⑱ **La Nacional Spanish restaurant.** This is part of La Nacional-Spanish Benevolent Society, a cultural institution founded in 1869 to serve the Spanish community in the New York area. It is historically important because it is the oldest Spanish cultural institution in the country. For many years, it helped thousands of immigrants start their new lives in the United States. Visit this community-operated restaurant if you have time. It often provides accommodation for some of Spain's best chefs in return for their services.

In the past, this street would have been at the center of the fes-

tivities held during the Hispanic feast day of St. James in June (held into the mid 1990s). Over the last few years many of the nearby Hispanic residents and their shops and businesses have disappeared. Ironically, although De Niro is associated with Italian heritage, he grew up here, surrounded by Hispanic culture.

Next door ❶ **No. 241** is the **Andrew Norwood House**, a registered landmark that was built in the mid-1840s when this part of Chelsea had just become a fashionable residential area. It was still largely rural in the decade before Norwood, a prosperous merchant, built three homes at Nos. 239, 241 and 243, incorporating Greek Revival and Italianate designs.

Continue on to **No. 245**, the former **KGB Espionage Museum** ❷ that was, for a brief period, one of the quirkiest museums in the city. It was opened in 2019 and was built around the personal collection of KGB spy equipment owned by Lithuanian historian Julius Urbaitis. It featured thousands of examples of Russian KGB espionage equipment, including assassination devices such as the "kiss of death" lipstick gun and an umbrella with a poison syringe inside. It was forced to close because of Covid and the collection was sold.

Continue to Eighth Avenue. There are two fine buildings on the opposite side of the intersection. The first ❷ houses the **Museum of Illusions** but was originally built for The New York County National Bank and dates from 1907. It was designed by De Lemos & Cordes—also responsible for the Siegel Cooper Dry Goods building seen earlier and Macy's Department Store (1901).

On the other side ❷❷ is a CVS drug store housed in another old bank building, this one constructed for **The New York Savings Bank** and dating from 1896. Enter the drug store, pretending you are interested in finding cotton balls but secretly admire the beautiful domed ceiling. They don't build banks like these anymore.

Turn right, walking north up Eighth Avenue and stop at the next intersection of West 15th Street. On the right ❷❸ is a five-story building with a flat roof notable for the amazing variety of **decorative stone faces** it contains, all unique. From the looks of their expressions, some may have been modeled on stressed-out New Yorkers of the past.

Opposite, on the west side, is ❷❹ a vast Art Deco building completed in 1932 for The Port Authority of New York. It was used for warehouse space for incoming freight and offices for Port Authority staff. The Authority moved out in the early 1970s (to the World Trade Center). More recently, the building was bought by **Google**, confirmation that this area has become desirable for technology firms, who in the past would not have considered moving to Chelsea.

Now walk westward down West 15th Street, with the Google building on the right.

Stop next at ❷❺ No. **346 West 15th Street** on the left. This was Beat poet Allen Ginsberg's home after he moved to the city in 1951, paying $4.50 a week. During his stay here—about a year—he met fellow poet Gregory Corso in the Village, and introduced Jack Kerouac to Corso for the first time at this address. He mentions this area in some of his poems, and you are following in the footsteps of Ginsberg and his poem "345 W. 15th St." which includes the lines:

"I came home from the movies with nothing on my mind,

Trudging up Eighth Avenue to 15th almost blind,

Waiting for a passenger ship to go to sea.

I live in a rooming house attic near the Port Authority."

Continue on, walking through the famous Meatpacking District. In 1900 this area was home to hundreds of slaughterhouses, meat-related businesses, and other industries. Nobody with any money would have chosen to live amid such conditions. Everything has changed in recent years. Evidence of this is obvious when you reach Ninth Avenue with the popular ❷❻ **Chelsea Market** on the opposite side.

The building fills an entire block, and from the 1890s, this area was dominated by the baking industry and The National Biscuit Company (later renamed Nabisco). Nabisco moved out in 1958. In a sign of the times, Google's parent company, Alphabet Inc., acquired the Market for $2.5 billion in 2018 (having spent $1.77 billion on the old Port Authority building you passed earlier). It was one of the most expensive real estate deals in New York history, although hardly surprising as the enormous site incorporates 19 former factory buildings.

If you go inside, you likely will want to spend some time here in the food hall and visiting the shops. Fortunately, the developers left many original details in place, which makes it worth a look inside. The site is now also home to offices and media firms on the upper floors.

Then continue down **West 16th Street**, stopping at **No. 408** ㉗ outside an elegant three-story brick building. Dating from 1906, it was used as a horse-stable for a whisky firm, and wagons would have come in and out of this building. It was later acquired by Nabisco.

Continue on, soon passing under ㉘ the **High Line**, one of the city's most popular visitor attractions. It extends for 1.45 miles and occupies part of the former New York Central Railroad's West Side Line that ran along the west side of Manhattan.

In the mid-19th century, railroad tracks were built along Tenth and Eleventh Avenues. However, collisions with other road users were common and by 1910, an estimated 540 people had been killed. For many years the "West Side Cowboys"—men waving red flags—walked down Tenth Avenue to warn pedestrians of freight trains. This led to the nickname "Death Avenue."

Something had to change, so plans were laid to construct an elevated railway line for freight traffic. Up high, it could run through buildings and avoid congestion down below. This allowed, for example, a train to stop inside the Nabisco factory (in what is now Chelsea Market) to deliver flour. The first freight train ran in 1933, however over the years the line began to struggle against the competition from interstate trucking. The last train (carrying frozen turkeys) ran along the line in April 1980 and after that it was abandoned, and was due to be demolished.

In 1982, a train buff and Chelsea resident named Peter Obletz walked along the abandoned line. He was inspired to fight demolition plans and ended up buying two miles of track (for $10). He dreamt of turning it into a passenger line, but the plan did not work out and Obletz died in 1996.

However, the track was saved and Joshua David and Robert Hammond founded the Friends of the High Line. This group is largely responsible for transforming the old line into the tourist attraction you see today. Ironically, a little-loved freight line that ultimately failed has—after its demise—helped revitalize Chelsea by drawing millions of visitors every year.

Continue on to Eleventh Avenue and the Hudson River to the west. Ahead is **Pier 57**, built in the early 1950s for shipping by the chemical business W. R. Grace and Company and later used as a bus station.

In 1837, Thirteenth Avenue was constructed beside the Hudson River, but it was an unlucky road and in the early 20th century it was removed in order to build Chelsea Piers that would accommodate the biggest and most luxurious ocean liners of the era. By the second half of the 20th century, the golden age of ocean liners was over, and the piers began to deteriorate.

Chelsea Piers are associated with some of the great dramas of maritime history. Pier 59 was where ocean liners of the White Star Line were berthed, and the *Titanic* was due to have arrived here on April 17, 1912. Instead, many survivors of the best-known shipping disaster in history were brought by Cunard's *Carpathia* to Pier 54. The *Lusitania* left Pier 54 before being sunk by a German submarine in 1915.

Today the piers complex ❷❾ is used for a sports village that includes a pool, a golf-driving range, skating rink, bowling alley, restaurants and bars. It is a nice place to come for a drink at sunset and look over the Hudson River. This place has been gentrified in recent years. In the 1970s and 80s it had a very different vibe, and was a popular gay cruising zone. Watch Nelson Sullivan's short documentary *The Piers in New York City in 1976* to get some insight.

Follow the map along the Hudson River Greenway path, passing piers 59 to 62. Look for the remnants of old pier structures out in the water. There are also a number of gleaming office buildings

constructed on the east side of Eleventh Avenue but look for **㉚** a sombre eight-story brick building on the corner of West 20th Street.

This is the former **Bayview Correctional Facility**, constructed in 1931 as a YMCA for sailors, when thousands would have come off ships at local piers every day. It was used as a women's prison in the 1970s, when this part of Chelsea was so rough and unpopular that having a prison in the neighborhood went largely unnoticed. At the time of writing, the building is empty, but no doubt—as this is hyper-gentrified Chelsea of the 21st century—it will be redeveloped soon into a gallery, luxury apartment building or restaurant. Despite the name, it is unlikely that prisoners ever had a nice view over the water—for years, the West Side Elevated Highway ran past here before it was demolished in the 1970s.

Now turn right down West 21nd Street. Stop outside the **㉛ Paula Cooper Gallery** at **No. 521**. This is a significant building in Chelsea

because in the late 1990s the trendier art galleries began to move here from their previous heartland in SoHo.

As the galleries moved in, the area between Tenth and Eleventh Avenues and 18th to 28th Streets became known as the Chelsea Arts District. Hundreds of galleries, artists, and those in the arts industry have since opened up businesses here, often attracted by the large, high-ceilinged old factories and warehouses that could be converted for new use. Paula Cooper is representative of this change, as she opened one of the first art galleries in SoHo (on Prince Street) in 1968, and relocated to Chelsea in 1996.

Follow the map, passing under the High Line again, to reach Tenth Avenue. Just to the south of here along West 21st Street ❷ are warehouses that were used to store uranium imported from Canada—also used during the **Manhattan Project** that ultimately produced the Nagasaki and Hiroshima bombs in 1945.

At the intersection is the ❸ **Catholic Guardian Angel School**, housed in a pretty Sicilian Romanesque-style church that dates from 1930. The original parish church was dedicated in 1888, and was frequented by workers on the nearby piers, with the original school opening in 1911. There is no church to see now—it was demolished to make way for the High Line in the 1930s.

Opposite is ❹ **192 Books**—a very Chelsea bookshop. If it feels very arty and cool, you might not be surprised to learn gallery owner Paula Cooper owns this with her husband.

If you are hungry, just a block down from here ❺ at 22nd Street and Tenth Avenue is **The Empire Diner**. Constructed in 1946, it is

perhaps best known for a scene-stealing appearance in Woody Allen's film *Manhattan* (1979). It also appeared in many other films and on the cover of the Tom Waits album *Asylum Years*.

Otherwise, head down West 21st Street on the other side. The streets around here are full of historic houses and buildings. First, stop outside ❸ **No. 467**, which is a fine example of the upscale residential buildings constructed in Chelsea in the mid-19th century.

This building is notable for two things: in 1900 it became home to the Sulphur and Mercurial Vapor Baths, described as "A clean and effective method of treating Syphilis and parasitic skin diseases." In 1966 it became the home of *Psycho* star Anthony Perkins (1932-1992). Despite being homosexual, Perkins married actress, photographer and model Berinthia "Berry" Berenson (1948-2001), sister of actress Marisa Berenson, and lived here for a few years with their two children. She died on American Airlines Flight 11 on September 11, 2001.

On the south side of this street is ❸ **The General Theological Seminary of the Episcopal Church** of New York. The Seminary was founded in 1817 with the purpose of educating young men designed for holy orders. Clement Clarke Moore (1779-1863), the grandson of Major Thomas Clarke who christened his landholding (and so this district) "Chelsea," donated 66 acres of land to the Seminary, much of which was covered by apple orchards. The Seminary has occupied the land here since 1827.

Moore was a respected writer and academic who would later teach at the Seminary. He will always be known for penning the Christmas poem "A Visit from St. Nicholas," better known today as "T'was the Night Before Christmas." The poem has become part of the Christmas tradition for many Americans, although debate continues as to whether he really was the poem's author.

Continue along, passing more beautiful houses. In this part of historic Chelsea, houses regularly sell for more than $7 million, and condominiums in more recently built properties can sell for much more than that.

At the end of the street, follow the map up West 20th Street. When Clement Clarke Moore inherited the estate of Chelsea in 1813, it was still open land covering what is now the area between 19th Street and 24th Street, and from Ninth Avenue to the Hudson River. After he gave land for the construction of the General Theological Seminary in the mid-1820s, new streets were developed here in the familiar grid pattern of the Commissioners' Plan.

The seven houses **37** at **Nos. 406-418** are the oldest homes in the district, completed in 1840. They are known as **Cushman Row**, after developer Don Alonzo

Cushman. At the time only the very rich could afford such houses, however, by the mid-20th century the elite of the city no longer lived in Chelsea, and it was a much more working-class area.

Walk up to ❸❾ No. **454 West 20th Street.** Jack Kerouac, often broke and still unknown, lived here in the early 1950s. This is where he completed his most famous book, *On the Road.* Had he lived to see it, I wonder what Kerouac would have thought of someone paying $2.4 million (in 2001) for the 120-foot scroll upon which he wrote an early draft.

Retrace your steps to Ninth Avenue and cross over to continue along West 20th Street to visit ❹⓪ **St. Peter's Episcopal Church**, or St. Peter's Chelsea. The current building featuring a Gothic design dates from 1838 and looks like something you would find in the English countryside. It also provides a continuous historical link with old Chelsea. The Church also appears in the little-known film *Guru the Mad Monk* (1970). Director Andy Milligan was also responsible for horror gems such as *The Rats are Coming! The Werewolves Are Here!* (1972).

Carry on down West 20th Street, passing the ❹❶ **Linda Gross Theater**, part of the Atlantic Theater Company. It is located within the former Parish House of the church and seats 199 people. Given its reputation for putting on new plays, I suspect Kerouac would have been a regular had he still been around.

To give a sense of how upscale this part of Chelsea has become since Kerouac's bohemian era, **No. 334** beside the theater is a five-bedroom property marketed recently at around $25 million.

Walk down to Eighth Avenue, turning left then left again onto West 21st Street. Stop outside **42** **No. 305** looking for a street-level representation of the man in the moon with a rocket in his eye. Odd? It is certainly unique. It is a

homage to **George Méliès' 1902** film *La Voyage dans la Lune (A Trip to the Moon)*. In the earliest days of cinema, this ground-breaking sci-fi film was only eight minutes long but became famous. Documentary filmmakers who worked in this building commissioned the design in 1997.

Hollywood has dominated filmmaking for so long it is hard to imagine a time before it existed. However, Chelsea was an important center for films in the early 20th century, with studios located on 21st and 23rd Streets. One of the first big film stars, Mary Pickford, appeared in films made in Chelsea.

Retrace your steps to Eighth Avenue. Look across to **43** the **"We Love NY" mural** featuring Albert Einstein on the corner. This is the work of **Eduardo Kobra (b. 1975)**, the Brazilian street artist known as

Kobra. You can find his murals all around the world, including Portugal, Russia, Poland, Japan and India.

Continue up Eighth Avenue to reach West 23rd Street. On the northwest corner ⑭ once stood the **Grand Opera House**. Entrepreneur Samuel N. Pike (1822–1872) spent the then astonishing sum of $1 million constructing the Opera House in the late 1860s. Able to seat 1,800 people, Pike's Opera House represented a high-risk attempt to draw away the city's elite from The Academy of Music on 14th Street. The gamble failed, and Pike's Opera House only lasted a year. It was bought by Jay Gould and Jim Fisk, who rebranded it as The Grand Opera House and put on productions that had a broader appeal. Over time 23rd Street became a theater district, so Pike had anticipated the promise of Chelsea but had invested too soon.

"Big Jim" or "Diamond Jim" Fisk (1835-1872) was one of the most controversial, unscrupulous and colorful characters in New York during the mid-19th century. His attempts to corner the gold market, bribery of politicians and judges, and keeping a mistress, were just some of the reasons why he was vilified by respectable society. A married man, Fisk began an affair with Josie Mansfield, an unemployed actress he met in a brothel. However, he made the mistake of introducing her to his business colleague Ned Stokes. Mansfield and Stokes entered into an affair of their own, and this led to a bitter quarrel that ultimately led to Stokes shooting Fisk dead at the Grand Central Hotel in 1872. Twenty thousand people visited the Opera House to see Fisk's body that was laid out for public view. The Opera House later became an RKO cinema and was pulled down in 1960.

The apartment block **45** at **No. 323** was where punk rocker Nancy Spungen (1958-1978) lived. She will always be known as the girlfriend of Sex Pistol Sid Vicious and for her murder in the Chelsea Hotel (seen shortly). Vicious was charged with her murder but died of an overdose before the case came to trial.

Head east along West 23rd Street to reach **46** the **Chelsea Hotel**, one of the most famous in the world. Hard to imagine today, but when this 12-story Gothic-inspired masterpiece was built, it was the tallest building in New York and remained so until 1899.

It has been home for hundreds of well-known artists and rock stars, including Patti Smith, William Burroughs, Arthur Miller, Tennessee Williams, Allen Ginsberg, Mark Twain, Bob Dylan, Jack Kerouac, Arthur C. Clarke, Stanley Kubrick, Jim Morrison, Chet Baker,

Joni Mitchell, Madonna and Janis Joplin. The goings-on here since the hotel was completed in 1885 has been the subject of numerous films, books, songs, and documentaries. Some of the most famous, or infamous, room numbers include 205, where Dylan Thomas was staying when he died in 1953. Arthur Miller lived in room 614 after his divorce from Marilyn Monroe, and Robert Mapplethorpe took early photographs in room 1017 (which he shared with Patti Smith). Bob Dylan wrote songs such as "Sara" (about his first wife) in room 211. Twenty-year-old Nancy Spungen bled to death on the bathroom floor of room 100 on October 12th, 1978. On a happier note, Janis Joplin and Leonard Cohen had a famous tryst in her room at 415, and it would later inspire his song "Chelsea Hotel."

The hotel became better known to the wider public after the success of Andy Warhol's 1966 film *Chelsea Girls*, which captured the lives of some of his circle (including Edie Sedgwick) who stayed here. Recently, the redevelopment of the hotel and eviction of long-term residents caused a great deal of controversy. The hotel's past and present is explored in the documentary *Dreaming Walls: Inside The Chelsea Hotel* (2022). A very different view of the hotel can be seen in the 1981 BBC Arena documentary, *Chelsea Hotel*.

From here, continue along to the 23rd Street subway station you started from. There is one final hidden gem here at ❼ **71 West 23rd Street**. This is Grand Lodge of the Free and Accepted Masons of the State of New York. Headed by a Grand Master, it traces its history back to 1782 although the secretive freemasonry movement was probably introduced by the British to New York by the 1730s. There are around 800 lodges and 60,000 men subject to the general jurisdiction of the Grand Lodge, including those within ten Manhattan districts. Many of the lodges have their own intriguing names, including Norsemen, Holland, Mariners, Manhatta, Pyramid, Publicity, All Seeing Eye, Knickerbocker, King Solomon-Beethoven, St. John's and Sibelius-Bredablick.

This is where the walk ends. From here you can continue to Seventh Avenue and the 23rd Street subway, where the walk ends. Alternatively, you can continue on straight ahead to reach the subway station you started from.

8 HELL'S KITCHEN WALK

START AND FINISH: Port Authority Bus Terminal Main Entrance at 42nd Street & Eighth Avenue
SUBWAY STATION: 42 St/Port Authority Bus Terminal  Ⓐ, Ⓒ, Ⓔ

HELL'S KITCHEN

Distance: 5.6 Miles

1. The New York Times Building
2. Port Authority Bus Terminal
3. Holy Cross Church
4. Theatre Row
5. Chez Josephine
6. Threshold Recording Studios
7. Catholic Church of Saints Cyril & Methodius and St. Raphael's
8. Lincoln Tunnel
9. Sean Kelly Gallery
10. The Spiral
11. Vessel
12. High Line
13. West Side Yard
14. 35 Hudson Yards
15. Jacob K. Javits Center
16. 538 West 38th Street (Stable)
17. Ventilation Tower for the Lincoln Tunnel
18. "Battle Row"
19. Michael J. Quill Bus Depot
20. Consulate General of China
21. Gotham West Market
22. Landmark Tavern
23. Former Auerbach Chocolate Factory Building
24. Juan Alonso Community Garden
25. Irish Arts Center
26. The Daily Show Studio
27. Clinton Park Stables
28. "Doughboy" Statue
29. Former Centro Maria Women's Residence
30. Oasis Community Garden
31. Church of the Sacred Heart
32. Site of The Sunbrite Bar
33. Stella Tower
34. Hermetic Society
35. Former Polyclinic Hospital
36. One Worldwide Plaza
37. Mickey Spillane's
38. Clinton Community Garden
39. 657 Tenth Avenue
40. Site of Spot Bar and Grill
41. Clinton Court
42. Hartley House
43. Restaurant Row
44. Matthews-Palmer Playground
45. 596 Bar
46. The Actors Studio
47. Home of June Havoc
48. Manhattan Plaza

The walk starts at the 42nd Street Port Authority Subway station, so begin at the intersection of Eighth Avenue and 42nd Street. Eighth Avenue is generally regarded as the eastern boundary of Hell's Kitchen (the other boundaries being 30th and 59th Streets and the Hudson River). You are only a two-minute walk from Times Square, so—unsurprisingly—this is a very busy part of the city.

Walk south down Eighth Avenue, with the Port Authority Bus Terminal on your right. Opposite the Terminal, look for the distinctive signage that makes it obvious this is ❶ **The New York Times Building** (No. 620 Eighth Avenue), a 52-story giant whose main tenant is the famous newspaper. It is the same height as the Chrysler Building and was designed by Renzo Piano (b. 1937), the famous Italian architect also responsible for the Pompidou Centre in Paris, The Shard in London, and the expansion of the Pierpont Morgan Library on East 36th Street and Madison Avenue.

The iconic font of the Times signage dates from 1966, a redrawing of the previous style by Ed Benguiat (1924-2020). A legend of typography, he created hundreds of typeface designs, including Benguiat Gothic, and designed (or redesigned) logotypes for brands such as Coke, Ford, and even the original *Planet of the Apes* film.

On the opposite side is the ❷ **Port Authority Bus Terminal**. The first bus terminal was built in the early 1950s, and the complex has been rebuilt and extended several times since. **The busiest bus terminal in the world, this place is hard to love. In 2021** New Jersey Senate member Loretta Weinberg described it as **"a source of aggravation and great frustration for frenzied New Jersey commuters who know all too well its many shortcomings."**

However, for some, the Terminal carries a special significance, marking their arrival to the city and a new chapter in their life. This was captured in the film *Port Authority* (2019), a minor gem in which the character Paul arrives here from the Midwest, ready to start afresh in New York, and makes a connection with Wye (played by trans actor Leyna Bloom).

Leave the romance of the Bus Terminal behind and proceed up Eighth Avenue, turning left (west) along 42nd Street, famous for its association with the theater industry.

You pass ❸ **Holy Cross Church** on the right. It was founded in 1852 to serve thousands of Irish Catholics, many of whom had moved out of Lower Manhattan into Longacre Square (later renamed Times Square) and other streets in Hell's Kitchen. The current church dates from 1870 and retained its Irish identity up to the mid-20th century. It is best known for its association with former pastor Father Francis Patrick Duffy (1871-1932). He served as a chaplain in the Spanish-American War and later with the fabled and Irish-dominated "Fighting 69th Division" during World War I. He became the most highly decorated cleric in the army and later became known for his efforts in helping the less fortunate

of Hell's Kitchen. He was portrayed by actor Pat O'Brien in *The Fighting 69th*, a film from 1940 that celebrated the regiment and which starred James Cagney. A statue of Duffy stands in Times Square.

Continue across Ninth Avenue, passing on the left ❹ **Theatre Row**. This arts complex now houses five Off-Broadway theaters, but in the 1970s, this street was dominated by porn cinemas. In 1977 an initiative began to revitalize the area, replacing porn with legitimate theater. Jackie Kennedy Onassis played a vital role in the initiative, and Theatre Row became a term used to describe a number of other small theaters lying between here and the Hudson River. Theatre Row features in scenes from the film *Tootsie* (1982) starring Dustin Hoffman.

Next door is ❺ **Chez Josephine**, founded in 1986 by Jean-Claude Baker, who struck up a long-term friendship with the trail-blazing entertainer, civil rights figure, and French Resistance agent Josephine

Baker (1906-75). He met her while working as a teenage bellhop in a Parisian hotel and later worked with Baker and co-authored a biography of his "second mother."

Turn left down Dyer Avenue, its name a reminder of the importance of tunnels to New York. Major General George R. Dyer (1869-1934), a member of a prominent Rhode Island family, had a successful career as a soldier and businessman. He also served as chairman of the New York Bridge and Tunnel Commission and played a key role in the project to build the Holland Tunnel.

Turn right into West 41st Street, passing on the southwest corner of an ❻ anonymous building with an exciting story. Recently it has been home to **Threshold Recording Studios** NYC. Artists who have recorded here since the studios were founded in 1997 include The Strokes, Foreigner, Slash, Duran Duran, The Black Keys, Cyndi Lauper, and Carlos Santana as well as many Broadway musical cast recordings.

Continue down West 41st Street, a run-down, fairly desolate area compared to the busy streets you saw at the start of the walk. Bland, uninspired, modern buildings are interrupted only by ❼ the **Catholic Church of Saints Cyril & Methodius and St. Raphael's.**

This Gothic Revival style building was completed in 1903 and—originally as the Church of St. Raphael—served a largely Irish Catholic community. Later, the construction of the first "tube" of the Lincoln Tunnel in the 1930s changed this immediate area dramatically as 19th-century tenement streets were demolished. As the Irish population faded away over time, the less well-known Croatian community took over the church in the 1970s (hence why it has a complicated dedication—Cyril and Methodius were 9th century A.D. Byzantine Christians). The church looks entirely out of place here, dwarfed by the modern buildings nearby. In the early 20th century, many Croatian immigrants settled around Eleventh Avenue between West 30th to West 50th Streets, working in the nearby rail yards, docks, and manufacturing.

Now proceed down pedestrian-unfriendly Galvin Avenue, named for John F. Galvin, chairman of The Port of New York Authority in the late 1920s. Bear left to find the recently opened Croatian Center. In the 1940s and 50s Jack Kerouac would set off from Manhattan and travel through the Lincoln Tunnel before beginning his many adventures that inspired his writing. "As we rode in the bus in the weird phosphorescent void of the Lincoln Tunnel we leaned on each other with fingers waving and yelled and talked excitedly, and I was beginning to get the bug like Dean," *On the Road* (1957).

If you look down the narrow strip of land between the road and the Center, you can see the bedrock everything man-made in Manhattan rests upon.

The Center is an essential place for the religious and cultural life of the Croatian community in New York, New Jersey, Connecticut, and Pennsylvania. The Croatian Franciscan Sisters are also based here.

Passing the Center on your left, you soon rejoin Tenth Avenue. It is hard to believe you are just over 2/3 of a mile from Times Square. The intersection of West 40th Street is the approximate location where three streams converged that formed part of the "Great Kill"—a river that ran along what is now West 41st Street before emptying into the Hudson River. A local neighborhood was even called Great Kill until the late 19th century. The name is a corruption of *kille*—a Dutch term for riverbed. By the 1880s, the river had been filled in.

No one is certain why Hell's Kitchen got its name. One local legend is that two policemen were walking around the crime-ridden slums of the area in the 19th century, and one remarked the area was like being in hell, to which his colleague replied that it was more like being in hell's kitchen. Alternatively, a man named Heil had a well-known

Croatian Center   Astro's Community Dog Run   Lincoln Tunnel

kitchen here, and his surname was corrupted when people described the area. Another theory is that an infamous den of vice on 39th Street was described as Hell's Kitchen by newspapers in the early 1890s, and the name stuck.

What is certain is that over time prominent people in the community despaired of the name, believing it discouraged attempts to attract investment. For decades there were efforts to change it, but it was not until 1959 that campaigners succeeded, and Hell's Kitchen became Clinton. You will find out more about the tragic catalyst for the change later on. However, recently the Hell's Kitchen name has acquired a certain cachet and has become widely used again. It is certainly more memorable than dull-sounding "Clinton."

Turn right at the intersection, walking south down Tenth Avenue. Just under the bridge is Astro's Community Dog Run—a reminder of how New Yorkers can make something out of the most unpromising strip of land. Continue along, with the ❽ **Lincoln Tunnel** running beneath your feet. The entrance is just over the wall on the left-hand side.

Connecting Midtown with Weehawken, New Jersey, the first "tube" of the Tunnel opened in 1937, with two more following in 1945 and 1957. Along with the Holland Tunnel that opened a few years before, it represents one of the most ambitious feats of engineering to have taken place in the history of the city.

Less well known is Omero Catan—or "Mr. First." He spent his adult life trying to be "first" at more than 500 public openings. He was the first member of the public to drive through the new Lincoln Tunnel in 1937 (at 4 a.m. on December 22). His other feats included being the first to skate at Rockefeller Plaza and cross the George Washington Bridge.

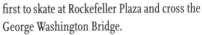

Another memorable moment occurred in May 1971, when a strike on the railway forced several stranded elephants and other animals to be led through the Tunnel to get to their destination at a circus in Madison Square Garden.

Walk on, passing the **Sean Kelly Gallery** on the right ❾, which champions contemporary artists. Its roster includes David Claerbout, José Dávila, Candida Höfer, Ilse D'Hollander, Hugo McCloud, Mariko Mori, Liu Wei, and Sun Xun. It is housed in a fine building dating from 1914.

With the gallery on the corner, turn right down West 36th Street and then left down Hudson Boulevard East.

You are entering the Hudson Yards development—a real estate development covering 28 acres that has completely transformed this part of the city. If New York had won the right to stage the 2012 Summer Olympics, a stadium would have been standing here, but the city's attempt failed, so developers pounced.

Walk straight ahead, passing Bella Abzug Park, named for "Battling Bella" (1920-1998), a lawyer, politician, and leading feminist activist. The daughter of Russian-Jewish immigrants, she was the epitome of the anti-establishment New Yorker, opposing everything from the Vietnam War to Senator Joseph McCarthy's anti-communist witch hunt.

On your left is ⓿ **The Spiral**, a striking 66-floor skyscraper that is the 14th tallest building in the city, and one of several enormous structures that have appeared recently in this area. Many will sit within the neighboring Hudson Yards redevelopment, the largest private real estate development in US history. Eventually, it will cover 28 acres, and this vast development is built on top of active railway lines.

This has been described as a final frontier in Manhattan and

the last major area of undeveloped land in Midtown. The only recent precedent is the construction of Rockefeller Center, but Hudson Yards has so far not received such a positive reception in many quarters. Described as an example of the "hyper gentrification" of the city, and as a "billionaire's playground," the expensive apartments, restaurants and office space have changed the character of this area completely.

New York Magazine critic Justin Davidson wrote (in 2019), "I can't help feeling like an alien here, as though I've crossed from real New York, with all its jangling mess, into a movie studio's back-lot version. Everything is too clean, too flat, too art-directed. This para-Manhattan, raised on a platform and tethered to the real thing by one subway line, has no history, no holdover greasy spoons, no pockets of blight or resident eccentrics—no memories at all."

Is this a corporate city-state or a genuine improvement to a previously neglected part of densely populated island of Manhattan? With some penthouses selling for around $60 million, most members of the public are likely to experience only a fraction of what this development contains.

The most memorable feature amongst the skyscrapers is ⓫ the

Vessel, the 150-foot-high honeycomb structure you can walk up that was designed by British designer Thomas Heatherwick (b. 1970). He is responsible for other public works around the world, from Singapore to Shanghai and London. If you visit London you may even travel on a red public bus he designed. Unfortunately, the Vessel has had to close to visitors recently, after it has become the site of a rash of suicides.

The Shed arts center nearby is the first major such development in the city since the foundation of Lincoln Center in the 1960s. To the east of the Vessel is 30 Hudson Yards, the tallest building in the development, the sixth tallest building (and second tallest office tower) in New York. In a sign of how Hell's Kitchen has changed, this building has attracted illustrious tenants such as KKR, Facebook, and Wells Fargo and offers the knee-trembling observation deck called "The Edge" that is located on the 100th and 101st floors.

Continue ahead, coming out onto a stretch of the hugely popular ⑫ **High Line**—the 1.4-mile elevated park built on the old New York Central Railroad line that ran up the west side of the city. The elevated track was first used in 1934, and to clear its path, around 640 buildings were demolished. If you combine that with streets cleared for the

Lincoln Tunnel, few sections of the city have undergone such a major transformation in modern times.

A decline in freight traffic (largely caused by the growth of trucking), and the construction of the nearby Javits Center caused the High Line to stop operating by the 1980s, and it was due to be demolished. Thankfully Joshua David and Robert Hammond founded Friends of the High Line that fought to transform the deserted line into what is now one of the city's most popular attractions. Its popularity contrasts sharply with the lukewarm reception of the Hudson Yards redevelopment.

Take the exit staircase leading down from the High Line to the street below. Turn right into West 30th Street, then walk a short way before turning right (north) up until Eleventh Avenue, passing the other side of the Hudson Yards site. If you walk on the sidewalk on the left (west) side you can see over the wall ⓭ the 26-acre **West Side Yard** used to store commuter trains. It gives you a better sense of the railway infrastructure the skyscrapers to your right are balanced on top of. On the right-hand side, just north of The Vessel, is ⓮ **35 Hudson Yards**. In the HBO hit show *Succession,* this is where the uber-wealthy character Kendall Roy

(played by Jeremy Strong) has a luxury apartment. The actual apartment was on the market for $54 million in 2021.

It is hard to love this stretch of New York, apart from the High Line, but carry on, passing the ⑮ **Javits Center** on the left, named for Senator Jacob K. Javits This is one of the biggest convention centers in the country, and opened in 1986 after seven years of construction. It is vast, with an interior space of 3.3 million square feet.

However, perhaps of more interest to the reader is that the construction—plagued by a series of delays and problems—was allegedly controlled by organized crime. In 2008 *The New York Post* reported how "New York state got overcharged some $12 million for the concrete used to build the Jacob Javits Convention Center because a mob cartel led by Anthony "Fat Tony" Salerno controlled the business and no legitimate firms would bid against the mob."

Hell's Kitchen's most notorious gang in modern times were the Irish-American Westies, described by *The New York Times* in 1987 as "a gang long known to law enforcement officials, if not to the public, as one of the most savage organizations in the long history of New York gangs." The Westies were involved in over 100 murders from the 1960s to the mid-1980s. They had links to the Mafia and were involved in contract killings, racketeering, and drug trafficking.

The most high-profile gangster in Hell's Kitchen was Mickey Spillane (1933-77). He controlled many aspects of criminal enterprise in the district in the 1960s and early 70s. He managed to keep the Mafia out of his area of control, but this led to an Irish-Italian mob war. One of the main disputes was over the Mafia's desire to get a piece of the action as tens of millions of dollars were being spent constructing the Javits Center. The war with the Mafia, and challenges from younger

and more aggressive mobsters in Hell's Kitchen, led to Spillane being shot dead in Queens at age 43. By this time he had been forced out of his territory by ultra-violent Hell's Kitchen resident Jimmy "C" Coonan. Coonan, aided by brutal killers such as Mickey Featherstone, forged an alliance with the Gambino crime family and acted as boss of the Westies until being sentenced to 75 years in prison in 1988.

Turn right down West 38th Street, cars zooming along the Lincoln Tunnel directly underneath your feet. On the right is the Rosewood Theater—not Off-Broadway but a strip club (according to the club's marketing: "The women are in charge. Act like a gentleman at all times"). Stop outside ⓰ the West Side Livery Stables at **No. 538**. This is part of the answer if you wondered where the carriage horses in Central Park stay. It has housed horses since the 1860s, originally used to transport ice wagons and vegetable carts before the Central Park trade arrived in the 1940s. Hay is kept on the fourth floor, and the horses live on the two floors below. Today only four such stables exist in the city for carriage horses. By contrast, in the late 19th century, New York was home to around 200,000 horses and thousands of stables, but the resulting hygiene problems with all the horse manure on the streets helped push the way for steam and electric-powered transport alternatives.

Retrace your steps to Eleventh Avenue, turning right to continue north. You pass ❶⑰ an elegant but formidable-looking brick **ventilation tower for the Lincoln Tunnel** below. If you had stood here in 1850, the area covered by the Javits Center and Lincoln Tunnel would instead be home to an enormous timber basin.

On the right, you pass West 39th Street, which—between Tenth and Eleventh Avenues—was once as a notorious slum known as ⑱ **"Battle Row."** Long before the Westies, the 500-strong Irish American Gophers gang controlled the area from the 1890s until around 1910, finding rich pickings by stealing from the nearby train yards and freight yards.

The Gophers, full of memorably-named criminals such as The Killer, Stumpy Malarkey, One Lung, and Goo Goo Knox, also had a female contingent called the Lady Gophers. One of their members was the feared "Battle

243

Annie" Walsh, infamous for her ability to hurl bricks and known as the "Queen of Hell's Kitchen." She could raise a force of hundreds of women armed with clubs and hung out at the Gopher's favorite bar—the Battle Row saloon run by Mallet Murphy.

Continue, and before turning left down West 40th Street, to your right is the ⑲ **Michael J. Quill Bus Depot**. The building is not of much interest, but the person it is named after is. Quill (1905-66) was the sort of hard-boiled trade union leader you rarely find today. Born in Ireland, he was involved with the IRA, then came to New York where he became

a close ally of the communist party, a founder of the hugely powerful Transport Workers of America (TWU) union, and retained his Irish Republican roots.

He was normally on the right side of the argument, supporting racial equality, the Civil Rights movement, and other progressive causes at an early stage. When a transport workers' strike brought the city's subway and bus lines to a halt in 1966, "Red Mike" was among those imprisoned for contempt of court. After Quill died, Martin Luther King Jr., said "Mike Quill was a fighter for decent things all his life—Irish independence, labor organization, and racial equality. . . Negroes had desperately needed men like Mike Quill, who fearlessly said what was true even when it offended. That is why Negroes shall miss Mike Quill."

This area was once dominated by industrial sites: breweries, piano factories, gas storage facilities, coal yards—and slaughterhouses. The latter were so prevalent that the area between Eleventh and Twelfth Avenues and West 39th Street was called Abattoir Place. In those distant days, this street would have felt almost unimaginably busy compared to today. You would see cowboys unloading cattle and sheep from ships at the piers, thousands of workers in the slaughterhouses and other businesses while hundreds of horse-drawn carts would pass by transporting every sort of imported good into the heart of New York. There also used to be two underground passages allowing cattle to cross Twelfth Avenue (one at West 34th Street, the other at West 38th Street).

When you reach the waterfront, you can see another ventilation building over the Lincoln Tunnel to your left. Cross over, turning right, walking northwards along the riverfront, passing Piers 81, 83, and 84 and Hudson River Park. Hard to believe today, but by 1900, the port of New York was busier than all the other ports in the country combined and the largest single port in the world in terms of cargo and passenger numbers. Manufacturers wanted to be near here and the new railroad lines on the west side of Manhattan because efficient transport links saved time and money. However, the port was in decline after World War II, particularly after the port of New Jersey became a major com-

Piers 81, 83 and Intrepid Museum

petitor, able to offer facilities better suited to the new age of super-large container ships.

Cross over Twelfth Avenue, heading down West 43rd Street. To your right is ❷⓪ the imposing-looking **Consulate General of China**. When Chinese diplomats arrived in New York after their country joined the U.N. in 1971, they had no consulate and rented a hotel floor near the U.N. building. The Chinese economy was then about the same size as Canada's and smaller than Italy's. Today China has the second-largest economy in the world and is likely to overtake that of the United States in the next few years.

This Consulate has attracted considerable controversy. In 2020 Mike Pompeo, then-Secretary of State, told *The New York Post* that the Consulate was a center of Chinese communist espionage efforts—"They're engaged in activities where they're crossing the line from normal diplomacy to the kinds of things that would be more akin to

what spies are doing . . ." Whatever the truth of this, China's influence on the city is immense—more than 1 million Chinese tourists visit every year while at least 150,000 Chinese students study here. Many of the new skyscrapers you see all around have also been funded partly through Chinese investment.

Now walk down West 43th Street to reach Eleventh Avenue again and turn left (north). A great place to stop for something to eat or drink is ㉑ **Gotham West Market** food hall at No. 600—one of a number of new attractions that have transformed Hell's Kitchen as it has become increasingly gentrified.

Keep heading up Eleventh Avenue, stopping on the right (at the corner of West 46th Street) where you see ㉒ the atmospheric **Landmark Tavern**, a famous Irish pub founded in 1868. The third floor was used as a speakeasy during the Prohibition era and was frequented by members of the Westies, dockworkers, and merchant seamen. It is also said to be haunted, including by the ghost of actor George Raft (who grew up nearby), a Confederate soldier, and an Irish immigrant girl. In the late '70s Jimmy Coonan and Mickey Featherstone met an official from the International Longshoremen's Association (ILA) here to discuss a decision by the Manhattan leader of the ILA to stop paying bribes to the Westies. Coonan threatened murder, and—unsurprisingly—payments continued.

Why did Hell's Kitchen become associated with the Irish? The railway, tanneries, docks, and other industries offered low-paid jobs that attracted many poor Irish immigrants, many of whom had arrived penniless in the mid-19th century after escaping the Great Famine in their homeland.

Keep heading north, passing on the right at ㉓ **No. 636**, the former **Auerbach chocolate factory building** constructed in 1913, a

relic of Hell's Kitchen's industrial heritage. Recently it was home to a very different kind of tenant—the advertising giant Ogilvy & Mather. When the firm arrived in 2009, this area was described as the "NYC equivalent of Siberia." Continue on this anonymous stretch dominated by luxury car dealerships, auto repair shops and bland architecture. Eleventh Avenue never seems to please New Yorkers. In 1911, a letter to the editor of *The New York Times* complained about the Avenue, asking why it could not be developed into "a beautiful roadway, helpful to all the residents of the nearby unattractive street . . ." and "instead of noise, dirt and an absolute lack of any point of interest" it could to be made into a tree-lined boulevard, with parks, model tenements, a Carnegie library and garden plots."

A bit farther, on the corner of West 51st Street, you reach the tiny ㉔ **Juan Alonso community garden**. Once the haunt of drug addicts when Hell's Kitchen really did deserve its name, it was transformed in 1993 into this community space and is named for a local resident and devoted gardener.

Continue up Eleventh Avenue, looking on the right for ㉕ the **Irish Arts Center**, a cultural hub founded in 1972 when the Irish

community's presence was more evident than it is today. Apart from putting on performances, the Center hosts classes in everything from Irish Gaelic to Irish dancing and traditional music.

Opposite the Center at **No. 733** is ㉖ the studio where The *Daily Show* is made. This late-night satirical news show began in 1996 and was made famous by long-time host Trevor Noah.

Take the next left onto West 52nd Street to reach DeWitt Clinton Park. The park was created in 1906 on what had been two farms in the 18th century.

Walk along the south side and stop by ㉗ another carriage horse stable—the **Clinton Park Stables** (No. 618) that occupies a building dating from the 1880s. Just past here at No. 624 is where Westie killer Mickey Featherstone used to work in the mid-1980s.

Take some time to walk around the park. The west side originally had good views over the Hudson River. Subsequent construction of roadways and piers sliced a chunk off the park, ruining the view. Look for the ㉘ **"doughboy" statue** commemorating the ordinary soldiers of Hell's Kitchen who died during World War I. The plinth contains a quote (actually a

misquote) of Lieutenant Colonel John McCrae's famous wartime poem *In Flanders Fields* (1915). McCrae died in 1918, just before the war ended.

The park is named for DeWitt Clinton (1769-1828), a governor of New York who did a great deal to secure the construction of the Erie Canal that helped secure the city's future as a global trading center and port. He was also a senior Freemason and helped establish the Grand Encampment of the Knights Templar. The Erie Canal trade connection helped stimulate the economy of the waterfront, explaining why Clinton was popular in this part of the city and why, in the late 1950s, many local people wanted to rename Hell's Kitchen after Clinton and this park.

Like many parts of the city, Hell's Kitchen has been the scene of race riots over the years. Many African-Americans had settled in Hell's Kitchen by 1900 but faced considerable hostility from other ethnic groups, mainly because of competition for low-paid jobs. This sparked a race riot in the summer of 1900 after an African American man stabbed an undercover policeman trying to arrest his girlfriend. The racial tensions in the area encouraged many African-Americans to move north to Harlem, which, by the 1920s, became famous as the capital of Black America.

Tensions rose also among other ethnic groups. In July 1911, *The New York Times* reported on a "Hell's Kitchen Race Riot" involving "old-timers" of the area who "watched with increasing anger the encroachments of Austrian immigrants into the neighborhood" and how "yesterday . . . the old fighting spirit of the kitchen flared up once more," with a score of youths attacking a group of Austrians armed with paving stones picked up off Eleventh Avenue. There were "a dozen

broken heads, one man was shot, and the saloon of an Austrian, the resort of his country-
man . . . had been wrecked almost to destruction." Austrians rarely feature in accounts of
New York's bitter history of race relations.

Leave the park and continue down West
54th Street, passing on the left ❷❾ a Gothic Revival style building dating from 1910 that was,
until recently, the **Centro Maria women's residence**, run by the Catholic Order of the Sisters
of Mary Immaculate. For decades it provided a
cheap, safe place to stay for around 80 women
from different countries who came to study
in New York. The building was originally the
church of St. Ambrose, which was founded
in 1897. It was reported in the media that the
home had to shut in 2021 because the Arch-
diocese of New York needed to raise funds to
fight sex abuse litigation claims.

Walk on and turn right on Tenth Avenue
where it intersects with 52nd Street, flanked
by five- and six-story buildings of the old
Hell's Kitchen that stand in sharp contrast to
the glitzier skyscrapers passed earlier.

52nd Street and Tenth Avenue

Take a right along West 52nd Street and
stop shortly on the right at ❸⓪ the **Oasis Community Garden**, its name accurately describing this pleasant spot. It often hosts commu-

nity events and volunteer days that allows locals to meet each other and make new connections

Retrace your steps and continue down Tenth Avenue. The next stop is left down West 51st Street to visit ❸❶ the **Church of the Sacred Heart**. Many social events connected to Irish mobsters took place here, including christenings, marriages, and the inevitable funerals. On August 27, 1960, around 200 people attended the wedding of leading mobster Mickey Spillane. The church was dedicated in 1885, and up until 1920, most of the congregation was still Irish, later replaced by Italian immigrants. By the time of Spillane's marriage, the church already represented a rare connection between the remaining Irish community and Hell's Kitchen's past.

Return to Tenth Avenue and continue along.

Shortly on the left is ❸❷ No. 736 Tenth Avenue, the former location of **The Sunbrite Bar**, an infamous Westies hangout. Watch *State of Grace*, a 1990 film starring Ed Harris, Sean Penn, and Gary Oldman, if you want to get a sense of what crime-ridden Hell's Kitchen was like. A minor classic, the plot is based on the Westies and their interaction with the Italian Mafia.

Local gangster Eddie "the Butcher" Cummiskey (1934-1976) worked for Mickey Spillane, but later switched his allegiance to Spillane's rival Jimmy Coonan. Cummiskey was a regular at The Sunbrite and committed murder here when he shot a bartender who had insulted him. Cummiskey was an expert at cutting up and disposing of bodies. Westie gangster Mickey Featherstone also shot someone dead inside the bar. Cummiskey met his own end at The Sunbrite in 1976, shot dead by "Mad Dog" Sullivan (the hit ordered by the Mafia).

The Sunbrite Bar later changed its name under a new owner, and in the early 1980s, Bruce Willis worked as a bartender here. Willis lived nearby on 49th Street and Tenth Avenue in a "$175-a-month railroad flat," and was regularly seen rollerskating in the area. He would soon leave bartending behind after starring in the hit series *Moonlighting*.

Head left down West 50th Street to reach
㉝ **Stella Tower**, on the left at **No. 425**. Dating from 1930, this art deco gem is one of the finest buildings in Hell's Kitchen (which doesn't have many great buildings) and was designed by architect Ralph Walker. It was built for the New York Telephone Company and later named for Walker's wife when it was converted into residential apartments. Walker was a prolific architect best known

for several spectacular Art Deco buildings in New York. Frank Lloyd Wright described him as "the only other honest architect in America." Walker (1889-1973) died when he shot himself with a silver bullet he had made himself.

Next door ❸ at No. **423 West 50th Street** is the home of the mysterious **Hermetic Society**, occupying a townhouse dating from 1870. Trying to explain in detail what the Hermetic Society does is beyond the scope of this book, but it centers upon pagan religious beliefs and philosophy that claims to trace its origins to ancient Greece. If you think you can do better than that in one sentence, let me know!

Cross over Ninth Avenue, where you will see more restaurants and theaters, and the streets getting busier. Stop at 345 West 50th Street ❸. This grand building was once the **Polyclinic Hospital** that treated many celebrities in the past; however, it will be forever best known for being where Rudolph Valentino (1895-1926) died on August 23 when he was a patient in the eighth-floor suite. It is difficult today to comprehend how popular Valentino was, especially with women, and the mass distress that erupted when news emerged of his death even led to people committing suicide. It has been estimated that 100,000 people lined the streets of the city to pay their respects on the day of his funeral. Others treated here included Peggy Lee, Marilyn Monroe, Mary Pickford, and various gangsters. The hospital closed in the 1970s, and the building was—you guessed it—converted into residential apartments.

Continue along West 50th Street, passing the Worldwide Plaza complex on your right. The public plaza here is a nice place to sit if you need a rest. Soon you reach Eighth Avenue, where on the right (west side) is the giant **㊱ One Worldwide Plaza** office tower. The Worldwide Plaza complex was completed in 1989 and comprised this building, Two Worldwide Plaza and Three Worldwide Plaza.

One Worldwide Plaza occupies the site of the third Madison Square Garden that played host to legendary sports and other entertainment events between 1925-68 before being pulled down. Perhaps

the most extraordinary event at the old venue took place on March 9, 1943, and was called "We Will Never Die." A group of Jewish writers and entertainers, including Kurt Weill, had been shocked by reports that 2 million Jews had been killed by the Nazis in Europe and wanted to stage a public performance that would keep the tragedy in the minds of the public. Twenty thousand people came to the performance, and entertainers who took part

included Edward G. Robinson and Frank Sinatra.

The Worldwide Plaza development helped transform this part of the city, which was previously—as described by *The New York Times*—"more red light then blue chip."

Now turn right off Eighth Avenue to head up West 49th Street, with ❸ **Mickey Spillane's** bar on the corner. It is named after the Hell's Kitchen mobster mentioned previously.

Head down Ninth Avenue and then right onto West 48th Street, passing ❸ the **Clinton Community Garden** on the left. Founded in 1978, it was built on a derelict lot. In 2001 the garden hosted a benefit concert for firehouses in Hell's Kitchen that had lost 38 firefighters on 9/11.

Years ago, gang members used to mug police officers for their coats (which were then altered by gangster girlfriends to wear), forcing policemen to walk

around in pairs. The gritty reputation of Hell's Kitchen, combined with a pretty cool name, has inspired many films over the years, including *Hell's Kitchen* (1998—starring Angelina Jolie among others), the *Streets of New York* (1939) and *Hell's Kitchen* (1939) starring the Dead End Kids.

At the end, turn left down Tenth Avenue, passing Hell's Kitchen Park on the left where many of the Westies gang used to play hockey together in the early 1970s. Look for 39 **657 Tenth Avenue** on the right-hand side. James J. Braddock (1905-74) was born into a poor Irish-American family in Hell's Kitchen. A longshoreman and journeyman boxer, he surprised everyone when he beat Max Baer to become heavyweight champion of the world in 1935. He came here in February 1937 to give a speech at the Boys Athletic League. A thousand excited children and adults turned up, creating such a commotion and noise that Braddock had to flee for his own safety. Braddock's life was immortalized in the 2005 biopic *Cinderella Man* starring Russell Crowe.

Continue down to 46th Street, where on the corner 40 (currently Mud Matters) used to stand the **Spot Bar and Grill**. On December 9, 1939, David "The Beetle" Beadle was shot dead outside here after a taxi pulled over and two gunmen got out and killed the longshoreman who had mob connections. His corpse, lying on the sidewalk surrounded by

policemen and the press, was captured in a photograph by the famous crime photographer Arthur Fellig—better known as Weegee.

Walk left down West 46th Street to ⓸ **Clinton Court**, on the right-hand side. Sadly, the tiny passageway on the right of 422 West 46th Street is not accessible because of a gate, but at the end is a tree-line courtyard and a former carriage house (No. 422 ½) that may date from the 1870s, although it could be much older. It is commonly described as belonging to George Clinton, governor of New York and relative of DeWitt Clinton mentioned earlier. It would almost certainly have stood here when the surrounding area was still largely farmland and undeveloped. Woody Allen used the building in two movies—*Bullets Over Broadway* and *Deconstructing Harry,* although the scenes filmed here did not make it onto the screen.

Continue on, passing very desirable late 19th century houses. **No. 413** is **Hartley House** ⓸. This institution has been helping people in Hell's Kitchen since 1897 and founded by Marcellus Hartley to help promote social reform through education, volunteerism, and charity. Many residents of Hell's Kitchen needed help, living in slum

conditions in overcrowded tenements. Hartley House has a range of programs, such as after-school activities for children to bingo for the elderly. They are always looking for volunteers if you are interested (www.hartleyhouse.org/volunteer).

You soon reach Ninth Avenue. On the other side of West 46th Street, leading to Eighth Avenue is ⓭ **Restaurant Row**—so-named because of all the eateries serving the many people visiting nearby theaters and other local entertainment spots.

Unless you are hungry, turn right down Ninth Avenue and right along West 45th Street. Walk for a few minutes to reach ⓮ the **Matthews-Palmer Playground**. This was the scene of two murders that helped lead to Hell's Kitchen being renamed as Clinton.

Salvador Agron was a teenage member of the Puerto Rican gang The Vampires. He was called the "Capeman" after the cape he wore on his shoulders. On August 30, 1959—like a scene out of *West Side Story*—he came here for a "rumble' with an Irish-American gang called the Norsemen. When the Norsemen failed to appear, Agron stabbed to death two 16-year-old bystanders. The so-called Capeman Murders shocked the city, particularly after Agron said, "I don't care if I burn. My mother could watch me." At the time there were around 2,000 street gangs, and the outrage helped campaigners who wanted to rename Hell's Kitchen as Clinton.

Walk on, turning left down Tenth Avenue and stopping on the left at **⑤** the former **596 bar** at No. 596. This was Westie leader Jimmy Coonan's bar between 1972-79. During the 1970s, mobsters signified their switch in allegiance to Coogan's gang by moving here from Mickey Spillane's White House Bar (No. 637 Tenth Avenue). In February 1982, local hoodlum Richie Ryan walked into the bar and shot dead former friend Tommy Hess (he shot him in the rectum).

Retrace your steps up Tenth Avenue, taking the next right down West 44th Street. About halfway down on the right is **⑥ The Actors Studio**. Founded in 1947 by Elia Kazan, Cheryl Crawford, and Robert Lewis, it is best known for its method-acting coach Lee Strasberg (1901-1982), who worked here from 1951 to 1982. It has occupied this former church since 1955, and actors who have attended classes here include Robert De Niro, Al Pacino, Sidney Poitier, Marilyn Monroe, Anne Bancroft, Dustin Hoffman, Jane Fonda, Paul Newman, Joanne Woodward and Marlon Brando. Strasberg was nominated for an Oscar for his portrayal of Hyman Roth in *The Godfather Part II* (1974).

Almost next door ❼ at **No. 428** was the **home of actress June Havoc** (1912-2010), sister of the famous exotic dancer Gypsy Rose Lee. Each sibling wrote a memoir: *Gypsy—A Memoir* (1957), which became the basis of the successful musical and film—and *Early Havoc* (1959).

Havoc once danced in a marathon for 3,000 hours as a young woman, winning second place. It inspired her own play *Marathon '33*, which premiered in 1964 (and which Lee Strasburg worked on, too). The house is said to be haunted by a ghost named "Hungry Lucy."

Continue and turn left down Ninth Avenue, passing on your left ❽ **Manhattan Plaza**. Opened in 1977, 70 percent of its 3,500 tenants are people who work in the performing arts industry, including many local theaters. When the Plaza was created, a large proportion of apartments were subject to controls on how much a tenant could pay as a proportion of their income. Tennessee Williams was one of many notable people who lived here. In 1979 the then managing director commented, "Tennessee doesn't care what, say, a doctor in North Carolina thinks about his plays . . . He likes to be with actors, to know what the people who perform his plays feel."

Samuel Jackson was a security guard here, Alicia Keys was born in the Plaza, and Larry David lived opposite Kenny Kramer, the inspiration for Cosmo Kramer in Seinfeld. Terrence Howard, Mickey Rourke, and Angela Lansbury were also tenants once, and a great documentary about the Plaza was made in 2017 titled *Miracle on 42nd Street*.

Turn down West 42nd Street. This general location was the site of a barricade put up by rioters during the infamous Draft Riots in mid-July 1863. The rioters assembled a long barricade of obstacles, angry about rules governing the draft for the Union Army during the Civil War. It turned into a race riot, and the city became a war zone as white, mainly working-class rioters attacked and killed African-Americans and assaulted the police and soldiers.

Fifty buildings were destroyed and perhaps 120 people killed, with 2000 wounded (although no one knows the exact figures). The violence caused many African-Americans to move out of Manhattan for fear of their lives, and all the while, Lincoln was trying to defeat the slave-owning South. It was the largest urban disturbance in US history.

Follow the map to reach the end of the walk at the subway station you started from.

9 MIDTOWN WALK

START AND FINISH: Grand Army Plaza
SUBWAY STATION: 5 Av/59 St **N**, **R**, **W**

MIDTOWN

Distance: 3.7 Miles

1. Grand Army Plaza and the Pulitzer Fountain
2. Plaza Hotel
3. Kennedy's Apartment
4. The Park Lane Hotel
5. 40 Central Park South
6. The Ritz-Carlton
7. Trump Parc
8. James Carpenter's Building
9. 120 Central Park South
10. Hampshire House
11. JW Marriott Essex House
12. The New York Athletic Club
13. Alwyn Court
14. The St. Thomas Choir School
15. Engine Company No. 23
16. 220 Central Park South
17. Central Park Tower
18. Carnegie Hall
19. The Osborne
20. Art Students League
21. 220 West 57th Street
22. Hearst Tower
23. Site of Studio 54
24. Site of Bell Sound Independent Recording Studio
25. Ed Sullivan Theater
26. Site of The Birdland Jazz Club
27. Hampton Inn
28. Worldwide Plaza
29. St. Malachy's Roman Catholic Church
30. Brill Building
31. Hotel Edison
32. Morgan Stanley Headquaters
33. Statue of Francis P. Duffy
34. The Lyric Theater
35. One Times Square
36. The Town Hall
37. Algonquin Hotel
38. New York Yacht Club
39. Harvard Club
40. Penn Club
41. The General Society of Mechanics and Tradesmen
42. Site of Colored Orphan Asylum
43. MMC Plaza
44. Site of Peppermint Lounge
45. News Corporation and Fox News
46. Pronto Pizza
47. Rockefeller Center
48. Site of Hurley's
49. Radio City Music Hall
50. 21 Club
51. St. Thomas Church
52. The University Club
53. St. Regis Hotel
54. Trump Tower
55. Tiffany & Co.

This walk starts at Grand Army Plaza, near the Fifth Avenue, 59th Street subway station. Midtown is the beating heart of New York—busy, exhausting, and full of the sort of attractions that draw tourists from every corner of the earth: Times Square, the Theater District, the Empire State Building, Rockefeller Center, Trump Tower, Radio City . . . the list is almost endless. This walk will focus on places that have featured in moments of great cultural change in America, as well as the grand hotels, exclusive clubs and celebrity haunts of the past.

Come out of the subway station and look for the golden statue of William Tecumseh Sherman—a general at the American Civil War. The square at the southeast corner of Central Park is ❶ **Grand Army Plaza and the Pulitzer Fountain**. The fountain located in the south-

ern part of the square is named for Joseph Pulitzer (1847-1911), a major media figure in his time and owner of the *New York World* newspaper.

Pulitzer, from a Jewish-Hungarian family, arrived as a teenager in America in 1864 to fight for the Union Army during the Civil War, even though he spoke hardly any English. He would later become a pioneer of a form of sensationalistic news reporting known as "Yellow Journalism." In the 1890s he fought a bitter circulation war against rival William Randolph Hearst's *New York Journal.* The techniques of Yellow Journalism developed by Pulitzer and Hearst are still used today, even if their newspapers are long gone. Pulitzer died a multi-millionaire, and his fortune would fund his most famous legacy—the Pulitzer Prize, established in 1917, a year after the fountain was opened.

Next door to the fountain is the legendary **Plaza Hotel ❷**—one of several upscale hotels overlooking Central Park. This has the appearance of a French Renaissance chateau in the heart of the city.

The hotel opened in 1890, the heyday of The Gilded Age in the city. The current building dates from 1907 and contains 800 luxurious rooms, a ballroom and offers some of the finest amenities found in any hotel in the world. It has had many owners over time, including Donald Trump who acquired it in 1988 and placed his (later ex) wife Ivana in charge. He sold it a few years later after running into financial difficulties. It is just the first of several Trump connections you will encounter on this walk, and whatever your political views, it is hard to ignore Trump's impact on the city's real estate over the last few decades.

At the time of writing, one night in the Grand Penthouse overlooking Central Park would cost you around $40,000.

Everyone who is anyone has stayed here, from Marlene Dietrich, Frank Lloyd Wright, Enrico Caruso, F. Scott Fitzgerald and, of course, Eloise, the heroine of Kay Thompson's children's book series.

John, Paul, George and Ringo arrived here on February 7, 1964, and 50 policemen had to patrol the perimeter of the hotel to keep screaming fans out. They stayed in the Presidential Suites on the 12th floor and conducted press conferences inside. The band's rise to fame was astonishing. No British pop group had made it big in America before, and just 12 months prior to their stay at the Plaza, The Beatles were playing small gigs in provincial towns in their homeland.

Their world and that of millions of teenagers in America changed forever on February 9, 1964, when The Beatles first appeared on the Ed Sullivan Show. Despite their success, the Plaza refused to let them stay when they next came to New York (instead, The Beatles stayed at the nearby Warwick Hotel).

The Plaza features in many films and television programs, including *North by Northwest, Home Alone 2* (in which Donald Trump has a cameo), *The Way We Were, Arthur, Crocodile Dundee, Sleepless in Seattle, The First Wives Club, Friends, Splash, The Sopranos* and *Sex and the City*. It is also mentioned a number of times in F. Scott Fitzgerald's *The Great Gatsby*. Fitzgerald and his wife Zelda spent several weeks in room 644 in 1922, and *The Great Gatsby* was published three years later. Madonna was also photographed outside The Plaza in June 1990 while visiting Warren Beatty here, the relationship then attracting media interest around the world.

Continue along Central Park South, passing ❸ **No. 24**, where the **Kennedy dynasty** kept an apartment for many years. On May 24, 1963, Robert F. Kennedy, then Attorney General, met with James Baldwin

and other prominent African-American figures such as Harry Belafonte and Lena Horne. The purpose was to discuss the Civil Rights cause, and while it was a rancorous meeting, it is credited with helping Kennedy become more supportive of the African American community.

Keep walking, passing ❹ **The Park Lane Hotel** (36 Central Park South). It was built in the early 1970s for real-estate magnate and billionaire Harry Helmsley (1907-1997). Helmsley and his wife Leona—nicknamed "The Queen of Mean"—were both charged with tax evasion (he was judged too frail to plead, however, Leona spent time in jail). A fellow real estate mogul was not a fan of Leona's influence on her elderly husband and wrote an extraordinary open letter in 1989 describing her as "a disgrace to the industry and a disgrace to humanity in general." He also said without "the veil of Harry Helmsley, you would be a nonentity. You would not be able to randomly fire and abuse people in order to make yourself happy." The author, so concerned about people being fired or abused, was Donald Trump.

Farther along at ❺ **No. 40** is an apartment building where Lady Gaga, Lance Armstrong and Liza Minnelli have lived. Gaga's two-bed-

room apartment was later offered for rent at $33,000 a month. Mobster Meyer Lansky lived here in apartment 14C—he would also live in the Essex House (seen shortly). Lansky was the inspiration for Hyman Roth in *The Godfather: Part II* (played by acting legend Lee Strasberg).

Next door at No. 50 ❻ is another upscale hotel—**The Ritz-Carlton**, formerly the Hotel St. Moritz. The building dates from 1930, and Donald Trump also owned this in the late 1980s, having purchased it from Harry Helmsley. In its glamorous Hotel St. Moritz heyday, it was home to the St. Moritz orchestra and attracted guests such as Marlene Dietrich. The architect was Emery Roth (1871-1948), and like Pulitzer, another person of Hungarian-Jewish heritage who had a big impact on New York. He designed many of the most significant apartment blocks and hotels built here in the 1920s and 30s. After his death, his sons continued the prominent architectural practice Emery Roth & Sons, also responsible for the Park Lane Hotel.

Farther along, is ❼ **Trump Parc** (No. 106), another Art Deco building also dating from 1930. It was used by British Royal Navy officers during World War II. Trump bought this in 1981 and then engaged in a bitter and highly public battle with tenants he wanted to evict. At one point, he threatened in newspaper advertisements to house homeless people here as part of the battle. It was another early sign of his willingness to use the media to fight his opponents.

Walk on, passing ❽ **No. 110**—designed by **James Carpenter** (1867-1932). This building, dating from the early 1900s, was just one of many luxurious apartment buildings Carpenter designed in New York, and Emery Roth was in some ways his successor.

Keep going to **No. 120** ❾, home until 2013 of the influential movie-making couple Kathleen Kennedy and Frank Marshall. Closely associated with Spielberg and Lucasfilm, if their names are unfamiliar to you, the films they have helped create between them will not be. These include *Schindler's List, Raiders of the Lost Ark, Jurassic Park, Back*

to the Future, The Sixth Sense, E.T. and the *Bourne* films.

The exclusiveness of Central Park South has ensured it has become home to countless celebrities, gangsters, artists and politicians over the years, including Meyer Lansky (40 CPS), Larry Hagman and LaToya Jackson (both at 106), Billy Joel and Christine Brinkley (128), George Burns, Bing Crosby and Betty Grable (all at 160) and Raquel Welch (200).

Hampshire House  is at No. 150. Past residents include Ingrid Bergman, John Wayne, Greta Garbo, Frank Sinatra, Ava Gardner, Marilyn Monroe, Joe DiMaggio, and Art Garfunkel. If there was a fantasy Hampshire House singing competition, you might think Garfunkel stood a good chance of winning, but—unfortunately for him—his rivals would include the Three Tenors—Domingo, Pavarotti and Carreras—who have each owned apartments here. At street level, it is difficult to see how imposing these buildings are, but from up high or a

distance, you get a better sense of their enormous size, with hundreds of windows giving fantastic views over Central Park.

No. 160, **JW Marriott Essex House**, ⑪ has a stunning art deco exterior, and on top has the famous "Essex House" red sign. Like so many buildings along here, it opened in the early 20th century—in this case 1931.

Why did so many buildings date from around the time of the Great Depression? It was not on purpose—construction here began a day after the Wall Street Crash in 1929 and the economic fallout delayed completion by many months. A fantasy resident's talent competition here would be interesting too, as past residents include Igor Stravinsky, David Bowie and Oasis frontman Liam Gallagher. For many years it has also been popular with visiting Major League Baseball teams. At the time of writing, one apartment at 160 was on the market for around $20 million, so that view of Central Park does not come cheaply.

Ownership of these high-profile real estate sites overlooking the Park changes frequently. The idea of owning such prestigious buildings does not always translate into commercially successful ventures. In recent decades Chinese and Middle Eastern investors, as well as global hotel chains, have competed with each other to buy these buildings, then renovate them in an attempt to squeeze even more money from wealthy visitors and residents.

Continue on to ⑫ **The New York Athletic Club** at No. 180. This is one of a number of the city's prestigious private social clubs seen on this walk. This club was founded in 1868 and became the main amateur sports body in the country, pioneering the organization of many sports and producing rulebooks. Today it fields 22 teams for sports such as judo, tennis, track and field, and lacrosse. Inside this building, facilities include basketball and squash courts, a swimming pool, and fencing and wrestling rooms.

The club has been involved in controversy in recent decades over its "men only" policy and widely held perception it discouraged any

members who were Jewish or of color. In 1964 demonstrators stood outside protesting about the lack of African American and Jewish members. Muhammad Ali held a press conference here in 1981 and—testing the microphone before it started—joked, *"Ladies and Gentlemen, the Jews and n****** and all the other members of the NAACP welcome you to the NYAC."* It eventually allowed women to join in the 1980s but only after being involved in a legal case against elitist clubs and their sexist membership restrictions.

Now you turn away from Central Park, heading left down Seventh Avenue and stopping outside ⓭ the impressive façade of **Alwyn Court** on the corner of West 58th Street. Look closely to admire the elaborate terra-cotta decorations that feature crowns and salamanders. It was designed in a French Renaissance style and, when completed in 1909, represented the ultimate in luxurious apartment living for the city's residents.

It is inspired by the architecture favored by the early 16th century French King Francis I, and the crowned salamander—with its fabled magical properties—was the chosen emblem of that monarch. The building stands 13 stories tall, small compared to the apartment buildings and hotels you have just passed, most of which were built a few decades later. As New York grew, the demand for ever taller buildings increased. It is currently occupied by Petrossian—caviar lovers can stop here—which, appropriately, given the French connection, traces its origins to a café founded in Paris in 1920. Past residents include Liam Neeson and other celebrities.

Now walk west along West 58th Street (Central Park is to the north). On the left, stop outside ⓮ **The St. Thomas Choir School**. Founded in 1919, the boys at this boarding school are age 8 to 14, and regularly sing at the nearby Episcopalian St. Thomas Church, as well as other prestigious venues in the US and abroad. A boarding school for male choristers is rare, and only a few exist around the world. They have occupied this building since 1987, and one former pupil is Kit Culkin (b. 1944), father of actors Macaulay, Rory, and Kieran, and sister of Bonnie Bedelia (who played Bruce Willis's wife in the *Diehard* films). Kit was a child actor himself, with an uncredited role in *West Side Story* (1961), and appeared on stage alongside Richard Burton and Laurence Olivier.

A little farther ahead on the right is ⓯ the home of **Engine Company No. 23**, first organized as a fire fighting unit in 1865 and located

here since 1906. There are photos of horse-drawn fire engines leaving this building in 1907, almost hard to imagine today as the location is dwarfed by the enormous early 21st century skyscrapers on all sides. Firefighters from here responded when a plane crashed into the Empire State Building in 1945, while 12 men lost their lives during a blaze in 1966. Look for the memorial to firefighter Mark P. Whitford who "made the supreme sacrifice" on September 11, 2001.

The firehouse is dwarfed by **⓰ 220 Central Park South**, a residential tower completed in 2019. It cost around $1.5 billion to build, and residents include many company CEOs, hedge fund managers, and musicians. The sale of one apartment for $238 million in 2019 by hedge fund manager and multi-billionaire Kenneth C. Griffin was then the most expensive home ever sold in the country. Others have sold for over $100

million. It seems unlikely any billionaires living here nearby have volunteered for Engine Company No. 23.

This is just one of a handful of super-tall, "pencil tower" apartment buildings that have sprung up in this area in recent years. Most are on or around 57th Street, giving rise to the nickname "Billionaires Row." These include One57 (157 West 57th Street), 111W57/ Steinway Tower (111 West 57th Street), 252 East 57th Street, Central Park Tower (225 West 57th Street), 520 Park Avenue and 432 Park Avenue.

The lack of affordable housing in the city for "ordinary" people has long caused tensions, and the rise of Billionaire's Row has led to much discussion about the future of Manhattan. From an architectural point of view, the new buildings are also revolutionary. The city's building code regards buildings as slender if the width to height ratio is 1:7. Some of the apartment buildings on Billionaire's Row have pushed this to unheard-of extremes—111 W 57 has a width-to-height ratio of 1:24, making it the thinnest skyscraper in the world. The irony is you can pay hundreds of millions for an apartment with a view over Central Park but feel yourself

swaying as the towers are affected by strong winds. One can only imagine what Jane Jacobs would have thought of it all.

On the south side of the street is ❼ **Central Park Tower** (or Nordstrom Tower), which reaches 1,550 feet and is the second-tallest building in the US and cost around $3 billion to construct. The extraordinary and controversial cantilever over the Art Students League of New York's building will be more obvious to see later on in the walk.

Retrace your steps to Seventh Avenue, with the world-famous **Carnegie Hall** on the left-hand side ❽. It opened in 1891 and is named

for Scots-born industrialist and philanthropist Andrew Carnegie (1835-1919) who funded the construction. There is a famous joke that Russian violist Jascha Heifetz was stopped by a pedestrian and asked how to get to Carnegie Hall to which the musician answered "practice!"

Turn right onto West 57th Street. At ❾ is **The Osborne** at No. 205, which dates from the mid-1880s and—like the more famous Dakota building of 1881—is an early example of the grand apartment buildings that would come to play such an important part in the city's development. Past residents include composer and conductor Leonard Bernstein (1918-1990). He conducted many concerts at Carnegie Hall, including several world-premieres of modern classical works. Apartments here can cost more than $6 million.

This street is not very old and was only laid out and opened in 1857. Over the next few decades, respectable New York families began moving to grand houses along the new streets south of Central Park. By the mid-1880s, the houses around here were regarded as being among the best in the city. The opening of Carnegie Hall helped attract many artists, art societies, piano stores, and art galleries, giving the area a Bohemian reputation that is hard to imagine today.

Continue on to ⑳ No. 215, home of the **Art Students League of New York**, a prestigious art school founded in 1875. It has around 2,500 students and among the many artists who have studied here are Georgia O'Keeffe, Jackson Pollock, Mark Rothko, Louise Nevelson and Ai Weiwei. The French Renaissance-style building is special, dating from 1891. It was designed by Henry Hardenbergh (1847-1918), a pioneer of the skyscraper and responsible for dozens of important New York buildings of which the Plaza Hotel and the Dakota are just two examples.

Opposite at ㉑ **220 West 57th Street** is another French Renaissance-style building dating from 1897 and designed by Cyrus L.W. Eidlitz, best known for One Times Square when *The New York Times* was based there. Originally this was home to the American Society of Civil Engineers. If you cross over to 220 and look back you can get a better view of Central Park Tower and how part of it hangs over the Art Students League Building. This

has raised concerns about how such tall towers will cast shadows over Central Park and neighboring streets. *The New York Times*, commenting about the proliferation of the new mega-residential structures, stated, "the new towers, with their luxury apartments designed for foreign investors and the superwealthy, can feel like a feat of inequality."

Continue along, crossing Broadway. In the early 20th century, this area up to Columbus Circle was known as Automobile Row on account of the large number of car showrooms that existed.

You now reach Eighth Avenue where—on the other side ㉒—is the striking **Hearst Tower**. This odd building looks like a jack-in-the-box that has been sprung. The bottom section dates from 1928, and the modern section from 2006—designed by Norman Foster, one of the most influential architects of recent times. It is named for William Randolph Hearst (1863-1951), Pulitzer's great rival and media tycoon whose equally extraordinary life helped inspire Orson Welles's classic film *Citizen Kane* (1941).

Continue south down Eighth Avenue, the dividing line between Midtown and Hell's Kitchen to the west. After a few minutes, turn left onto West 54th Street and stop outside ㉓ **No. 254**. This is the site of **Studio 54**, arguably the most famous nightclub in modern history.

The building dates from 1927 and was used for opera productions and then by CBS for television radio right into the 1970s. It was after this that Steve Rubell and Ian Schrager opened up the iconic club (in 1977), the most exclusive, hedonistic spot in the age of disco. Celebrities who flocked here included Mick and Bianca Jagger, David Bowie, Woody Allen, Halston, Salvador Dali, Andy Warhol, Liza Minnelli, Grace Jones and John Belushi.

People were so desperate to get inside that one man was found dead inside an air vent after having tried to  sneak in. Its heyday ended with a closing party in 1980 after the founders were convicted for tax evasion and later imprisoned. It reopened a few years later but never recaptured its heyday. President Barack Obama pardoned Ian Schrager in 2017 (Steve Rubell died in 1989).

Like punk-dominated CBGB, Studio 54's legendary status continues to grow as the years go by, and it continues to feature in films, television series, documentaries and films. Today the building is occupied by The Roundabout Theatre Company.

On the other side of the road at **237 ㉔** was the location of the **Bell Sound independent recording studio** from the mid-1950s to the 1970s. In its heyday, artists who recorded here included Bill Haley and the Comets, Buddy Holly, Ike Turner, The Everly Brothers, Ben E. King, Dionne Warwick, Ray Charles and Wilson Pickett.

Continue down West 54th Street, and turn right onto Broadway, with ㉕ the **Ed Sullivan Theater** on the right. It opened in 1927 and has been used by CBS since 1936. Over the decades, many of the most

famous names in show business have appeared here, but it was appearances by Elvis, and then The Beatles that represented turning points in popular culture that continue to impact us today.

On September 9, 1956, Elvis made his first appearance on the popular Ed Sullivan Show, and over 60 million people tuned in to watch. Elvis's enormous popularity would help spread Rock'n'Roll's global phenomenon. Oddly Sullivan did not present this seminal show—he was recovering from an automobile accident and British actor Charles Laughton stood in as host. Elvis was not actually here either—he was filming at the time in Hollywood, so was beamed in live from CBS's West Coast studio.

On February 9, 1964, 72 million would watch The Beatles make the first of three appearances on the show that month. The band represented a revolution in how popular music was made, as they wrote and performed their own songs rather than relying on professional song-writers. Within a few months, The Beatles would be filling stadiums across America, giving rise to the modern era of rock and pop. Today, the theater is home to CBS's *The Late Show* (at the time of writing hosted by Stephen Colbert).

Walk on, stopping outside ㉖ **1678 Broadway**—approximately where the parking sign is today. This venue has an equally important place in modern music culture as its basement was home to **The Birdland Jazz Club** from 1949 to 1965. It was named for jazz pioneer and saxophonist Charlie Parker (1920-1955), whose nickname was "Bird." Birdland attracted all the great performers—Miles Davis, John Coltrane, Dizzy Gillespie, Billie Holiday, Ella Fitzgerald, Duke Ellington and Nina Simone. On a good night the finest jazz musicians of their generation performed in front of celebrities such as Frank Sinatra, Judy Garland, Marilyn Monroe, Joe Louis and Marlene Dietrich.

However, as with many jazz clubs, there were often racial tensions under the surface, and the police were often heavy-handed with Black performers. In August 1959 Miles Davis had just released the iconic album *Kind of Blue*, which would go on to become the highest selling jazz record in history. He was outside the club smoking a cigarette when a white policeman told him to move on. Miles refused, answering "Move on, for what? I'm working downstairs. That's my name up there!" and pointed to his own name in lights above. He was attacked by two policeman and arrested, photographed covered in blood. Davis could handle himself, a keen boxer who was given boxing lessons by the great Sugar Ray Robinson in Harlem.

Head right up West 52nd Street—once the heart of the city's jazz scene and part of it became known as "Swing Street" (originally, this

term was used for 133rd Street in Harlem until the ending of Prohibition in 1933 encouraged jazz clubs to move here). In recent times only the 21 Club survived from this era (seen later). You are now very much in the Theater District. The first theaters appeared in Midtown in the 1880s, and despite ups and downs over subsequent decades, it remains a world-famous area for live entertainment. You will pass the August Wilson and Neil Simon theaters. The marketing blurb from an apartment block on this street boasts, "If you're looking for that classic old New York feel, this is the place to be. From jazz clubs to gastropubs, this vintage area flaunts the dense urban vibe you crave."

At the end, turn left onto Eighth Avenue. On the right ❷⓿ is the **Hampton Inn**. It was at a hotel on this address that activist Angela Davis (b. 1944) was arrested by the FBI on October 13, 1970. She had been on the run for two months on murder and kidnapping charges.

President Nixon thanked the FBI for its "capture of the dangerous terrorist Angela Davis." Davis would eventually be found not guilty of the charges and would go onto pursue a high-profile and often controversial academic and political career. Reference to her arrest here is made in the Aretha Franklin biopic *Respect* (2021) and the Rolling Stones dedicated a song to her, "Sweet Black Angel," on their famous 1972 album *Exile on Main Street*.

Now walk for a few minutes down Eighth Avenue, passing ㉘ **Worldwide Plaza** on the right. This stands on the site of the old Madison Square Garden.

Now turn left onto 49th Street, stopping on the left ㉙ at **St. Malachy's Roman Catholic Church**. Known as The Actors' Chapel, it was founded in 1902. From the 1920s it became known for attracting many people from the theater community. Thousands of people crowded the street outside when the New York funeral was held for 31-year-old movie sensation Rudolph Valentino in August 1926. Mary Pickford and Gloria Swanson were among those in attendance.

Douglas Fairbanks, Jr. and Joan Crawford were married here in 1929 (he was 19, she was five years older). The marriage did not last long— Crawford's affair with Clark Gable helped its demise. Others who have worshipped here include Spencer Tracy, Bob Hope and Perry Como.

The church has survived many changes in this area, particularly when many of its congregation drifted away as local streets became plagued by prostitution, crime, drugs, massage parlors and the sex entertainment business in the 1970s and 80s. In 1972 it was reported that this immediate area was home to 30 hotels such as The Raymona that "catered to" prostitution. There were also 41 massage parlors used by sex workers, six bars used by pimps, and around 50 adult movie cinemas. Things got even worse as the 70s continued, and if you watch Martin Scorsese's bleak film *Taxi Driver* (1976) you will get a sense of how downtrodden this part of Midtown had become.

Continue along, passing the Ambassador and Eugene O'Neill Theaters, and turning left onto Broadway. On the corner is the ❸⓿ art deco **Brill Building** constructed in 1931. It was originally the Alan E. Lefcourt Building. Alan was the son of property developer Abraham E. Lefcourt who had named other buildings for his family. It became known as the Brill Building after a haberdasher who later came to own the building. The Brill Building also became a byword for the music industry that grew up in this immediate area, and covered other offices (for example at 1650 Broadway).

From the 1930s to 1960s this was the heart of the country's music industry, home to hundreds of music publishers, record pluggers, writers, lyricists and composers. These included Burt Bacharach, Gerry Goffin, Carole King, Neil Sedaka, Paul Simon, Neil Diamond, Jerry Leiber, Mike Stoller, Phil Spector, Frankie Valli, Liza Minnelli and The Drifters. So, what happened? The Beatles helped change the music industry, as teenagers now wanted to worship bands that wrote their own material. Almost overnight the Brill Building factory system became uncool. Brill Building stalwarts such as Carole

King, Neil Sedaka, and Neil Diamond developed their own performing careers instead of writing songs for others.

The bust of a young man above the entrance carries a sad story. It depicts Alan Lefcourt, who died at age 17 in 1930. At the same time, his grieving father, Abraham, had to cope with the disastrous impact of the Wall Street Crash on his real estate empire. He died, possibly a suicide, in 1932, his multi-million dollar fortune having disappeared. The large bust up high is also believed to represent Alan.

Continue south down Broadway (the Brill at your back) and then turn left onto West 47th Street to stop outside ❸➊ the **Hotel Edison**. This is another art deco masterpiece, dating from 1931 and named for the famed inventor Thomas Edison (who switched on the lights at the opening). Why is this so important? Because no New York walk is complete without a Godfather connection. Luca Brasi walks along the rear entrance hallway before being murdered in *The Godfather* (1972). Scenes from *Birdman* (2014) and Woody Allen's *Bullets over Broadway* (1994) were also filmed here.

Retrace your steps, now passing the global headquarters for **Morgan Stanley** on the left ❸➋. On all sides you are surrounded by hotels, theaters, tourist shops and restaurants, so one of the world's most powerful financial firms in such a busy area seems unusual.

When you reach Broadway again, turn right to continue into Times Square. Considered by many to be the heart of the city, it is also known as the "Crossroads of the World." If you suffer from agoraphobia, you may need to calm yourself before carrying on.

Times Square was originally called Longacre Square. It was renamed in 1904 after *The New York Times* moved into a new headquarters at the Times Building—now called One Times Square. Why

Longacre? Because this used to be the center of the city's horse and carriage trade, and was named after Long Acre in London, which traditionally had the same role.

On the north side is Duffy Square, and walk over to see the ❸❸ **statue of Father Francis P. Duffy** (1871-1932). A Catholic priest and military chaplain, he served with the "Fighting 69th" in various conflicts, including World War I. Many of the soldiers he looked after were Irish-Americans from New York, and Duffy later worked as pastor of the Holy Cross Church near here. His reputation and fame ensured he was portrayed by actor Pat O'Brien in the movie *The Fighting 69th* (1940) that starred James Cagney.

By the 1890s, this area had already become a place for entertainment, but it really took off after World War I when cinemas began to open alongside grand theaters and restaurants. After the area became sleazy in the 1960s and 70s, it went into a major decline, reaching a nadir in the early 1980s. However, successive mayors, developers, politicians and corporations such as Disney, invested huge sums to revitalize Times Square. While this has certainly reduced crime and brought back tourists, for some New Yorkers the "Disneyfication" of the district in recent times has not been welcomed. In the last few years, however, Times Square has once again begun to appear in the media about the city's

Times Square

growing crime problem, although it is nowhere near as bad as it used to be.

Continue down Seventh Avenue, turning right onto West 43rd Street. Continue along to ㉞ **The Lyric theater** at No. 214. The story of The Lyric is typical of this area, opening in 1903 in the golden age of new theater construction. In the 1920s its shows involved famous composers and performers such as Cole Porter, the Gershwins, Fred and Adele Astaire and the Marx Brothers. However, it went into decline and was a movie theater from 1932 to 1992. In the film *Taxi Driver*, this is where Bickle (Robert de Niro) takes Betsy (Cybill Shepherd) to see a porno film on a date. The date was not a success.

This area was revitalized in the 1990s through investment in modernizing (and demolishing) many of the old theaters. The Lyric building was pulled down although the façade was retained for the new theater constructed here.

Retrace your steps, passing ㉟ **One Times Square**. This iconic building, underneath the neon signs, has at its core the landmark skyscraper built in 1903 for *The New York Times*. The newspaper's owner Adolph Ochs persuaded the city authorities to rename Longacre Square as Times Square, and it was during this era the famous "New Year's Eve ball drop" tradition began.

Follow the map to turn right (east) along West 43rd Street, passing on the left ㊱ at No. 123 **The Town Hall** performance space. Look up to see signage on the exterior that recalls a very different purpose for this building. It refers to The Town Hall being founded by the League for Political Education.

The League was founded in 1894 to support the cause of women's suffrage and democratic values. The 19th Amendment that gave women the vote was ratified in 1920 and The Town Hall opened the following year. The auditorium was used for speeches and gatherings by the League and associated causes, but over time it became better known for the artistic events held here.

The rather plain Georgian Revival style of the design was specifically chosen because it was felt at the time to symbolize the League's grassroots democratic ideals. The Town Hall Club, which promoted political discourse among the public was also based here. For decades many famous people performed or talked at The Town Hall, including Sir Winston Churchill, Paul Robeson, Marian Anderson and the Von Trapp family (immortalized in *The Sound of Music*). Famous jazz concerts were also held here too, including one in June 1945 that involved Dizzy Gillespie, Max Roach, Charlie Parker and others that would become a milestone in the emergence of bebop, and Billie Holiday making her first solo concert performance the year after.

Continue up, turning left up Sixth Avenue then right onto West 44th Street. At the time of writing, there are 41 "Broadway" theaters, usually understood to be theaters within Manhattan's Theater District that can seat 500 or more people. Five date from 1903-1910, eleven from 1911-1920, nineteen from the 1920s, and only six were built after 1965. That gives an idea of when theater construction was at its more frenzied. By one estimate, there are around 85 "Off-Broadway" theaters (defined as seating 100 to 499 people) and 120 "Off-Off-Broadway" theaters (99 seats or less).

This stretch contains some of the most prestigious clubs in the city, but first you pass ❸❼ the **Algonquin Hotel** that opened in 1902. Under Frank Case, it became popular with guests from the entertainment world, and hosted what became to be known as the Algonquin Round Table. During the 1920s, some of the city's most influential writers, critics, actors and journalists met over lunch to exchange gossip, news, and ideas and impress each other with sparkling witticisms.

Regular members included Dorothy Parker, Harpo Marx, Ruth Hale, Harold Ross, and Tallulah Bankhead. The Round Table members were also keen poker players and even staged their own revue, "No Sirree!" in 1922.

Other regulars at the hotel included William Faulkner (he wrote his acceptance speech for the 1949 Nobel Prize for Literature while staying here). Alan Jay Lerner and Frederick Loewe wrote songs for the musical hit *My Fair Lady* while staying in suite 908 in 1956.

Next you pass The Iroquois Hotel on the same side (where James Dean lived on an off between 1950-53) before stopping at ❸ **The New York Yacht Club**. It will be forever associated with the America's Cup (the club had the longest winning streak in sports history from 1851 until 1983). The club was founded in 1844 and has been based here in this fantastic Beaux-Arts building since 1901 (it also has a base in Newport, Rhode Island). Look for the three windows designed to resemble the bows of 17th-century Dutch yachts.

This is another private invitation-only club. Past members include the great and the good of New York, including J. P. Morgan, various Astors, Vanderbilts, Rockefellers, Kennedys, Roosevelts and some the club would prefer not to celebrate (Bernie Madoff).

This area around 43nd and 44th Streets has long been known as Clubhouse Row, and popular with Ivy League private alumni clubs in particular.

Next door ❸ is the **Harvard Club**, founded in 1865 and based here since 1894. Past members include John F. Kennedy, Franklin D. Roosevelt and Theodore Roosevelt, Reginald Lewis, and Major Michael Bloomberg. The club fought hard to stop women from becoming members, but its membership finally agreed by a vote in 1973 to

change its historic policy in the face of anti-discriminatory legislation.

Opposite the Harvard Club is  the **Penn Club**, an alumni club of the University of Pennsylvania. Another private alumni club, The Williams Club, is also based here.

Next door is  **The General Society of Mechanics and Tradesmen of the City of New York**. Founded by, and for the benefit, of skilled tradesmen in 1785, it mirrors other trade organizations that existed in America and Europe at this time. As labor practices changed in later years, many trade bodies became obsolete, however, the Society survived by becoming focused on charitable and educational endeavors. Andrew Carnegie supplied funds for the clubhouse building, expanding the existing building in 1903. If you have time, visit the John M. Mossman Lock Museum inside, with its unique collection of locks, keys, and tools from all eras of history.

Within a short walk of here are other exclusive clubs such as the Cornell Club, Yale Club, Dartmouth Club, Columbia University Club of New York, and the Princeton Club. Look out for confident-looking, well-heeled club members strolling these streets on their way to their club—probably going to a cocktail party.

Follow the map to reach Fifth Avenue. On the right at ㊷ is the approximate site of the **Colored Orphan Asylum**. Founded by Quakers in 1836, it was located near here in 1863 when one of the most shameful episodes in the city's history took place here during the Draft Riots.

The riots were triggered by the anger felt by many working-class New Yorkers against draft laws that allowed rich residents to escape serving in the Union Army by paying $300. However, the mob contained a significant racist element and a white mob attacked the orphanage, setting it on fire. Around 233 children were lucky to be led away just in time to escape with their lives. The riots resulted in around 120 people being killed over several days, including many African-Americans who were murdered. Many traumatized African-Americans would flee Manhattan for safer districts, a reminder that the Confederate South was not the only place where deep-seated racist attitudes could be found in America.

Head north up Fifth Avenue, turning left onto West 45th Street. On the right is ㊸ the half-acre **MMC Plaza**, where you can sit and rest, while admiring the Japanese pagoda trees and Tony Smith's sculpture *Throwback*. Smith (1912-1980) was a major figure in the early days of American minimalist sculpture. Trivia lovers may also appreciate the fact that Tennessee Williams was the sole witness at Smith's wedding to opera singer Jane Lawrence in 1943.

Carry on ㊹ to **No. 128**. The car park entrance is approximately the site of the **Peppermint Lounge**, a legendary disco that operated between 1958-65, and which was frequented by The Beatles, Frank Sinatra, Audrey Hepburn, Marilyn Monroe, Truman Capote, Norman

Mailer, Jackie Kennedy and even the reclusive Greta Garbo. Many came because of the club's fame as the birthplace of the "Twist" dance that swept the world in the early 1960s.

The Peppermint Lounge was Mob controlled and run by **Johnny Biello**, capo of the Genovese crime family. Biello was murdered in Miami in 1967 after opening a Peppermint Lounge there.

Retrace your steps, and turn left (north) up Sixth Avenue, also known as Avenue of the Americas. You pass the offices of ㊺ **News Corporation and Fox News**, part of the media empire controlled by Rupert Murdoch and his family. Murdoch, like Pulitzer and Hearst before him, has done much to shape the political discourse in this country.

Continue north up Sixth Avenue, passing on the east side the famous Diamond District that dominates West 47th Street between here and Fifth Avenue.

Next head down West 48th Street to No. 62 on the right ㊻, occupied by **Pronto Pizza**. It is notable because in September 2021 a lucky person went in for a slice of pizza and ended up buying a Mega Millions lottery ticket. The ticket happened to be a winner—for $432 million. Pronto Pizza also got a $10,000 bonus

for selling the ticket and the place must be lucky—another ticket sold here by the same member of staff was worth a $3 million prize. The mystery buyer has not been publicly identified but may just about be able to buy an apartment on Billionaire's Row. You might want to buy a ticket here before you carry on.

On the other side of the road is Christie's auction house, where billionaires buy their art. In 2021 a Picasso sold here for $103 million.

Retrace your steps, continuing up Sixth Avenue, passing the 22-acre **⑰ Rockefeller Center** on the right. Most of the site, featuring 14 art deco buildings, was constructed in the 1930s. The project was driven by John D. Rockefeller Jr. (1874-1960) whose father founded Standard Oil.

On the northeast corner of 49th Street is **⑱** a four-story building dwarfed by everything around it. Until 1999 this was home to the famous **Hurley's restaurant**. It was owned for many years by the Irish Hurley brothers, who operated it as a speakeasy during Prohibition and—against all the odds—resisted having their restaurant demolished to make way for Rockefeller Center.

Hurley's became a favorite watering hole for people working at the Center, and local media companies such as NBC, and The Associated Press. It was even known as Studio 1H among NBC technicians. The multi-millionaire recluse Howard Hughes used to drop in to eat hamburgers.

Continue along, admiring the striking art deco figures on the exterior of Rockefeller Center, and the site of NBC's long-running *The Tonight Show* currently hosted by Jimmy Fallon.

Soon you reach ❹ the legendary **Radio City Music Hall**, headquarters for the Rockettes, which opened in 1932 as part of Rockefeller Center.

Turn right onto West 52nd Street to reach ❺ the former **21 Club** (at number 21). This is another legendary venue that arrived here in 1929, although its origins go back to Greenwich Village in 1922. It was also a speakeasy during Prohibition and employed a lever system that could tip shelves full of booze away if the police raided the premises.

Many celebrities stored their wine collections at the club, including John F. Kennedy,

Frank Sinatra, Mae West, Judy Garland, Richard Nixon and Marilyn Monroe. John, Paul and Ringo from The Beatles came here on their first visit to New York in 1964 for dinner and later were given a tour to see the city's landmarks. In more recent years, it was a favorite dining spot of Donald Trump, and he is said to have sat at table 11 (also the favored location of President Gerald Ford). He held a reception party for his wedding to Ivana here in 1977.

At the end of the block, turn left up Fifth Avenue to stop at ❺❶ **St. Thomas Church**, a Gothic masterpiece consecrated in 1916. This is where boys from the St. Thomas Choir School, visited earlier, regularly perform. In August 1921, *The New York Times* reported how "the dollar sign over the door of St. Thomas's Church drew larger crowds than ever yesterday . . ."—a quirky feature of the design.

Continue up Fifth Avenue, turning left onto West 54th Street to see ❺❷ **The University Club** of New York, yet another exclusive private social club. The club was chartered in 1865, and this clubhouse opened in 1899. Members call it "The U," and the Italian Renaissance style building is one of the finest clubhouses in New York.

Continue north, turning right onto East 55th Street to reach ❸ the **St. Regis Hotel**. John Lennon and Yoko Ono lived here for a while, and it was in October 1971 in his room here that he recorded a demo of "Happy Xmas (War is Over)." The hotel opened in 1904, founded by John Jacob Astor IV. The Astor family and other prominent city dynasties had invested in hotels farther to the south, but as fashionable society moved closer to Central Park, luxury hotels began to open in this area. Its construction was controversial at the time, seen as being "disrespectful" to the private mansions owned nearby by families such as the Vanderbilts.

John Jacob Astor overcame opposition to the hotel, although his victory was short-lived as he died on the Titanic in 1912. It has had many famous guests, including Alfred Hitchcock, Marlene Dietrich, Salvador Dali and Nikola Tesla. The King Cole Bar is famous, and where the Bloody Mary was invented (originally called the "Red Snapper"). The hotel has also been featured in many films, including *The Godfather, Hannah and Her Sisters, The First Wives Club, The Devil Wears Prada* and *Taxi Driver*.

Continue up Fifth Avenue, passing ❸ **Trump Tower**, the headquarters of the Trump

Organization, and where Donald Trump keeps a penthouse. It was completed in 1983. Other people reported to have lived here in the past include Bruce Willis, Michael Jackson, Andrew Lloyd Webber, Paul Manafort, and Donald Trump's parents. Trump Tower has also, unsurprisingly, made it into films, including Batman epic *The Dark Night Rises* (2012).

Just past the Trump Tower is ⑤⑤ **Tiffany & Co.** This has been the luxury jewelers' flagship store since the building was completed in 1940. The location famously appears in the 1961 film *Breakfast at Tiffany's*, with Holly Golightly portrayed by Audrey Hepburn. The film was based on Truman Capote's novella of the same name published in 1958 and actually set in 1943.

If you are having a bad day, you may wish to take Holly's advice on dealing with angst: "I've tried aspirin, too. Rusty thinks I should smoke marijuana, and I did for a while, but it only makes me giggle. What I've found does the most good is just to get into a taxi and go to Tiffany's. It calms me down right away, the quietness and the proud look of it; nothing very bad could happen to you there." In the film Hepburn, wearing that famous little black dress, sunglasses and pearls, looks through the window at Tiffany's while holding a coffee and eating a croissant. When the scene was filmed, hundreds of onlookers stood nearby, causing Hepburn to keep making mistakes.

You can now continue up Fifth Avenue to reach Grand Army Plaza again and where this walk ends.

10

UPPER EAST SIDE WALK

START: Grand Army Plaza
SUBWAY: 5 Av/59 St
FINISH: INTERSECTION OF 77TH STREET AND LEXINGTON AVENUE
SUBWAY: 77 St 6

8

UPPER EAST SIDE

Distance: 2.5 Miles

1. Metropolitan Club
2. The Harmonie Club
3. Site of Copacabana
4. The Pierre Hotel
5. Knickerbocker Club
6. Former Home of Ernest Hemingway
7. Fifth Avenue Synagogue
8. Fabbri Mansion
9. The Links
10. 40 East 62nd Street
11. The Browning School
12. The Colony Club
13. The Halston House
14. The Leash Club
15. Daniel
16. Sara Delano Roosevelt Memorial House
17. Apartment in *Being John Malkovich*
18. Park Avenue Armory
19. 110 East 66th Street
20. The Cosmopolitan Club
21. St. Vincent Ferrer Roman Catholic Church
22. Site of Hamilton Square
23. Hunter College
24. 116 East 68th Street
25. The Union Club
26. Explorers Club
27. 730 Park Avenue
28. 740 Park Avenue
29. St. James' Church
30. Herbert N. Straus House
31. The Gertrude Rhinelander Waldo House
32. Former Woody Allen home
33. Former Paul and Bunny Mellon home
34. Holly Golightly's apartment in *Breakfast at Tiffany's*
35. The Buckley School
36. Church of the Resurrection
37. Temple Israel of the City of New York
38. Lenox Hill Hospital

Exit the subway at East 60th Street, with Central Park to the west. If you stood here around 1830, there would be little to see other than fields, streams, and the occasional house, farm, or church. Central Park would not exist for almost another 30 years, and there would be no clues that this urban district would become—arguably—the most exclusive in New York. It is a place of largely discreet privilege: members-only clubs, mansions, apartment buildings, hotels, restaurants, and schools that are—de facto—closed to the average New Yorker.

To get the first glimpse of this exclusive world, walk east down East 60th Street (the Upper East Side's southern border is at 59th Street, and 96th Street to the north). On the left ❶ is the grand gated entrance of the **Metropolitan Club**, a bastion of the city's "Old Money" dynasties.

It was founded in 1891 by J.P. Morgan and various members of Manhattan's elite clans (Whitneys, Vanderbilts, Roosevelts, etc.) in protest against the strict admissions policy of existing social clubs, ironic given how impossible it is for ordinary people to join today. The clubhouse was designed by the legendary architect Stanford White. Past and present members include Bill Clinton, Salman Rushdie, Richard Nixon, and Ronald Reagan. From the sidewalk you can get a tantalizing glimpse of the opulence inside, but to visit the beautiful Gilded Age ballroom in the West Lounge you have to have contacts to invite you, or be able to afford to hire one of the club's luxurious rooms for a function.

Opposite is ❷ **The Harmonie Club**, another Stanford White design (he was the architect for a number of social clubs). The Harmonie was founded in 1852, making it the second oldest social club of its kind in the

city. Founded by German immigrants, many of whom were Jews, its origin story is similar to that of many social clubs, as its founders felt excluded or discriminated against by existing institutions so decided to set up on their own.

This building has been Harmonie's home since 1905. While its non-Jewish membership has increased recently, the perceived lack of diversity caused Michael Bloomberg, billionaire businessman and later Mayor of New York, to resign from here in 2001. He also quit the

Racquet and Tennis Club not far from here for the same reason. Einstein was among those who held events at the club to raise awareness of the plight of the Jews in Nazi-controlled Europe. Like many elite social clubs founded in the 19th century, the Harmonie was originally based farther south in Manhattan (on 42nd Street) before moving to the Upper East Side.

Next door to the left if you face The Harmonie is the former location at **No. 10** East

60th Street of the ❸ legendary **Copacabana** nightclub, one of the great New York nightclubs for decades after it opened in 1940. Partially owned by mobster Frank Costello, many of the outstanding performers of their time appeared on stage here—from Frank Sinatra, Marvin Gaye, The Supremes, The Temptations, Dean Martin and Jerry Lewis, Sammy Davis Jr., and Harry Belafonte. The latter headlined here years after being refused entry at the door as a customer because of the "whites only" policy. The Club was immortalized in Barry Manilow's 1978 song "Copacabana" and featured in numerous films, including

Raging Bull (1980), *Tootsie* (1982), *Goodfellas* (1990), and *Carlito's Way* (1993). In the 1940s, it was probably the most famous nightclub in the world and was the subject of the film *Copacabana* (1947), starring Groucho Marx and Carmen Miranda. The nightclub moved to different locations later on and closed finally in 2020.

Why did the Upper East Side become synonymous with wealth and privilege? During the mid-19th century, the construction of streets envisaged in the Commissioners' Plan of 1811 crept northwards, but it was the creation of Central Park (which opened in 1858) and new transport links that encouraged wealthy New Yorkers to move uptown. Many immigrants also came here from Germany, Hungary, Bohemia, Ireland, and other places. In 1888 Fourth Avenue was renamed Park Avenue, and stately mansions were constructed along Fifth Avenue and nearby streets. This attracted the city's upper-class families, such as the Vanderbilts, Rhinelanders, and Astors, as well as "new" money millionaires such as

Andrew Carnegie. Exclusive clubs such as the Knickerbocker, Colony, Union, Harmonie, and Metropolitan Club all moved to the area. By the early 20th century the open land was gone, a whole new district was carved out of the earth, and it became home to perhaps the highest concentration of millionaires in the world.

Retrace your steps along East 60th Street, heading towards Central Park and turning right (north) up Fifth Avenue. On the right, you pass ❹ **The Pierre Hotel**, a luxurious establishment founded in 1930 with Corsican links. Charles Pierre Casalasco worked at his father's restaurant in Corsica before learning how to cook in Monte Carlo and London before arriving in New York, where he established himself as an outstanding chef before founding the hotel. It went bust in 1932 and was owned for some time by the billionaire oil tycoon J. Paul Getty. Guests have included everyone from Audrey Hepburn, Lucille Ball, Aristotle Onassis, Frank Sinatra to Mikhail Gorbachev.

In the 1970s, Led Zeppelin regularly stayed here, hosting the premiere of their concert film *The Song Remains the Same* at the hotel in 1976. John Lennon also stayed here during his "Lost Weekend" with May Pang, and used to visit David Bowie when the latter was a guest. In the 1930s, an FBI team used a room at the hotel to conduct surveillance on NKVD spies operating at the Russian consulate opposite (7 East 61st Street), including the "Puppetmaster," Gaik Ovakimian, who helped recruit several top spies in the US before he was arrested by the FBI and returned to Russia in 1941.

Continue up Fifth Avenue, turning right into East 62nd Street to reach on the right ❺ the **Knickerbocker Club**, at **No. 2**. Known as "The Knick," it was founded in 1871 and is possibly the most exclusive private members club in the country.

The Knick's founders started the club in 1871 because they were alarmed at what they thought were the declining admission standards of the Union Club, the oldest private club in the city. This building was completed in 1915, and past members include many famous European aristocrats and those from New York's elite with surnames such as Roosevelt, Vanderbilt, and Rockefeller. Douglas Fairbanks, J.P. Morgan, John Jacob Astor, and Franklin D. Roosevelt were members. It is still a male-only club, is said to have a secrecy code, and don't bother trying to find a club website. You could walk past this innocuous-looking building and have no idea it is home to some of the most powerful and wealthiest men in the world.

What is the origin of "Knickerbocker"? It is traditionally a name for New Yorkers, particularly those who can trace their lineage back to the original Dutch settlers, and so is often associated with the patrician class who inhabit clubs such as this one. Wider usage of the name can be traced back to Washington Irving's hugely popular and satirical book

A Knickerbocker's History of New York (1809). He wrote under the pen name Diedrich Knickerbocker, meant to be a fictional Dutch historian. Irving may have taken the name from his friend Herman Knickerbocker, a descendant of Harmen Jansen Van Wijhe—later Harmen Jansen Knickenbacker—who arrived in New York in the 1670s. The name Knickerbocker may be derived from a Dutch surname meaning "baker of marble"— "knikker" means marble and "bakker" means baker. It may also be linked to the loose-fitting breeches (or knickers) worn by the Dutch. In any case, the Dutch settler "Father Knickerbocker" character became popular in the city from the 19th century, often portrayed in knickered pants and wig and three-cornered hat. The name was incorporated into everything from beer brands to sports team names, including in 1845 for the "New York Knickerbockers" baseball team. The Knicks basketball team is the most famous derivation of the name today.

Opposite at **❻** at **No. 1** East 62nd Street is the **former home of Ernest Hemingway** (1899-1961), who moved into a fourth-floor apartment in 1959. His writing career and personal life were both in a steep decline by then, and during this time he worked on *A Moveable Feast*, published after his death. Hemingway also had a Russian connection as he was recruited as a spy for the Soviet Union under the code-

name "Argo" in 1941. He committed suicide in Idaho in 1961, and his widow, Mary Welsh, kept the New York apartment until she died in 1986.

Next to Hemingway's home is ❼ the **Fifth Avenue Synagogue** at **No. 5**. Founded in 1958, its unusual design stands in sharp contrast to the ❽ **Fabbri Mansion** two doors up at **No. 11**. The latter is an elegant Beaux-Arts French-style mansion dating from 1899 and designed for Margaret Louisa Vanderbilt Shepard, scion of the Vanderbilt dynasty. She was wealthy enough to build mansions for family members, and this one was for her daughter Edith Shepard and her husband Ernesto Fabbri.

This was a house built to entertain at the highest level with a ballroom and 42-foot long dining room. It was later rented out to Alfred G. Vanderbilt and other wealthy members of New York society over the decades. In 1998 it was sold for $21.5 million to the Japanese government, then the highest price paid for a townhouse on the island. It is said Michael Jackson was a potential buyer at the time.

The Fabbri Mansion and synagogue both appear in Woody Allen's film *Hannah and Her Sisters* (1986). The architect David (played by Sam Waterston) takes Holly and April (Dianne Wiest and Carrie Fisher) on a memorable tour of his favorite buildings in Manhattan. Holly admires the Mansion: "Oh, its so romantic. I just want to put on a long gown . . ." but is less impressed by its neighbor, "It's really terrible . . . And it ruins everything else . . ."

Ponzi-scheme fraudster Bernie Madoff was a prominent member of this synagogue, and *The New York Post* reported in December 2008, "Members of a posh Upper East Side synagogue suffered a \$2 billion bloodbath in Bernie Madoff's epic Ponzi scheme." Madoff died in prison in 2021, at age 82.

Carry on down East 62nd Street, crossing over Madison Avenue, named for James Madison Jr. (1751-1836), the fourth president of the United States. It was built in the 1840s and would become popular with the upper classes for residential living. From the 1920s, it became associated with the advertising industry that had offices here, although in recent years many have moved elsewhere.

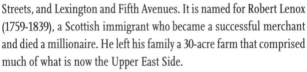

This area is also part of Lenox Hill, which stretches between East 60th to East 77th Streets, and Lexington and Fifth Avenues. It is named for Robert Lenox (1759-1839), a Scottish immigrant who became a successful merchant and died a millionaire. He left his family a 30-acre farm that comprised much of what is now the Upper East Side.

Continue along East 62nd Street, passing ❾ **The Links** on the right at **No. 36**, housed in an elegant Neo-Georgian revival townhouse. Hard to believe perhaps, but this is one of the most elite golf clubs in the world, even though it does not own a golf course (which would admittedly be a challenge to maintain on the Upper East Side). The Links was founded in 1917 by C.B. Macdonald, a prominent society figure who wanted to mirror the ethos of the Royal and Ancient Golf Club of St. Andrews in Scotland, the spiritual home of the game, and keep a low profile. However its members are anything but low profile, and include those within the highest echelons of the country's business, military, political and social elites.

Dwight D. Eisenhower was a member, and the club contains a painting of the President wearing his Links patterned tie. While the purpose of the club is to promote the game of golf, it is not without reason that it has been suggested its heavy-hitting membership qualifies it as the most powerful club in the world. Like many clubs, the use or even display of cell phones inside the common areas is prohibited and jacket and tie "or equivalent dress for ladies" are required at all times. To join you need five members to sponsor you, the kind of restriction that will continue to keep clubs like this exclusive for decades to come.

Next door at **No. 40** is a ❿ beautiful neo-medieval condominium building whose façade includes terra cotta and stone features and dates from 1911. Look for the griffins above the entrance and other features such as shields that were inspired by medieval castles. A three-bedroom apartment here will likely cost you over $4 million.

Where does the Upper East Side elite educate their children? One place is next door, at ⓫ **The Browning**, **No. 52**. It is one of several schools in the Upper East Side that caters to the next generation of the elite, typically charging fees of over $50,000 per annum. The Browning School was founded in 1888, and alumni include various Rockefellers, politicians, diplomats, financiers, newspaper proprietors, and media figures. Particularly notable are John D. Rockefeller Jr., Percy Avery Rockefeller, *Little Miss Sunshine* actor Paul Dano, J.P. Morgan boss

Jamie Dimon, *Sesame Street* composer and lyricist Jeff Moss, General Douglas MacArthur's son Arthur MacArthur, and Peace Corps pioneer and Kennedy clan member Robert Shriver Jr. (who was, for a while, Arnold Schwarzenegger's father-in-law).

Walk on to reach Park Avenue, where at **No. 564** on the north-west corner of East 62nd Street is ⓬ **The Colony Club**. While male members of the city's elite decided to found male-only clubs, women chose to look after their own interests and founded The Colony Club in 1903. It was the first of its kind, and today men can only come as guests. This is another Neo-Georgian design, and the building was completed in 1916 (the first clubhouse was by Stanford White and still stands at 120 Madison Avenue).

It was cofounded by Florence "Daisy" Harriman (1870-1967), a true member of the elite whose wedding was attended by J.P. Morgan, Cornelius Vanderbilt, and John Jacob Astor IV. She led an extraordinary life, from leading women's suffrage marches, taking part in the Versailles Peace Conference, to having a diplomatic role in Norway when the Nazis invaded.

Inside the club are squash courts, a pool, ballrooms, three dining rooms, and many guest bedrooms. The surnames of past members tell a familiar Upper East Side story—Morgan, Harriman, Astor, Rockefeller, and Vanderbilt.

Turn left to walk north up Park Avenue, then cross over to head right down East 63rd Street. Shortly on the left ⓭ is **The Halston House** at **No. 101**. It is incredibly hard to join any of the clubs you have already passed, but getting into a party at this residence in the late 1970s would have been equally unthinkable for "civilians."

That is because this was the party-house residence of the legendary fashion designer Halston. Roy Halston Frowick (1932-1990) became an internationally famous designer in the 1970s, best friends with Liza Minnelli, Bianca Jagger, and Andy Warhol, and host of many wild parties that took place here—often followed by a visit to Studio 54.

After designing Jackie Kennedy's iconic pillbox hat (worn to JFK's inauguration in 1961), he became well-known and founded an international fashion brand. His often chaotic, excessive lifestyle was immortalized in the 2021 Netflix series *Halston* (Ewan McGregor played the lead). The 1991 book *Simply Halston* by Steven Gaines is a great read if you want to find out more. He describes how, "101 was the clubhouse for the Studio 54 crowd."

The original 1870s carriage house that once stood here was largely replaced by the famous architect Paul Rudolph's design (completed by 1967). Halston purchased the property in 1974, calling it "101" after the street number. Typical guests at a "Halston Happening" might include Lauren Bacall, Angelica Huston, Elizabeth Taylor, and Truman Capote, while Bianca and Liza sometimes lived in the top-floor suite. After Halston sold the house, it was owned by German photographer and art collector Gunter Sachs, and it was reported to have been bought by another fashion designer, Tom Ford, for $18 million in 2019.

Return to Park Avenue, crossing over to walk down to **No. 41** East 63rd Street, home to ⓮ **The Leash Club**. Founded in 1925, the club was ostensibly a place for dog lovers of the elite to meet and promote the scientific study of breeding dogs. During the Prohibition Era, members would hide alcohol in lockers bearing the names of their dogs.

Why do people join clubs? One former club owner summed it up in *The New York Times* in 2015: "There is a commonality of interests, backgrounds, and rituals. There are all sorts of things that make you part of that club, and you don't have to explain yourself when you're inside." If you can get inside this seven-story townhouse, you can dine under paintings of dogs on the walls.

Go back to Park Avenue, turn left, and walk north for a couple of blocks to then turn left onto East 65th Street. Look out for the offices of therapists, plastic surgeons, and other professionals who earn a good living servicing the residents of the Upper East Side. Immediately ⓯ on the left at **No. 60** is **Daniel**, a restaurant owned and run by Daniel Boulud. Like Pierre before him, Boulud forged his early career in France before coming to conquer New York. At the time of writing, Daniel had 2 Michelin stars and had been rated as one of the top ten restaurants in the world. If you cannot get into one of the exclusive member's clubs seen on this walk, you may be able to book a table here, although it won't be cheap.

This was also the site of Le Cirque, for years the glitziest restaurant in New York. It was founded in 1974 by Italian Sirio Maccioni. During its glory days, Le Cirque was at the epicenter of Upper East Side society, and on a typical evening, you might see a Hollywood A-lister, Donald Trump, or several billionaires. The recovery of the city from its economic nadir in the 1970s was reflected in the rising fortunes of Le Cirque. It became particularly popular with wealthy, well-connected diners during the Reagan years, an era whose excesses were captured in Tom Wolfe's satirical novel *The Bonfire of the Vanities* (1987). Daniel Boulud, David Bouley, pastry chef Jacques Torres (who went on to open his own chocolate shops), and other great chefs worked at Le Cirque.

Le Cirque moved to a new location in 1997, and over time suffered as the tastes of New York's elite changed. As other areas of the city became more gentrified and popular with the super-rich, new restaurants opened that competed with the traditional haunts of the elite on the Upper East Side. Le Cirque closed in 2018 and seems unlikely to return.

A little farther down East 65th Street on the right is ⓰ the **Sara Delano Roosevelt Memorial House (Nos. 47-49)**, another Upper East Side residence with an extraordinary history. This Neo-Georgian design was the work of architect Charles A. Platt, and was completed in 1908 for Sara Delano Roosevelt (1854-1941), mother of President Franklin D. Roosevelt. Sara had a reputation as a domineering mother and difficult mother-in-law, for example, she took young Franklin away on a cruise in a failed effort to persuade him not to marry his distant cousin Eleanor.

She did not stop the marriage but built this house—living at No. 47 while the newly-wed bride had little choice but to live in Sara's wedding present to them—No. 49. Franklin spent months on the fourth floor in the early 1920s trying to recover after being afflicted with polio, being watched over by his mother and wife. The couple stayed here until they moved into the White House in 1933. Nearby Hunter College later bought the house.

You are in foreign consulate country right now—within a five-minute walk of the consulates of Indonesia, Pakistan, India (interestingly opposite each other . . .) and those of France, Russia, Italy, and many others not much farther away. Why so many here? The mansions of affluent Upper East Siders of the past are large enough to accommodate diplomats (and spies . . .), and the United Nations building is less than two miles away.

Return to Park Avenue and turn left (north). The first building on the left, **620 Park Avenue**, was ⓱ the site of John's apartment in the brilliant 1999 film *Being John Malkovich* starring . . . Malkovich, John Cusack and Cameron Diaz. Today 620 is home to a plastic surgery center, helping Upper East Siders stay (or at least appear) youthful.

Cross over Park Avenue to reach the ⑱ **Park Avenue Armory** build-ing, today a leading cultural and arts institution, but originally, as its name suggests, it had a military purpose. The 7th New York Militia Regiment was based here and took pride in being the first militia to respond to President Abraham Lincoln's demand for troops in 1861 at the start of the Civil War.

This grand Gothic Revival style building from 1880 was a familiar place to the sons of the great families of the Upper East Side during the Gilded Age (c. 1870 to 1900). Roosevelts, Vanderbilts, Harrimans, Livingstons, and Stewarts were officers in what became known as the "Silk Stocking Regiment," on account of the upper-class composition of the unit. The Regiment played a role in suppressing riots in New York over the years, including the infamous Astor Place Riot of 1849 and Draft Riots of 1863.

Walk down East 66th Street (with the Armory building on your left). Stop at **No. 110** on the right, ⓳ the location of two former horse stables dating from the early 1880s, a time when this street was lined with stables that belonged to wealthy local residents who lived in grand houses and travelled by carriage. Today, you would need to be a millionaire to buy a carriage house once regarded being suitable only for servants and lowly workers employed by wealthy Upper East Siders.

Continue along, stopping next at ⓴ the **Cosmopolitan Club** at **No. 122**. This is another women-only club, and Eleanor Roosevelt was a member here, no doubt eager to escape the close monitoring of her mother-in-law at Roosevelt HQ nearby. It was founded in 1909 and was aimed at women interested in the arts, philanthropy, science, and education. Many members were involved in the women's suffrage movement. The great African-American singer Marian Anderson (1897-1993) was also a member. She sang in an open-air concert attended by a crowd of 75,000 beside the Lincoln Memorial in 1939 after she was denied the right to perform at Constitution Hall because of the "whites only" policy. Eleanor Roosevelt helped organize the concert—an early victory for the Civil Rights movement.

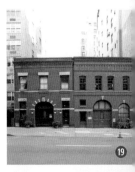

Carry on to reach Lexington Avenue. On the other side ㉑ is the **St. Vincent Ferrer Roman Catholic Church**. If it is open, try and visit as the interior is superb. Its origins go

back to the establishment of a presence here by the Dominicans in the 1860s. The French Neo-Gothic church you see is the second on the site, dedicated in 1918 with 50,000 people in attendance. One regular worshipper here was Andy Warhol, who lived on the Upper East Side for many years. Another local was Ivana Trump. Her funeral service here in 2022 was attended by her ex-husband Donald Trump and other members of the Trump dynasty. At the time of her death, Ivana was living on East 64th Street. The Dominican order is still based here and traces its own history back to 1216 in France.

Walk north up Lexington Avenue. If you stood here in the 1830s, you would be on the site ❷ of the 18-acre square that never was—**Hamilton Square**. It was named for Alexander Hamilton, whose estate gifted the land to the city for use as a park or army parade ground. An open space was contemplated in the famous 1811 Commissioners' Plan that formed the basis of the New York grid system. Disputes with owners of lots delayed the construction of the square, and it was used as pasture land and almost became the site of a grand 425-foot high monument to George Washington. However, in the second half of the 19th century, the development of Central Park nearby spelled the end of any desire to create a public square here, and the site was developed for public institutions such as the Normal College (founded in 1870 and later renamed Hunter College after its first president, Thomas Hunter).

Continue up Lexington Avenue, dominated on the left by ❷❸ the **Hunter College** campus, originally for women students when founded. Today it is a constituent college of the City University of New York. It has some famous names among its alumni—including Harry Connick, Jr., Ellen Barkin, Bobby Darin, Vin Diesel, Peter Carey, and members of The

Strokes Nick Valensi and Nikolai Fraiture. Many famous artists also played here in the late 1960s, such as The Doors, Canned Heat, and Jefferson Airplane. Janis Joplin had her last gig with Big Brother and the Holding Company at the College's auditorium on November 15, 1968.

The renowned architect Rosario Candela (1890-1953) not only designed some of the city's finest and most expensive apartment buildings but was a gifted code-breaker who wrote a book about the subject that attracted the interest of the US intelligence services. He taught a night course on cryptology at Hunter College, running his architectural practice during the day. During World War II, Candela even had a role with the US intelligence services.

Turn left, walk up East 68th Street looking out for an Art Deco gem on the left at ❷❹ **No. 116**, dating from 1931. This apartment block was built by John D. Rockefeller Jr. Look for the sculpted animal features staring down at you.

Now walk on to reach Park Avenue, where you turn right (north). Continue along to the right corner of East 69th Street to find ❷❺ **The Union Club** of the City of New York. Founded in 1836, it is the oldest

club in New York. Past members of this men-only institution include William Randolph Hearst, Harold Vanderbilt, Dwight D. Eisenhower, J. P. Morgan, J. Bruce Ismay (managing director of the White Star Line and Titanic survivor), Tom Wolfe, and Ulysses S. Grant. The club has been here since moving into the specially designed building in 1933. You may recall "The Knick" was founded by members of the Union Club who were unhappy with its admission policy.

Now cross over Park Avenue and head up East 70th Street to the ㉖ **Explorers Club** on the left at No. 46. Scientists and explorers have been meeting here since the club was founded in 1904. It has the stated purpose of promoting scientific exploration of land, sea, air, and space and sponsors expeditions around the world. Only a tiny number are deemed important enough to carry The Explorers Club flag—see the example hanging outside the club. Notable members include Edmund Hillary and Tenzing Norgay, Neil Armstrong, Buzz Aldrin, James Cameron, and Jeff Bezos. It allowed women to join in 1981, and members have been responsible for famous "firsts," such as climbing Everest, and standing on the moon's surface.

Return to Park Avenue, turning left and walking on, passing some of the best apartment buildings in the city. One is **730 Park Avenue**,  a classic Upper East Side apartment house built in 1929 by the eminent architect Lafayette A. Goldstone "offering white-glove service with a wonderfully attentive staff of 24-hour doormen, elevator attendants, and handymen." If that sounds like a high level of service, it is relative to the cost of apartments—one in 2021 sold for over \$38 million. In May 1968, *New York Magazine* contained an article on the city's most expensive apartment houses, describing how purchase prices at 730 ranged from \$200,000 to \$300,000. While in the last half-century prices have increased enormously, the article could equally apply today with its observation that "Ninety-nine percent of all the people who call themselves New Yorkers will never set hesitant foot in any of the city's best apartment buildings."

730 & 740 Park Avenue

Just farther along on the left (just past West 71st Street) **28** is **740 Park Avenue**. This has been described as the "Tower of Power" and "one of the most lusted-after addresses in the world." The life of the billionaires who live here is well-covered in a book, *740 Park: The Story of the World's Richest Apartment Building*, by Michael Gross (2005). The staggering wealth and privilege of residents described in Gross's book, in turn, inspired the 2012 documentary *Park Avenue: Money, Power and the American Dream*. This compared the very different life opportunities for those in Park Avenue with their fellow New Yorkers residing in the South Bronx.

Architect and cryptographer Rosario Candela was involved in the design of this art deco building, completed in 1929. Residents have included Jacqueline Kennedy Onassis (when she was a child—her grandfather built 740), John D. Rockefeller (who lived in arguably the best apartment in New York, combined apartments 15/16B), and a host of hedge-fund managers, bankers, and business CEOs that makes No. 740 the location of arguably the highest concentration of billionaires in America.

Take a left down East 71st Street to **㉙ St. James' Church** (Episcopal) on the right side. When it was founded in 1810 as a summer chapel in Hamilton Square, this part of the city was still open countryside. Many of the earliest residents of the area traveled to the chapel to worship. The church had to adapt and expand as the Upper East Side developed around it, and the current church opened in 1885. It was later transformed into a neo-Gothic building in the 1920s by architect Ralph Adams Cram.

This has long been a fashionable church with a well-heeled congregation. When writer John Steinbeck died in 1968, his funeral service took place here (he had requested a "Church of England" funeral), and actor Henry Fonda gave a reading from the bible.

Now cross over Madison Avenue and carry on up East 71st Street to **㉚ No. 9**. Known as the **Herbert N. Straus House**, after its original owner, it was completed in the 1930s and is thought to be the largest single private residence in Manhattan. The fancy façades of Upper East Side mansions hide many secrets and no more than No. 9. Notorious sex offender and financier Jeffrey Epstein (1953-2019) moved into the property in 2006. After his death in prison, it was bought by a Goldman Sachs banker for

$51 million. (Epstein's partner and convicted sex-trafficker Ghislaine Maxwell had her own house at 116 East 65th Street, which she sold for a reported $15 million in 2016).

Retrace your steps to continue left (north) up Madison Avenue, getting a better view of the main entrance of St. James' Church.

A little farther along on the right ㉛ at **867 Madison Avenue** is **The Gertrude Rhinelander Waldo House**, a fabulous French Renaissance-style building that was completed in 1898. It was built for Gertrude Rhinelander Waldo (1842-1914), a wealthy scion of the Rhinelander family that had been prominent in the city since the first German-born family member arrived in the 1680s. It is a superb example of the kind of building the elite of New York in the Gilded Age wanted to live in, a Loire Valley royal residence transported to the Upper East Side.

By most accounts, Gertrude never lived here, choosing instead to stay with her sister in a smaller house nearby. Why build a ballroom with 2,000 electric lights when it was rarely used? Only the very rich can answer that, although when Gertrude died, she left large debts and was described in one city paper as "of forceful manner and some un-usual views." Today it is a flagship store for Ralph Lauren.

Now head right down East 72nd Street, then right again down Park Avenue before turning left down East 70th Street to see grand houses of various styles. **No. 118 East 70th Street** (on the right) dates from 1901 and ❷ in 2005 was bought by Woody Allen for over $22 million.

No. 125 (on the left) was ❸ built by power couple Paul and Bunny Mellon. Paul was a scion of the hugely wealthy Mellon Bank dynasty. Bunny, a noted garden designer, was asked by President John F. Ken-nedy to redesign the White House Rose Gar-den. Her grandfather invented Listerine, and she was a close friend of Jacqueline Kennedy Onassis. She died in 2014 at age 103.

The Mellons were a classic super-wealthy Upper East Side couple, owning houses and estates around the world. The high-profile philanthropists amassed an art collection that, after their deaths, would be sold for hundreds of millions of dollars, far more than the mere $41 million this house cost in 2015.

At the end, turn left up Lexington Avenue, then right along East 71st Street, stopping outside ❸ **No. 169**. This house was used for the exterior shots of **Holly Golightly's apartment** in the film *Breakfast at Tiffany's* (1961). Other occupants of this house include the Cremin family, and Stephen Cremin walked into the exclusive Lambs Club one day in 1915 and cut his throat, his suicide note ending "Forgive me, fellow Lambs."

Holly was played by Audrey Hepburn, and the film was fairly loosely based on Truman Capote's book of 1958. The novel was set in the early 1940s, and Holly was originally called Connie Gustafson in Capote's early draft. Capote preferred Marilyn Monroe to have played Holly in the film, indicating how he saw the character but which nearly everyone now associates with Hepburn. In 2021 this townhouse, dating from 1910, was marketed as "The Hepburn" and available to rent to visitors. Another great writer, John Steinbeck, lived near here at 206 East 72nd Street.

Retrace your steps to continue up Lexington Avenue. You pass East 73rd Street, which is home ❸ to the elite **Buckley School**. Its alumni include three sons of President Franklin D. Roosevelt, Donald Trump Jr., (son of President Donald Trump), FBI Director Christopher A. Wray, and the fictional characters Pete Campbell (from the hit series *Mad Men*) and Sherman McCoy from Tom Wolfe's *Bonfire of the Vanities*.

Turn down East 74th Street to stop ❸ by the **Church of the Resurrection**, the oldest church structure in the district and completed in 1869. It was designed by James Renwick Jr. (1818-1895), a successful architect who also designed St. Patrick's Cathedral in Midtown Manhattan and the Smithsonian Institution in Washington. It describes itself as having a "small country church atmosphere" and has followed Anglo-Catholic doctrine since 1920. When it opened on the Upper East Side, it was known as the "Servants' Church," and the area would have still have had a countryside feel to it.

Return to Lexington Avenue, and next turn left down East 75th Street to find ❸ **Temple Israel of the City of New York**. This had its origins in Harlem when German Jewish immigrants founded a place of worship in the early 1870s above a printing shop. The synagogue later moved to the Upper West Side and then to this new Brutalist-design building (completed in 1967).

The Upper East Side is not only populated by the super-rich and members of the city's great families. Many immigrants settled here, mainly Germans who, from the late 1900s, moved to the Yorkville area of the Upper East Side from "Little Germany" or "Kleindeutschland" on the Lower East Side and the East Village. Other parts of the Upper East Side also became associated with immigrant groups from Europe, in particular, "Little Hungary" was focussed a few blocks from here on Second Avenue between 78th and 79th Streets. By 1940, New York's Hungarian population was around 125,000, the bulk living in Yorkville. They ran restaurants, newspapers, shops, churches, and entertainment facilities, all largely catering for fellow-Hungarians. A Czech community dominated life in a similar fashion on East 72nd Street and between First and Second Avenues. There are few visible remains of these once distinct communities, although the odd church, deli or bakery can be found.

Return to Lexington Avenue, passing on the left ❸ the **Lenox Hill Hospital**. The influence of the German community is evident here as this was founded as the German Dispensary in 1857, its purpose to help German

speakers in the city obtain medical care. It later moved to this site as The German Hospital of the City of New York in the 1860s. However, any connections with Germany caused problems during World War I, so it was renamed the Lenox Hill Hospital in 1918. It is ranked as one of the best hospitals in the country and was the subject of a Netflix documentary series, *Lenox Hill* (2020). Those whose last days were spent at the hospital include Ed Sullivan, actresses Myrna Loy and Natasha Richardson, lawyer Robert Morgenthau, alleged Soviet spy Alger Hiss and cosmetic entrepreneur Elizabeth Arden.

There was a mob hit just outside the hospital in April 1995. "Handsome Jack" Giordano, a capo in the Gambino crime family and close aid to John Gotti, was leaving the hospital when he was gunned down by a hitman in a passing car. The attack left Giordano paralyzed from the waist down, and he died in 2009.

You now reach the 77th Street station where this walk ends.

11
UPPER WEST SIDE WALK

START AND FINISH: Verdi Square
SUBWAY STATION: 72 St ❶, ❷, ❸
FILM WARNING: You've Got Mail (1998), Taxi Driver (1976), When Harry Met Sally (1989)

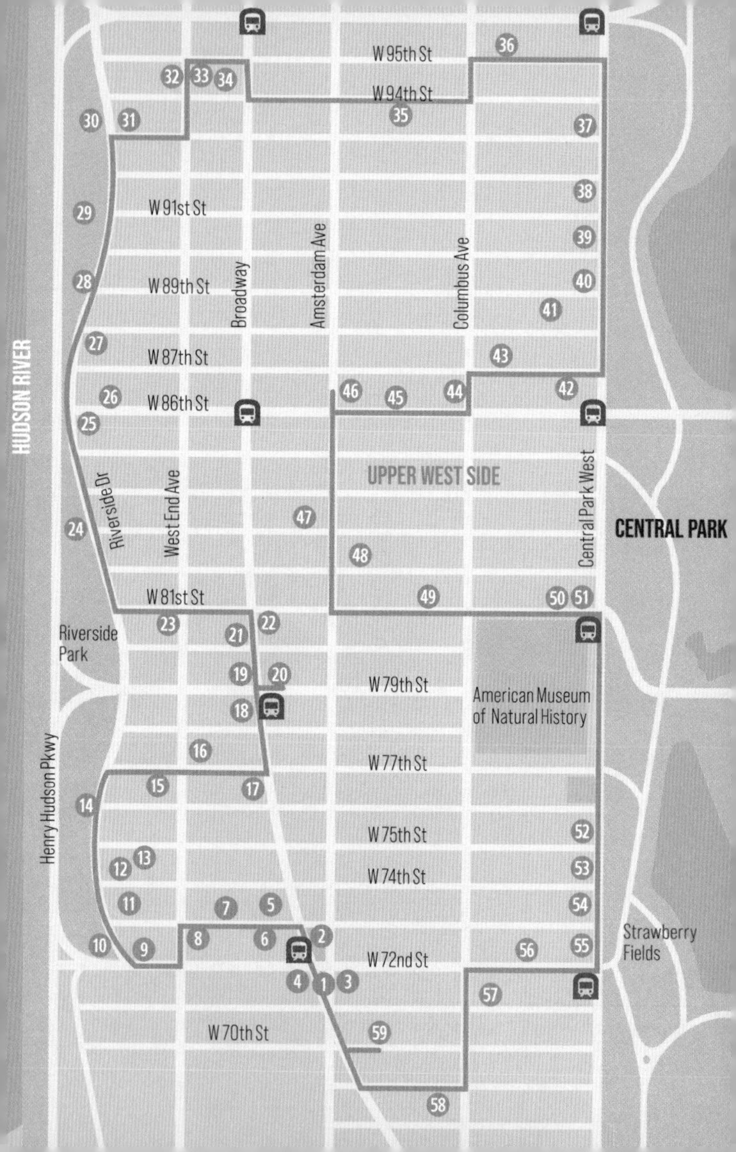

HUDSON RIVER

W 95th St
W 94th St

30 31
32 33 34
35
36
37

W 91st St
29
38
28 W 89th St
39
27 W 87th St
40
26 W 86th St
41
25
43
42

Broadway
Amsterdam Ave
Columbus Ave

46 45 44

UPPER WEST SIDE

47

48

Riverside Dr
West End Ave
Central Park West

CENTRAL PARK

24

W 81st St
23
49
50 51
22
21
20
19
18

Riverside Park

W 79th St
American Museum
of Natural History

16
17
W 77th St
15
14

Henry Hudson Pkwy

W 75th St
52
W 74th St
53
54

12 13
11
7 5
6
8 2
55
56

10 9
4 1 3
W 72nd St
57

59
W 70th St

58

Strawberry Fields

UPPER WEST SIDE

Distance: 5.4 Miles

1. 72 St Subway Station
2. Verdi Square
3. Gray's Papaya
4. Site of Colonial Club
5. The Ansonia
6. 246/248 West 73rd Street
7. The Level Club
8. Former Marlon Brando Home
9. Sutphen Family Mansion
10. Monument to Eleanor Roosevelt
11. The Schwab House
12. Home of Guinevere Sinclair
13. The Manhattan Day School
14. Robert Ray Hamilton Fountain
15. Home of Miles Davis
16. West End Collegiate Church
17. Hotel Belleclaire
18. The Apthorp
19. The First Baptist Church
20. "Boy with a Hammer"
21. Zabar's
22. Coffee Shop in *You've Got Mail*
23. Calhoun School
24. Warsaw Ghetto Memorial Plaza
25. Former Mansion of William Randolph Hearst
26. 349 West 86th Street
27. 155 Riverside Drive
28. Soldiers and Sailors' Monument
29. Little Garden in *You've Got Mail*
30. Joan of Arc Monument
31. 210 Riverside Drive
32. Home of Alexander Orlov
33. English Tudor-style buildings
34. Pomander Walk
35. Narrow Houses from 1890s
36. Uncle Rob's Home in *Home Alone 2*
37. The Turin at 333 CPW
38. The Ardsley at 320 CPW
39. El Dorado at 300 CPW
40. Dwight School (291 CPW)
41. Marie and Jess's Home in *When Harry Met Sally*
42. Billie Holiday's Last Home
43. West 87th Street Park and Garden
44. 546 Columbus Avenue
45. Jewish Center
46. Barney Greengrass
47. Café Lalo
48. 155 West 82nd Street
49. Seinfeld's Apartment
50. 15 West 81st Street
51. The Beresford
52. The Kenilworth at 151 CPW
53. The San Remo at 145-46 CPW
54. The Langham at 135 CPW
55. The Dakota
56. The Olcott
57. Site of Café La Fortuna
58. Site of *The Shop Around the Corner*
59. Pythian Temple

This walk starts at the **72nd Street subway**, where you exit into the triangle between Broadway and Amsterdam Avenue. There are two subway buildings, the older one ❶ on the south side dating from when the station opened in 1904—one of the first 28 subway stations in the city. For the sake of your sanity I would suggest watching (or re-watching) *You've Got Mail*, *Taxi Driver* and *When Harry Met Sally* before starting this walk.

Walk into ❷ **Verdi Square** by the northern subway building. Until the last quarter of the 19th century, the affluent Upper West Side area

you walk through today was still largely open ground, punctuated by a few country estates, farmhouses and shacks inhabited by people who were forced to move from their homes due to the development of Central Park.

The construction of the pioneering Dakota apartment building in 1884 (seen later) and the Ninth Avenue/Columbus Avenue elevated railway helped to transform the area. It encouraged developers and speculators to invest heavily in the construction of residential streets and higher end buildings in the hope of attracting the city's upper and middle-class residents.

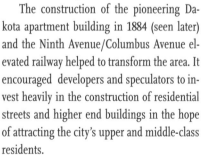

The Upper West Side (UWS) has had its difficulties. It never quite attracted the upper-class residents in the numbers the early developers hoped for. By the mid-20th cen-

tury many streets in the area had become run down, but revitalization (particularly encouraged by the construction of Lincoln Center in the 1960s) over the last few decades has ensured that this is once again a desirable and affluent area, generally regarded as cooler and artsier than the stuffy Upper East Side on the other side of Central Park. This divide was well captured in the classic series *Seinfeld*, itself set in the UWS, when Kramer remarks, "If you don't want to be a part of society, Jerry, why don't you just get in your car and move to the East Side?!"

The UWS has featured in many films, television series and books, hardly surprising given many creative people live here. As well as being Seinfeld-land, this is where many scenes in rom-coms such as *When Harry Met Sally* (1989) and *You've Got Mail* (1998) were filmed. Both were written by UWS resident Nora Ephron (1941-2012). Look over to the southeast corner for ❸ **Gray's Papaya**. In *You've Got Mail* this is where Joe (Tom Hanks) and Kathleen (Meg Ryan) sit by the window eating hotdogs. Joe runs a big-chain bookstore that forces Kathleen's own business to close—a rom-com with a secondary story about the *Starbuckization* of the UWS (that bird has well and truly flown . . .).

Inside Verdi Square is a monument to the great opera composer Giuseppe Verdi (1813-1901) that dates from 1906. If you are very cultured you may be able to recognize four other statues representing characters from his operas (Otello (east side), Falstaff (west side), Leonora (La Forza del Destino) and Aida (north side). The statue was just one of a number in the city's parks that commemorate famous Italians, and which were sponsored by the Italian-American community. Ten thousand Italian Americans attended the unveiling here, and between 1900-1910 around two million Italians emigrated to the United States.

On the southwest corner at ❹ No. **2073 Broadway** is a modern commercial building housing Trader Joe's and other businesses. This site was once home to the **Colonial Club**, an exclusive private members social club housed in a grand building completed here in 1892. The Upper East Side tended to attract the clubs favored by the city's elite, so the opening of the Colonial Club was a sign of how the UWS could compete with its snootier eastern cousin. However, financial difficulties

Colonial Club

forced the club to close in 1903 and the building was demolished in 2007. A very different view of life in this area is captured in the film *The Panic in Needle Park* (1971) starring Al Pacino in his first lead role. Based on a book of the same name by James Mills, it centers around the drug addicts who used to hang around Verdi Square and nearby Sherman Square.

Walk north up Broadway and turn left into West 73rd Street to see ❺ **The Ansonia** apartment building. If buildings could tell their secrets, this one would make for a fascinating listen. This iconic Beaux Arts landmark building opened in 1904, at the time the largest hotel in the city. In its early days it was so luxurious that seals swam in the lobby fountain and a bear, ducks and other animals were kept on the roof. It later became an apartment building, the thick walls providing soundproofing that attracted musicians such as Yehudi Menuhin, Toscanini, Stravinsky, and Caruso.

Others who have stayed here include Babe Ruth, Angelina Jolie, and Glinda the Good Witch of the North (Billie Burke from *The Wizard of Oz*). In late 1960s-1970s this was home to a gay bathhouse called the Continental Baths in the basement where Bette Midler and Barry Manilow performed. It was later home to an infamous swingers club called Plato's Retreat, the goings-on at which were immortalized in

Spike Lee's film *Summer of Sam* (1999). Today a four-bedroom apartment here might cost you around $9 million.

Why is it called The Ansonia? It is derived from the name of businessman Anson Green Phelps (1781-1853). His grandson William Earle Dodge Stokes (1852-1926) was the investor behind the construction of the building, and several others on the UWS. The Ansonia has appeared in many films including *Single White Female* (1992) and *The Sunshine Boys* (1975).

Opposite The Ansonia at ❻ **246/248 West 73rd Street** is a house dating from 1890, and fairly typical of the large family houses then being built for well-off middle class residents. Within a few years, there would be tension between those who wanted to retain large, private houses, and those who wanted to demolish them to make way for mega-apartment buildings such as The Ansonia. There are so many famous people who have lived on the UWS over the years it would be impossible to mention everyone linked with this route. However, the French artist Marcel Duchamp (1887-1968) lived at No. 246 around 1920, and Man Ray took a photograph of his studio here. Not long after Duchamp— one of the greatest artists of the 20th century—effectively retired to devote much of his energy to becoming a competitive chess player.

Walk down West 73rd Street, stopping outside ❼ **The Level Club** residential building on the right at **No. 253** (just after The Ansonia). Dating from 1927, this building looks like it should be in a Dan Brown novel. It was built for the Freemasons and this explains the many Masonic embellishments on the exterior such as the all-seeing eye, the level and hourglass.

Walk on to reach West End Avenue, the name for Eleventh Avenue between 59th and 107th Streets. Most of this was first laid out in the

1880s, the "West End" name reflecting the desire of real-estate developers to distinguish the new residential area from Eleventh Avenue.

On the corner is ❽ **No. 270** where actor Marlon Brando lived in his mother's apartment in the 1940s. Mae West may have lived next door at No. 266 with her sister in the 1930s. This is a lovely French-Renaissance style house from the 1890s.

Now follow the map heading down West End Avenue and then right up West 72nd Street. On the right is ❾ a mansion at No. **311 West 72nd Street**, built for the wealthy Sutphen family who were involved in real estate development on the UWS in the early days of its development. John S. Sutphen owned the entire block here (between 72nd and 73rd Street) and in the mid 1890s began to sell off plots for the development of mansions along Riverside Drive.

Ahead is a monument to ❿ **First Lady Eleanor Roosevelt** (1884-1962) that was sculpted by Penelope Jencks. It was unveiled in 1996 in the presence of another First Lady, Hillary Clinton, who gave the keynote speech. The monument stands at the beginning of Riverside Park that runs for four miles up to 158th Street, and was founded in the 1870s.

At that point most New Yorkers still lived below 23rd Street. As with Central Park, this space owes its existence to the parks movement that came to the fore in the mid-19th century and which was supported by many prominent New Yorkers.

Frederick Law Olmsted (1822–1903), best known for his work in the design of Central Park, was also involved with Riverside Park in its early years before being pushed out. Much of what you see today can be traced back to the 1930s when major reconstruction works were carried out under Parks Commissioner Robert Moses (1888-1981) and as part of his West Side Development Plan. The Park has been the subject of many bitter battles over its use and development over the years.

The West Side railway line runs underneath the park, however it is hard to ignore the Henry Hudson Parkway that runs parallel to the Hudson River and is another legacy of the controversial Moses. An old section of the railway south of here has become the popular High Line. The route under the park includes the "Freedom Tunnel," named for graffiti artist Chris "Freedom" Pape who did much of his work down below when the tunnel was out of use, and a haven for homeless people. Now used by Amtrak trains, the tunnel attracts urban explorers. The documentary film *Dark Days* (2000) by Marc Singer is worth watching to learn more about those who lived in the tunnel.

Now start to walk along Riverside Drive. In the last few years of the 19th century, the Drive failed to attract many very wealthy residents, yet remained out of reach of middle class residents. However, a number of mansions were built, soon followed by upscale apartment blocks—by 1910 there were 24 such blocks along the Drive. This was part of a mini-revolution in the city, as for much of the 19th century respectable members of society would never have dreamt of living in an apartment. One attraction here was of course the Park, and views over the Hudson. The Upper East Side, whose development began earlier than the UWS, was also getting "full." However, rail traffic and heavy industry along the shoreline led to friction with residents—one factor that led to Moses's expansion of the Park in the 1930s.

Just after 73rd Street at 11 Riverside Drive is ⑪ **The Schwab House**, built in 1950 and containing 636 apartments. It is named for millionaire steel magnate Charles M. Schwab and his grand mansion "Riverside" that once occupied this whole block. Expect to pay about $3.5 million for a decent apartment here.

Charles M. Schwab (1862-1939) overcame humble beginnings to become president of the United States Steel Corporation, a role that enabled him to fund a vast 75-room French chateau style mansion on this site. It was completed in 1906—the heyday of mansion development on Riverside Drive—and Schwab paid a then record sum of $865,000 to acquire the block from the New York Orphan Asylum (which was subsequently demolished). However, Schwab's subsequent history and mansion were not untypical of his time.

"Riverside"

The Schwab mansion ca. 1920

He lost a great deal of money during the Great Depression and died insolvent, living in a tiny apartment (like most other New Yorkers). His grand house was torn down in 1948 to be replaced by this mansion block. It is a shame as this was one of the grandest private residences ever built in Manhattan.

Continue along the Drive, stopping at ⑫ No. **323 West 74th Street**. Schwab lived here for a while to keep an eye on the construction of his mansion, which once stood opposite. Later it was the **home of Guinevere Sinclair**, a dancer who became the mistress of married millionaire George Gould, one of six children who inherited $72 million from industrialist Jay Gould. George had children with Guinevere, and later married her after his wife Edith died of a heart attack in 1921 as she was playing golf. She was found to be wearing a rubber suit, an attempt to lose weight and regain the attentions of George. When George died a few years later, the former showgirl married an English noble and became Lady Dunsford.

Carry on, passing by or near places many notable people have lived over the years including George Gershwin (33 Riverside Drive), Woody

Allen (311 West 75th Street), Mark Rothko (314 West 75th Street) and Fanny Brice (306 West 76th Street).

The Manhattan Day School ⓬ at 310 West 75th Street is an independent Jewish school founded in 1948, and the first sign on the walk of the large Jewish community on the UWS.

Walk on, next stopping on the left ⓮ by the **Robert Ray Hamilton Fountain** (opposite West 76th Street). Dating from 1906, it was funded by Hamilton, a wealthy businessman, UWS landowner and great-grandson of Alexander Hamilton. This ornamental delight was mainly used as a drinking trough for thirsty horses, a rare reminder of a lost age when thousands of horses tramped the streets of the city.

Now turn right down West 77th Street, stopping at ⓯ **No. 312** on the right. This was the **home of jazz legend Miles Davis** (1926-1991) for two decades after he moved into the former Russian Orthodox Church in 1961. These were the best years of his career, although he was mostly a recluse towards the end, before his career was revitalized by the 1981 album *The Man with the Horn*.

Continue to reach West End Avenue again, with ⓰ the **West End Collegiate Church** on

the other side. The church was dedicated in 1892, and was part of the early development of the UWS. It is part of The Collegiate Reformed Protestant Dutch Church that has its origins in the Netherlands in 1571. Dutch settlers in New Amsterdam brought their Protestant beliefs with them, first worshiping in the loft of a gristmill in 1628.

The Flemish-style church was inspired by a building from 1606 that still stands in Vleeshal in Haarlem, the Netherlands. Millstones from the New Amsterdam-era mill can be seen inside the church. The Collegiate School, founded by the church in 1638, has claims to be the oldest school in the country. It is certainly one of the finest academically and alumni include David Duchovy, Mark Ronson, Douglas Fairbanks Jr., John F. Kennedy Jr., Peter Bogdanovich and Cornelius Vanderbilt II.

Walk on down West 77th Street to Broadway. On the right hand corner is ⑰ the **Hotel Belleclaire**, another UWS landmark building where Babe Ruth, Mark Twain and Maxim Gorky have all stayed. It was built in 1903 and designed by Emery Roth (1871-1948), one of the finest architects of his era and responsible for other landmark apartment blocks and hotels in New York such as the San Remo, Hotel St. Moritz, The Ardsley, The Beresford, the Warwick Hotel and The El Dorado. You will walk past some of these later.

Turn left or north up Broadway. Just after West 78th Street on the left is ⑱ **The Apthorp** apartment building, built by the Astors and completed in 1908. Nora Ephron lived here for ten years, and was familiar with the nearby UWS locations that feature in the films she wrote the scripts for. She co-wrote a number with her sister Delia who also lived here. Other notable residents have included Joseph Heller, Jennifer Hudson, Al Pacino, Cyndi Lauper, and Lena Horne. The enormous Italian Renaissance-style building occupies a full block and was named for a local farm owner named Charles Ward Apthorp. It has featured in many films, including *Heartburn* (1986) (written by Ephron, starring Meryl Streep and Jack Nicholson and inspired by Ephron's real-life marriage breakup with journalist Carl Bernstein). The Apthorp has for decades been a popular movie location—in 1986 the *New York Times* reported, "Some 30 films are shot there each year, and many residents do not like it." Other notable films with scenes here include *Network* (1976) and *The Cotton Club* (1984).

Just after the Apthorp ⑲ is an unusual looking building that

serves as the sanctuary of **The First Baptist Church in the City of New York**. The building dates from the 1890s, but the congregation traces its origins back to 1746. The tall tower represents Christ, and the shorter one represents that the church will be incomplete until the return of Christ. Years ago the First Baptist Church was not welcoming to African-American worshippers, which led them to create the Abyssinian Baptist Church.

Cross over and go about 100 yards on the left down West 79th Street. Look closely at ground level for ⓴ a work by British graffiti artist Banksy. Known as *Boy with a Hammer*, it appeared suddenly in October 2013. The protective Plexiglas was placed here by the building's owners, the Zabar brothers, who own the famous Zabar's deli.

Retrace your steps and turn right to continue up Broadway. **Zabar's** deli is on the left ㉑ at West 80th Street. A true UWS institution, it was founded in 1934 by Lillian and Louis Zabar. Over the years, successive generations of the family have kept the high standards here, their history stating that back in the 1960s, "we introduced New York to brie, in the '70s we brought them sun-dried tomatoes and gnocchi, and in the '80s, we got so excited about caviar—and wanted everyone to taste it—that our prices set off a so-called 'Caviar War.' (Incidentally, we won)."

Lillian and Louis Zabar were both from Russia and escaped the persecution of the Jews there to start a new life in New York in the 1920s. Nora Ephron knew Zabar's well, and, unsurprisingly, it appears in a scene from *You've Got Mail* (when Kathleen has no money in the cash-only checkout line and Joe helps her out). Isaac (played by Woody Allen) and Mary (played by Diane Keaton) also share a scene here in the classic ode to the city, *Manhattan* (1979).

You've Got Mail

Opposite Zabar's on the corner (2239 Broadway) once stood H&H Bagels. It opened in 1972 and, until it closed in 2011, was the hippest bagel shop in New York. It gets a mention in *Seinfeld*, a classic episode when Kramer goes back to work at H&H after being on strike for 12 years. H&H also appeared in other films and television programs including a scene in *You've Got Mail* (Joe walks through a mist of flour being pumped into H&H). Recently, a new branch of H&H was opened on the UWS at 526 Columbus Avenue.

The **❷** Starbucks on the other side of **Broadway** (at **2252**) also features in *You've Got Mail* as Joe and Kathleen pass each other here (clearly she didn't care too much about independent coffee shops going out of business).

Now head back to Riverside Drive by turning left off Broadway and down West 81st Street (westwards). At West End Avenue you will see **❷** the prestigious **Calhoun School**. Founded in 1896, it has educated

generations of well-heeled Upper West Siders, including Peggy Guggenheim, Ben Stiller and actor Cooper Hoffman, son of Philip Seymour Hoffman. Right beside the school at No. 304 West 81st Street is a grand five-story house dating from 1898 that originally sold for $34,000. Why so special? Mick Jagger and Jerry Hall bought the house in 1982. It was later sold to the school in 2001. This is a survivor of a row of similarly designed houses built by the developer in the 1890s.

Continue down to Riverside Drive, passing more fine UWS brownstones and apartment buildings. Turn right down the Drive, and almost opposite West 83rd Street take the path down into the Park (Babe Ruth lived at 110 Riverside Drive near here).

As you enter the Park, bear right until you reach ㉔ the **Warsaw Ghetto Memorial Plaza** with a granite plaque in the middle. This was dedicated in 1947 with 15,000 people present. Survivors from Buchenwald and Dachau concentration camps also attended, and this was one of the first Holocaust memorials to be erected in the United States. Hundreds of thousands of Jews were deported from the Warsaw Ghetto by the Nazis, despite a heroic fight by Jewish combat groups in April to May of 1943.

Take the next path on the right to return to Riverside Drive. When you reach West 86th Street, turn right to see ㉕ the entrance to The Clarendon on the corner. This was once the main **home of publishing magnate William Randolph Hearst** (1863-1951). The inspiration for *Citizen Kane*, Hearst bought his first apartment here in 1905, and kept expanding it, eventually buying the whole building. His own mega-apartment had more than 30 rooms and is thought to have been the largest single apartment in the world at the time. His wife stayed here until 1937, after Hearst moved out to live with his mistress, Marion Davies.

How much does it cost to live around here? Turn around from the Clarendon's entrance to see ㉖ an elegant five-story mansion at **349 West 86th Street**, dating from 1910. It was marketed recently at $50 million and boasts 14 bathrooms.

Continue along Riverside Drive. When you reach West 88th Street, look at the apartment block on the corner ㉗—**155 Riverside Drive**. A rent-controlled ninth floor apartment here was Will Truman and (sometimes) Grace Adler's home in the hit television series *Will and Grace.* "Father of the atomic bomb" and physicist J. Robert Oppenheimer (1904-1967) lived at No. 155 when he was a child.

Now walk to ㉘ the Beaux Arts **Soldiers and Sailors' Monument**, which commemorates those who fought on the Union side in

328 West 89th Street

the Civil War. The opening ceremony in 1902 was officiated by President Theodore Roosevelt and attended by Civil War veterans marching along the Drive. From the 1920s the monument and Grant's Tomb (at 122nd Street) were focus points for a large gay cruising scene that took place in the Park.

Big fans of *You've Got Mail* may wish to make a small detour at this point to see 328 West 89th Street, the site where Kathleen lives in a pretty brownstone.

Otherwise continue along the Drive, although alternatively, you may wish to walk through the Park parallel to this route. **The little garden** where the ending of *You've Got Mail* takes place is found here ㉙ and is maintained by The Garden People volunteer organization.

If you stay on the Drive you pass ㉚ the **Joan of Arc monument**, which commemorates the 15th century French martyr and patriot. Dedicated in 1915, it is another sign of how keen the authorities were to make the Park an attractive and culturally interesting public space

in the early 20th century. Unusually for that era, it was the work of a female sculptor, Anna Hyatt Huntington (1876-1973). This was also the first monument in New York to commemorate a historical woman. Huntington was still producing public statues in the 1960s.

Now head down West 93rd Street. The first door on the left ③① is the side entrance of **210 Riverside Drive**. This serves as the exterior of Joe's apartment in *You've Got Mail* (even though in the film it has a sign indicating 152 Riverside Drive). If you have never watched this film, you really need to . . .

When you get to West End Avenue turn left, then continue along. On the left ③② is **711 West End Avenue**, once the **home of Alexander Orlov** (1895-1973). Before he defected in 1938, Orlov was one of Stalin's most effective spymasters. During the Spanish Civil War, he helped arrange the transport of 510 tons of gold from Spain's gold reserves to Moscow, and carried out operations in several countries. He fled to the United States with his family when he realized he was next on Stalin's hit list. Orlov lived on the seventh floor from 1953 to 1962.

Now turn right into West 95th Street. On the corner ㉝ look for some unusual two-and-a-half-story **English Tudor-style buildings**. They are just part of the mostly hidden ㉞ **Pomander Walk**. This residential complex, described once as the real-life Diagon Alley, was built in the early 1920s and contains 27 buildings all constructed in a similar Tudor style. It has an unusual history as it was inspired by a now-obscure play called *Pomander Walk*, a romantic comedy set in an imagined lane of that name in 18th century London. It features in a scene in Woody Allen's *Hannah and Her Sisters* (1986), and Humphrey Bogart lived here. You may be able to sneak a view of the interior if a gate is ajar, however, sadly the complex—which stretches out to West 94th Street—is not open to the public.

Now you will start walking a few blocks to explore the eastern edge of the UWS. If you are

getting tired, there are lots of places to stop around here. Turn right down Broadway, then left along West 94th Street, crossing over Amsterdam Avenue. This is really Tenth Avenue but Upper West Siders like to think they are different. It was commercial interests that pushed for the "Amsterdam" name, adopted in 1890, to give the developing UWS a little more cachet. It almost became Holland Avenue.

On the other side of Amsterdam Avenue you pass on the right  a row of fine, but **narrow houses, dating from the early 1890s**. It is hard to imagine just a few years before this would have all been open ground.

At Columbus Avenue turn left, and then right down West 95th Street. On the left **36** is **No. 51.** In *Home Alone 2: Lost in New York* (1992), this is the address where Kevin, played by Macaulay Culkin, looks for his Uncle Rob but finds the place deserted. In real life, sadly, a fake brownstone on a L.A. back lot was used for filming.

Soon you reach Central Park West (CPW), with Central Park on the other side. CPW is home to a number of the grandest apartment blocks in the city, and there are so many they warrant a full walk. Today you will learn just

a little about some of the most notable examples.

First up is ❸❼ **The Turin at 333 CPW**. Dating from 1909, it is noted for its relative shortness (just 12 stories) and Italian Renaissance design.

Next up is ❸❽ **The Ardsley at 320 CPW**, an Art Deco masterpiece built in 1931. Barbra Streisand lived here for 30 years, including with then-husband Elliot Gould. Lyricist Lorenz Hart lived in the same apartment in the 1940s, and with Richard Rodgers wrote standards such as "My Funny Valentine" and "Blue Moon." The architect was Emery Roth, who designed the Hotel Belleclaire you walked past earlier.

Next stop at **300 CPW** is ❸❾ the **El Dorado**, another Art Deco masterpiece that Emery Roth was involved in designing with Margon & Holder. It was completed in 1931. It has long been a favorite with writers and entertainers including Sinclair Lewis, Benny Goodman, Moby, Alec Baldwin, Carrie Fisher, Richard Dreyfuss, Bianca Jagger, Faye Dunaway, members of U2 and Michael J. Fox. Many apartments here sell for more than $10 million.

Continue to reach West 89th Street. On the corner at **291 CPW** is ❹❶ the prestigious

Dwight School, where Roy Lichtenstein, Truman Capote, Robert Moses, three members of The Strokes, Vanessa Trump, Fiorello H. La Guardia, and Paris Hilton went to school.

A little farther along (optional visit) is ④① the house at **32 West 89th Street** that features in *When Harry Met Sally.* Marie (Carrie Fisher) and Jess (Bruno Kirby) end up living here, and there is a classic scene in which Marie criticizes Jess's wagon wheel coffee table. Asked to umpire, Harry loses his temper. The film script described the location as "A nice West Side floor-through with a beautiful fireplace and a great deal of furniture . . . "

Continue down CPW, and then right up West 87th Street. The UWS has been home to many of the great figures in jazz, and on the left is ④② **No. 26**, where **Billie Holiday** (1915-1959) lived in the last year of her life. She died at age 44, her health in ruins and having difficulty working in New York after being subject to oppression from the police and city authorities. Built in 1910, this elegant brownstone was sold in recent years for around $10 million.

Continue up West 87th Street, passing No. 35 where Russian-born author Vladimir Nabokov moved into a tiny flat in 1940, 15

years before he wrote his most famous and controversial novel, *Lolita* (1955). Just past here is ㊸ the small, but pretty **West 87th Street Park and Garden**.

Walk on to reach Columbus Avenue again, turning left and then right up West 86th Street. On the corner, at ㊹ **546 Columbus Avenue,** is a building that appears in Martin Scorsese's *Taxi Driver* (1976). Travis, played by Robert De Niro, shoots a man dead who is robbing a small store. The store owner is grateful, telling Travis to go: "Don't worry about it man. I'll take care of it . . ." It is hard to imagine a film less like the rom-coms that tend to be filmed on the UWS.

On the right at **131 West 86th Street** is ㊺ the **Jewish Center**, a prominent synagogue founded in 1918. Look up high for the dates 1919 and its equivalent in the Hebrew calendar, 5680. The size of this building reflects how many wealthy Jews were moving to the UWS in the early decades of the 20th century.

When you reach Amsterdam Avenue, turn right where ㊻ you find

the UWS institution **Barney Greengrass**, "The Sturgeon King." If you have not been before, you must try the smoked fish specialties here and soak up the atmosphere. Greengrass founded his original Jewish deli in Harlem in 1908 and moved here in 1929. You probably guessed it, but the deli has appeared in many films and television programs, most notably *Seinfeld, Sex and the City, You've Got*

Mail, Deconstructing Harry, Revolutionary Road, 30 Rock, Extremely Loud and Incredibly Close, and *Billions*. Stars such as Meg Ryan, Tom Hanks and Leonardo DiCaprio have sat at these tables and read their lines.

Walk away from Barney Greengrass and south down Amsterdam Avenue, right down to West 83rd Street. A little farther up on the right 47 is **Café Lalo** (201 West 83rd Street). In *You've Got Mail* this is where Kathleen and Joe (she only knows his email name, NY152) are due to meet. When Joe realizes his date is his bookstore rival, he does not reveal this to Kathleen who believes she has been stood up.

Continue down Amsterdam Avenue, turning left down West 82nd Street to stop 48 at **No. 155** on the left. This is where an unknown 22-year old law graduate from Cuba stayed for three months with his wife on their honeymoon in 1948. The couple enjoyed everything the city had to offer, and the law graduate contemplated studying in New York. He would return for a second trip in 1955 to continue his love affair with New York, but Fidel Castro was also seeking to raise funds for his Cuban revolutionaries. His third visit in 1959 was quite different. He was now divorced, and a media star who could draw a crowd of 16,000 when he gave a speech from a Central Park bandstand. Castro's popularity in the United States was not to last. Opposite is the Ukrainian Orthodox Cathedral.

Return to Amsterdam Avenue and head left down West 81st Street, in recent years one of the most expensive streets in the city to buy an apartment. On the left  is **129 West 81st Street**, where **Jerry Seinfeld** lived in apartment 5A in the long-running series (Cosmo Kramer lives at 129 across the hall from Jerry). No filming took place here and the façade of the building seen in the show was that of a building in Los Angeles. However, fans continue to pay their respects here.

Grand apartment buildings can start to look remarkably similar, and sadly most of us will rarely (if ever) get a chance to look inside. However, two notable ones along here are  **15 West 81st Street** and **The Beresford** ⑤. The first is notable for being another design by Emery Roth and was completed by 1930. This remarkable architect was also working on The Beresford and San Remo at the same time. This features an Italian Renaissance-style design and a typical apartment here might cost around $5 million.

The Beresford on the corner dates from 1929 and its entrance faces Central Park. This was Roth's largest apartment building and is one of the most expensive addresses in New York. It is also a favorite of celebrities who love soaring ceilings, ballroom-sized rooms, and sheer opulence. The average price here is around $10 million, and some have sold for $40 million. The list of famous people who have lived here is very long but it includes Rock Hudson, John McEnroe, Diana Ross, Meryl Streep, Calvin Klein, mobster Meyer Lansky, Glenn Close and—inevitably perhaps—Jerry Seinfeld.

Turn right down CPW, passing the American Museum of Natural History and the New-York Historical Society. Why does the latter institution have a hyphen between "New" and "York"? When the Society was founded in 1804, the hyphen was commonly used in this way right up until the mid-19th century.

A little farther down ⑤ is **The Kenilworth at 151 CPW.** This French Second Empire-style delight was completed in 1908. Actor Basil Rathbone lived here and the greatest Sherlock Holmes used to go walking with the finest Frankenstein—actor Boris Karloff, who lived in the Dakota. Michael Douglas and Catherine Zeta-Jones also lived here. It is named after Kenilworth Castle in England.

Next up ⑤ is **The San Remo at 145-46 CPW.** It has been home to Dustin Hoffman, Raquel Welch, Barry Manilow, Diane Keaton,

The Langham, The San Remo and The Kenilworth (from left)

Bruce Willis, Bono, Rita Hayworth, Stephen Sondheim, Steven Spielberg, Tiger Woods, Demi Moore, Steve Martin, and Paul Simon. Madonna's application to live here made headlines when she was rejected by the co-op board. In 2019 it was reported that Demi Moore's old apartment was on sale for $50 million (she had sold it for $5 million less in 2017). Completed in 1930, this is another Emery Roth design.

Continue, passing **The Langham** ④ at **135 CPW**. Completed by 1907 at the cost of $2 million (try not to smile . . .), Maureen O'Sullivan and her daughter Mia Farrow lived here. Woody Allen (then Farrow's husband) included her apartment in his film *Hannah and Her Sisters* (1986). Other residents have included Robert Ryan and Carly Simon. Marilyn Monroe used to visit The Langham, both to see her psychiatrist and her friend and acting coach Lee Strasberg.

Walk on, passing ⑤ **The Dakota**—the most famous apartment building of them all. When it was built in 1881, this was a very unfashionable and remote part of New York. As you have seen over the last few miles, all that was soon to change. Books have been written about this iconic building but most people associate it with John Lennon and Yoko, and inevitably Lennon's murder here in 1980.

A fantasy residents' social night here includes Roberta Flack, Judy Garland and Yoko singing together (Imagine!), accompanied by Lennon on guitar and Leonard Bernstein on piano. Not to be outdone, Nureyev would be dancing around the room, with the coolest of them all— Lauren Bacall—gazing on through a fog of cigarette smoke. Melanie Griffith, Carly Simon, and Billy Joel would not be at the party—their applications to live here were rejected by the co-op board. The Dakota has featured in several films, most notably *Rosemary's Baby* (1968).

Now walk up West 72nd Street. The arched gateway of the Dakota facing onto the street is where John Lennon's killer Mark Chapman hung out for several hours on December 8, 1980. At about 5 p.m., Lennon and Yoko Ono came out of here to get into a limousine. Len-

non talked to Chapman briefly and signed a copy of an album for him. The couple went to the Record Plant Studio on West 44th Street, and returned here at around 10:50 p.m. When they got out of the limousine, Chapman shot Lennon, and then calmly sat down on the curb and began to read *Catcher in the Rye* before being arrested.

Lennon was rushed to Roosevelt Hospital by the police but was pronounced dead at

11:07 p.m. Each year thousands of people visit the memorial to Lennon in Strawberry Fields, located directly to the east of the Dakota in Central Park. The Liverpudlian is a reminder of how people born outside the city often make the biggest impression on New Yorkers.

Continue up West 72nd Street where—on the right ⑤ at **No. 27**—is **The Olcott** apartment building. It used to be the Olcott Hotel and features in *Taxi Driver* when Bickle drops off a fare here. It is also one of the locations Mark Chapman stayed in November 1980, a few weeks before he returned to New York to murder John Lennon in front of the Dakota.

Follow the map, turning left down Columbus Avenue then left onto West 71st Street. Stop at ⑤ No. 69 on the left, now a restaurant. This was **the site of Café La Fortuna** that was a local institution for three decades before it closed in 2008. It was a regular haunt of John Lennon, Yoko Ono, and their son Sean. On Lennon's last day he had breakfast here with Ono at their regular table. Afterwards he went to get a haircut, did a photoshoot at the Dakota and—as mentioned earlier—went to the recording studio before returning home to encounter his murderer.

Continue down Columbus Avenue, turning right onto West 69th Street. You pass on the corner ⑤ No. 106 (at the time of writing a dry cleaners). It used to be a cheese and antiques shop, but during filming for *You've Got Mail* the lucky owners were paid to go away for a few weeks while their shop was turned into a movie set. It would serve as Kathleen's independent bookstore—***The Shop Around the Corner***.

Continue to Broadway, and turn right, passing a real-life iconic UWS bookstore—Shakespeare & Co. It was the opening of a new Barnes & Noble store on 82nd Street that helped inspire *You've Got Mail*. Many Upper West Siders were unhappy that independent stores like Shakespeare & Co. would be severely affected and the controversy was picked up on by Nora and Delia Ephron. Fox Books was the fictionalized chain-store version.

The last stop on this walk is ⑤ the astonishing **Pythian Temple**, reached by turning right onto West 70th Street, **No. 135**. Dating from 1927, it was designed as the meeting place for Pythian lodges that existed in New York. There are decorative embellishments reflecting Babylonian, Assyrian, and Egyptian motifs.

The Knights of Pythias is a fraternal organization that has many similarities to Freemasonry although is centered around the Greek legend of Damon and Pythias. In the early 20th century, there were around a million Knights of Pythias, but in recent years this has declined to 50,000 or so. After the Knights moved out from here, this became a recording studio for Decca Records. Bill Haley and His Comets recorded *Rock Around the Clock* here in 1954, and the world was never the same again. Billie Holiday, Buddy Holly, and Sammy Davis Jr. also recorded here. It was converted—sadly—into yet another condo building in 1983.

Return to Broadway and continue up it to reach the end of the walk.

12 HARLEM WALK

START: Intersection of 110th Street and
Malcolm X Boulevard
SUBWAY: Central Park North [110 St] ② ③
FINISH: Schomburg Center
SUBWAY: 135th St ② ③

HARLEM

Distance: 3.5 Miles

1. Central Park
2. Placid and Saranac
3. Martin Luther King Jr. Playground
4. Martin Luther King Jr. Towers
5. 66-72 St. Nicholas Avenue
6. Mount Neboh Baptist Church
7. Fields Court
8. Wadleigh Secondary School
9. The Community Kitchen and Food Pantry
10. First Corinthian Baptist Church
11. Graham Court
12. A. Philip Randolph Square
13. Carrie McCracken Truce Garden
14. Minton's Playhouse
15. Harlem Hebrew Language Academy
16. Harlem Parish
17. Headquarters of the New York Chapter of the Black Panthers
18. The Castle
19. The Joseph Daniel Wilson Memorial Garden
20. Harriet Tubman Memorial
21. Police 28th Precinct Building
22. Hancock Park
23. "New York Amsterdam News" Building
24. Clayton Williams Community Garden
25. Apollo Theater
26. Site of Rivera Riot
27. Former Blumstein's Department Store
28. Former Hotel Theresa
29. Adam Clayton Powell Jr. State Office Building
30. The Harlem Alhambra Building
31. James Brown Way
32. Salem United Methodist Church
33. "Tree of Hope" Sculpture
34. Site of Lafayette Theater
35. St. Aloysius Catholic Church
36. Muhammad Ali Islamic Center
37. Bill's Place
38. YMCA building
39. Mother Zion
40. Strivers' Row
41. The Abyssinian Baptist Church
42. Salvation Army Building
43. Harlem Hospital Center
44. Schomburg Center for Research in Black Culture

As you exit, look south ❶ to see the northern edge of **Central Park**, the dividing line between the Park and Harlem. The cultural significance of the divide inspired the title of the crime film Across *110th Street* (1972). It depicts the struggle between Italian and African American gangsters and features Bobby Womack's song "Across 110th Street," which contains the forbidding lines:

> *"Across 110th Street*
> *Pimps trying to catch a woman that's weak*
> *Across 110th Street*
> *Pushers won't let the junkie go free*
> *Across 110th Street*
> *Woman trying to catch a trick on the street, ooh baby*
> *Across 110th Street*
> *You can find it all in the street."*

The song accompanies the opening credits of Quentin Tarantino's film *Jackie Brown* (1997) and also features in Ridley Scott's film *American Gangster* (2007) about legendary Harlem drug-trafficker Frank Lucas (1930-2019).

Harlem has been considerably gentrified since the early 1970s, as will be evident during this walk.

Follow the map up Malcolm X Boulevard—also known as Lenox Avenue. It was originally known as Sixth Avenue but was renamed in 1887 after the wealthy philanthropist James Lenox (1800-80). Nothing in New York stays static, however, and in 1987 it was co-named after Malcolm X, the civil rights activist who spent much of his life in Harlem. This is the primary north-south road through central Harlem.

Stop at the right-hand corner ❷ of West 111th Street to see the beautiful apartment buildings named the **Placid and Saranac**, designed by C.A.F. Miller and dating from 1899. They are just a taste of the many buildings in Harlem that are among the most pleasing in the city.

Dutch settlers came to the area in the late 1650s—originally, it was "Nieuw Haarlem," named after the city of Haarlem in the Netherlands, which had a population of only 40,000 or so in the mid-17th century. Farms dominated the area, and it remained largely undeveloped until the 1880s. In that decade elevated railway lines extended up Eighth and Ninth Avenues. New transport lines in a densely populated city inevitably attract speculators and developers, and row houses and later apartment buildings like these were constructed to attract wealthier white residents who could easily commute downtown.

The hopes of those early developers were overly optimistic, however. As other northern districts in Manhattan were also developed, there was an over-supply of residential buildings. Philip A. Payton Jr. (1876-1917), known as the "Father of Harlem," was an African American entrepreneur who persuaded many white landlords struggling to fill their buildings to accept African American tenants in the early years of the 1900s. Over the next few years, thousands of African Americans flocked to the relative safety

of Harlem to escape the racial and economic problems that had plagued them in the southern states and other parts of the city such as Hell's Kitchen. The effect was that most white residents began to move away, a reminder of the city's long-running racial tensions.

By 1914 it was estimated that three-quarters of New York's African American residents lived in Harlem. By 1920 the community numbered around 80,000 and over 200,000 by 1930, and from it emerged a golden age of cultural activity—the Harlem Renaissance. Harlem would become known around the world as the heart of Black America, and its artists, musicians, writers and activists would influence American society in ways that the African American community had never achieved before.

Continue along, turning right (after West 112th Street) to follow the map around ❸ the **Martin Luther King Jr. Playground**. To your right are ❹ **Martin Luther King Jr. Towers**. Harlem suffered badly in the Great Depression of the 1930s, and no one was building anything as memorable as the smart apartment blocks that had been constructed in the 1880-90s. The area to our right resulted from the regeneration of Harlem after World War II. In the late 1940s, the City Housing Authority carried out an ambitious plan of urban renewal, with housing projects like this aimed at helping poorer residents.

This involved tearing down buildings on dilapidated residential streets and replacing them with a vast new residential development. The Joseph family were the first to move in in May 1952, their address then being Stephen Foster Projects Houses, named for the "father of American music" Stephen Foster (1826-84). It was later renamed after Martin Luther King Jr., another reminder of the importance of the civil rights movement to many in Harlem.

Tragedy struck here in 1989 when two local children—Christopher Dansby (2 years old) and Shane Walker (18 months)—vanished on separate dates from the playground, presumably abducted. They have never been found, and the case was featured in the Netflix series *Unsolved Mysteries*.

Follow the map back onto Malcolm X Boulevard and turn left, crossing over to walk down West 113th Street. At the entrance to West 113th Street, you pass more examples of fine apartment buildings from the early days of Harlem's development as a new residential suburb. When you reach St. Nicholas Avenue, turn right. Steven Spielberg used these streets to film a number of scenes in his 2021 remake of *West Side Story*. The Upper West Side streets that feature in the classic 1961 movie had long since disappeared, demolished for the construction of the Lincoln Center complex.

When you reach the corner of West 114th Street, turn right where immediately on the right is ❺ **66-72 St. Nicholas Avenue**. Completed in 1915, the details of its impressive frontage with its lion faces is typical of the buildings in this area. Retrace your

Harlem-Lane (St. Nicolas Avenue) from Central Park to Manhattanville, 1865

steps, now crossing over to the other side of West 114th Street (heading west).

Harlem has been home to many different communities over the centuries, many of which are overlooked today given the area's more recent reputation as the Black Mecca of the world. Originally Native Americans lived here, followed by Dutch settlers in the 1600s. Nieuw Haarlem was incorporated as a stand-alone settlement in 1660 when Peter Stuyvesant served as leader of the New Netherland colony.

Nieuw Haarlem lay about eight miles north of New Amsterdam's boundary along Wall Street, and served as a useful bulwark against intruders heading down Manhattan island. The British later tried to rename Harlem as "Lancaster" but it never stuck. Several eminent New York families such as the Bleekers, de Lanceys and Rikers had landholdings here, however in the 19th century many local farms were struggling and some abandoned. Irish squatters arrived, followed by many other immigrant groups including German, Italian, Jewish and even Finnish.

On the right (as you approach Adam Clayton Powell Jr. Boulevard) is ❻ the **Mount Neboh Baptist Church**. Harlem was once home to about 175,000 Jews. In 2002 *The New York Times* noted, "On the map of the Jewish diaspora, Harlem is Atlantis. That it was once the third largest Jewish settlement in the world after the Lower East Side and Warsaw—a vibrant hub of industry, artistry and wealth—is all but forgotten. It is as if Jewish Harlem sank 70 years ago beneath the waves of memory, beyond recall." This church was originally a synagogue, one of around 50 once found in Harlem.

The size of the Jewish community declined steadily as the 20th century progressed, and the synagogues were demolished or sold to be converted into Christian churches. There is a clue to this church's origins on a ground-level cornerstone. It contains the foundation dates of 1908 and its equivalent 5668 in the Hebrew calendar. Above the entrance are Hebrew inscriptions on the sculpture of the ten commandments.

The front of the church faces onto Seventh Avenue, known as Adam Clayton Powell Jr. Boulevard north of Central Park. Adam Clayton Powell Jr. (1908-1972) was one of the highest-profile African American politicians of the mid-20th century and represented Harlem in the House of Representatives between 1945-71. He was also a prominent pastor at Harlem's famous Abyssinian Baptist Church (seen later on) and the first African American from New York to be elected to Congress. He emerged as a key figure in the emerging civil rights movement during the 1930s, representing a generation of activists before

the era of Malcolm X and Martin Luther King Jr.

Cross over from the church to continue down West 114th Street, but stop on the corner to admire ❼ **Fields Court**—a striking early 20th-century apartment building. By the 1970s, it was badly neglected and was taken over by the city authorities.

Continue along West 114th Street. On the right is ❽ the **Wadleigh Secondary School** For The Performing & Visual Arts. It occupies a fine building dating from 1902 and is significant for being the first public high school for girls in this part of Harlem. It is named for Lydia Fowler Wadleigh (1817-88), a pioneering educationalist and principal of the first public high school for girls in New York (in Greenwich Village). The building was designed by Charles B. J. Snyder, renowned for his innovative designs of 140 schools, with around 25 in Manhattan.

Adam Clayton Powell Jr., Frederick Douglass, James Lenox (from left)

As you continue along the street, look for the fantastic variety of details that adorn many of the buildings. Developers went to a great deal of effort and expense to make their buildings as attractive as possible.

Soon you reach Frederick Douglass Boulevard, where you turn right. Originally Eighth Avenue, the section north of 110th Street was renamed for the African American abolitionist, writer, and statesman. Douglass (1817-95) was one of the most extraordinary Americans of the 19th century, born a slave on a plantation in Maryland and overcoming near-impossible odds to escape to freedom. When he arrived in New York, he wrote, "I felt as one might feel upon escape from a den of hungry lions."

His books became bestsellers, and his anti-slavery speeches and campaigns in America and Europe did much to steer popular opinion against slavery.

Harlem has two little-known connections to Scotland. James Lenox (of Lenox Avenue) was the son of Robert Lenox, a Scottish merchant who emigrated to America when it was under British rule. Douglass's original name was Frederick Augustus Washington Bailey, but having escaped to New York in 1838, he had to be careful to avoid being tracked down by slave catchers. He changed his name to Frederick Johnson, but an acquaintance—who was reading Scottish writer Sir Walter Scott's popular poem *The Lady of the Lake* (1810)—suggested he adopt the surname Douglass. This was because there were two key characters in Scott's poem named Douglas. Perversely the poem's depiction of a burning cross to rally supporters of the Scottish king was later corrupted by the Klu Klux Klan.

Next turn right down West 116th Street, still part of South Harlem. On the right at **No. 252** is ❾ **The Community Kitchen and Food Pantry**, just one of several centers that does a great job helping local residents in need. Tensions continue to rise in Harlem due to concerns by locals about the impact of gentrification on everything from housing costs to what shops now stock. There are many more white residents living here now than a few decades ago, and by around the year 2000 the percentage of Harlem's population that were African American changed from a majority into a minority. The existence of food banks is a reminder that for many, the benefits of gentrification are few and far between.

Carry on, looking on the right at the intersection with Adam Clayton Powell Jr. Blvd. for the vast building that is home to ❿ the **First Corinthian Baptist Church**. The origins of the original African American congregation go back to 1933 when it met in a private home. It would move to this building in the 1960s.

This beautiful building was opened in 1913 as the 2,000 seater Regent Theater, an early example of the huge and lavish cinemas that would be constructed in New York and which hastened the decline of traditional vaudeville shows.

Today the congregation numbers around 10,000 people and includes a small but significant proportion of white people, reflecting changing Harlem. *The New York Times* noted in an article about the church in 2014, "This trend defies the racial norms of American Christianity. The Rev. Dr. Martin Luther King Jr. once called church time on Sunday morning 'the most segregated hour' in a racially divided nation." This church is a vibrant place, the hub for many community events.

On the other side of Adam Clayton Powell Jr. Blvd. is ⑪ **Graham Court**. This historic apartment building dates from around 1901, and was commissioned by William Waldorf Astor (1848-1919), a scion of the famous Astor family and the richest man in America. It has been described as Harlem's equivalent to the more famous Dakota facing Central Park and is a reminder of ambitious speculative construction that took place here in the early 20th century. Astor was an interesting figure who, among other things, moved to Britain, tried to fake his own death and died on the toilet.

Now head left, walking north up St. Nicholas Avenue. It is named for Saint Nicholas of Myra (c. 270-343). Devotion to St. Nicholas all but disappeared in Protestant Europe after the

Reformation, except in the Netherlands. The Dutch who settled in Manhattan in the 1600s brought this tradition with them, and St. Nicholas would become the patron saint of the city. St. Nicholas Avenue is believed to follow an old Indian trail.

On the right, you pass ⑫ **A. Philip Randolph Square**, named for African American civil rights leader and union activist Asa Philip Randolph (1889-1979) who used to live in Harlem. In the 1920s, he organized the first predominately African American labor union, and during the 1940s spearheaded campaigns to prevent segregation in the defence industries, leading to President Roosevelt passing the Fair Employment Act. He directed the famous March on Washington in 1963 where Martin Luther King Jr. gave his "I Have a Dream" speech in front of a crowd of more than 300,000 people.

As you continue up (north) St. Nicholas Avenue, just after the corner of West 117th Street on the left is the small ⑬ **Carrie McCracken Truce Garden**, one of many community gardens in Harlem that help local people make connections with one another.

Continue on, stopping at 210 West 118th Street on the right, ⑭ now the Cecil Steakhouse with Minton's Playhouse beside it. The original **Minton's Playhouse** in this building was a legendary jazz club opened in 1938 by saxophonist Monroe Henry Minton. Minton's is credited as being where the bebop jazz style emerged in the 1940s through sessions involving musicians such as Charlie Parker, Thelonious Monk, and Dizzy Gillespie. Sarah Vaughan, Ella Fitzgerald, Billie Holiday, and Miles Davis are just a few of the great jazz artists who played here.

The heart of the city's jazz scene would later move from Harlem, principally along 133rd Street, to 52nd Street after Prohibition ended in 1933. The original Minton's Playhouse closed in 1974. If you want to get a sense of the atmosphere of this club, listen to the album *Midnight at Minton's* (1941 recording) featuring Don Byas, Thelonious Monk and the great although largely forgotten singer Helen Humes.

Opposite ⑮ is the **Harlem Hebrew Language Academy**, where lessons are held in Hebrew. It is a rare link with Harlem's Jewish past, although it was only established in 2013. Perhaps, surprisingly, forty percent of its students are African American, and the third-largest group is Hispanic.

Turn left down West 118th Street, stopping at **No. 258** on the left, ⑯ a former Catholic church that is today occupied by the **Harlem Parish: arts and cultural space**. This was originally the Catholic Church of St. Thomas the Apostle, and the building dates from 1907. The parish was established in the late 19th century for Irish immigrants, and the neo-Gothic exterior is complemented by a stunning vaulted ceil-

ing. The stained glass came from Franz Mayer of Munich, a leading designer and manufacturer of stained glass that has supplied hundreds of Catholic churches and cathedrals around the world. Like many parts of Harlem, the congregation was Irish, then German and finally African American. The church closed in 2003 and has since been used for a variety of events, including the Amazon launch of the comedy series *Harlem* in 2021, focusing on a group of local women in their 30s.

The 7-foot, 2-inch NBA legend Kareem Abdul-Jabbar (b. 1947) was baptized here, and singer Harry Belafonte's family also had links to the church.

Now head down the other side of West 118th Street, looking for the architectural embellishments outside 164 St. Nicholas Avenue, and then turn left (north) up Adam Clayton Powell Jr. Boulevard.

Every third Sunday in September, this is crowded by bands, performers and spectators during The African American Day Parade held in Harlem. Its mission is to highlight African American culture, heritage and unity, showcase members of the community and commemorate the legacy of its ancestors. Groups from all around the US come to parade alongside Harlemites. The parade starts on West 110th Street and Lenox Avenue, and goes up this street before ending at West 136th

Street. The first parade was held in September 1969 and established as part of the Civil Rights Movement.

Adam Clayton Powell Jr. Boulevard was chosen by the parade's organizers as they regarded it as the focal point of the Harlem Renaissance that reached its zenith around 1926. Just a few figures associated with this golden age include Langston Hughes, Paul Robeson, Louis Armstrong, Zora Neale Hurston, Marcus Garvey, Countee Cullen, and Josephine Baker.

164 St. Nicholas Avenue

One of the key figures of this era was poet, writer, and social activist Langston Hughes (1901-1967). In his poem "Juke Box Love Song" he includes the lines:

"I could take the Harlem night/And wrap around you/Take the neon lights and make a crown/Take the Lenox Avenue busses,/Taxis, subways,/And for your love song tone their rumble down./Take Harlem's heartbeat."

Continue north up the Boulevard.

The next stop is on the left, just after the intersection of West 121st Street, at **No. 2026.** From 1969 ⑰ this was the **headquarters of the New York chapter of the Black Panthers**. At the time, the Black Panthers were demonized in the media, but here members worked with the community, helping children with homework, providing breakfast, and tenant-help programs. Murdered rapper Tupac Shakur's

mother Afeni Shakur was involved with the Panthers here.

In January 1968, Adam Clayton Powell Jr. gave a speech reflecting on "Black Power" and new groups like the Black Panthers. He said "Black power means we are developing a new breed of cats . . . you know when you read the Bible and you read about old Daniel going down in the lion's den . . . When they lowered down Daniel into that lion's den they might have been Black Panthers down there . . . We are a new breed of cats . . . We are finished with the old things." Clayton Power Jr. was an engaging public speaker—you can hear his speeches on YouTube.

Now head left down West 122nd Street, looking for the fine buildings on the left side ⑱ (**The Castle** at **No. 202**, built in 1910, stands out). This is an expensive area for real estate—apartments regularly sell for over $2 million in this part of Harlem.

Continue along West 122nd Street, looking on the right-hand side at **No. 219** ⑲ **The Joseph Daniel Wilson Memorial Garden**. This urban oasis is run by Project Harmony, Inc., a grassroots volunteer-driven group that for several years has cleaned up derelict lots and turned them into green spaces for residents. This one is named for a former resident who worked hard to get enough money to emigrate to Harlem from Guyana and loved horticulture.

Continue on to reach Frederick Douglass Boulevard and cross over to reach the ⑳ **Harriet Tubman Memorial**, a striking bronze created by Alison Saar and unveiled in 2008. Also known as "Swing Low," it commemorates Tubman (c. 1822-1913), another remarkable figure in American history. She escaped a life of slavery only to return and repeatedly risk capture by merciless slave catchers in order to free other slaves using the famous Underground Railroad network. She also worked for the Union Army, playing a leading role in a raid at Combahee Ferry in 1863 that helped free hundreds more. Her extraordinary life was the subject of the Oscar-nominated film *Harriet* (2019).

Continue north up St. Nicholas Avenue, passing ㉑ on the right the fortress-like **Police 28th Precinct building**, which covers the central part of Harlem.

In April 1957, an African American man was beaten by policemen near here (at the intersection of 125th Street and Seventh Avenue). A passing Nation of Islam member named Johnson X Hinton shouted, "You're not in Alabama! This is New York!" He was then beaten by the police, after which Malcolm X led hundreds of protestors to the 28th

Malcom X

Precinct to demand Hinton be treated for his injuries. It was a turning point in the historically unequal relationship between local people and the NYPD. It also increased Malcolm X's public profile, although one consequence was the beginning of surveillance by the FBI on the Nation of Islam. The incident is depicted in Spike Lee's 1992 film *Malcolm X*.

Continue, passing on the left ㉒ **Hancock Park**. It contains a bronze bust of General Winfield Scott Hancock (1824-1886), so skilled a leader of the Union Army during the Civil War that he was known as "Hancock the Superb." Despite being badly injured during Pickett's Charge at Gettysburg in 1864, he continued to lead Union forces. He later ran, unsuccessfully, for President in 1880. The statue was dedicated in 1893.

Walk on, turning right at the corner of West 125th Street, co-named Dr. Martin Luther King Jr. Boulevard. This street is the spiritual heart of Harlem. Langston Hughes, described as the poet laureate of

Harlem, even wrote a poem entitled "125th Street." While affected by gentrification in recent years, it remains a lively place, but be careful of the traffic—statistics show it is one of the most dangerous streets in the US for pedestrians. Former President Bill Clinton has an office on 125th Street (No. 55) and when celebrating 20 years in Harlem in 2021, he commented: "I'd look at the old Apollo Theater and the Cotton Club and all those places and wondered if I could've made it if I was a better musician . . . I'd say it always had a hold on me."

Turn left down Frederick Douglass Boulevard to stop outside **No. 2340**, a four-story narrow ㉓ building with the "New York Amsterdam News" sign. Founded in 1909, this newspaper was originally sited near Amsterdam Avenue—hence the name—and has occupied various locations since. It has been here since the early 1940s, and is famous for being one of the country's oldest and most influential African American focused newspapers (amsterdamnews.com).

Continue along, stopping at ㉔ the **Clayton Williams Community Garden** on the left on the corner of West 126th Street. The Garden is named after Williams, who grew up in Harlem before spending many years in prison. Upon his release, he devoted his life to helping other released convicts and other good causes (he died in 1999 at age 65). Look out for the apple trees—a rare sight in urban Harlem.

The garden stands on the site of the Braddock Hotel. In the mid-20th century, it was popular with many legendary musicians who

West 125th Street

played in Harlem clubs, bars and hotels. On a night out in the hotel bar you might have spotted Ella Fitzgerald, Billie Holiday, Dizzy Gillespie, and even Malcolm Little—before he spent time in prison and later became Malcolm X.

Tragedy struck here on August 1, 1943, when a policeman tried to arrest a female guest, and Robert Bandy—an African American soldier, intervened. The policeman shot Bandy, and while he was not severely injured, rumors of his death spread. The result was the Harlem Riot of August 1-2, 1943, one of several that have rocked the district (others include those of 1935 and 1964).

Dozens of largely white-owned businesses were attacked over a 12-hour period, with six Black residents shot dead and hundreds injured. Around 15,000 policemen and National Guardsmen were sent to keep order, and it marked a low point in relations between the local African American population and the police. At the time, many businesses remained white-owned, often refusing to employ African American workers despite the fact nearly 90 percent of Central Harlem's population was Black.

Retrace your steps and turn left, continuing east along 125th Street/Dr. Martin Luther King Jr. Boulevard. King visited Harlem, but Malcolm X was the civil rights campaigner with deep local connections. Born Malcolm Little in Nebraska in 1924, he moved to Harlem in 1943. It was while serving a prison term that he became a member of The Nation of Islam. He would progress to leading Temple Number 7 in Harlem in 1954, at No. 102 West

116th Street. He was assassinated in 1965 at the Audubon Ballroom just over two miles from here at 3940 Broadway.

Soon on the left you pass  the world-famous **Apollo Theater**. It began in 1914 as a whites-only venue called Hurtig & Seamon's New Burlesque Theater. As the demographics of Harlem changed, the venue began to allow African American customers to attend. Burlesque also became unpopular with city authorities, so in the early 1930s the theater's

Billy Holiday at the Apollo Theater, 1944

new owners changed to offering musical variety shows under the Apollo name. Over the following decades, the greatest entertainers in American history have performed here. Perhaps the golden years were in the 1930s, with talents such as Ella Fitzgerald making their debuts here (in her case, in 1934). Anywhere that has hosted Billie Holiday, James Brown, Sammy Davis Jr., Gladys Night, Bob Marley, Jimi Hendrix, and Aretha Franklin has to be special.

Opposite at **No. 256** is the **site where in March 1935, another major riot began** after a Puerto Rican teenager named Lino Rivera was apprehended by an employee of a shop and accused of shoplifting. Word spread Rivera had been beaten to death, and demonstrations began. These developed into violence that led to three deaths, around a hundred people injured, and millions of dollars of damage caused to largely white-owned businesses. It has been described as "the first modern race riot," with violence largely against property, not between racial groups. Together with the terrible impact of the Great Depression on Harlem, it helped mark the ending of the Harlem Renaissance era.

Carry on, stopping on the right outside the ㉗ once-grand five-story **former Blumstein's Department Store**, named for Louis Blumstein, who arrived from Germany in 1885 and initially worked as a street peddler. His first department store was replaced on this site by the current building in 1921 (the year after Louis died). It has been described as being designed in an "odd amalgam" of late Art Nouveau and early Art Deco style.

In the early 1920s, most white-owned businesses like Blumstein's only hired white workers, causing resentment with the African Americans who accounted for much of the store's customer base. Local African American religious and civic leaders campaigned for change, culminating in a picket line outside Blumstein's in mid-1934. Blumstein's management eventually capitulated, agreeing to hire some African Americans. Around 1,500 people celebrated in a parade outside. In 1943 Blumstein's had the first Black Santa Claus and led the way in Black models and mannequins.

Walk on, looking on the right for the ㉘ **"Hotel Theresa"** sign up high. If you could make an entertaining mini-series about a hotel, this would be a prime candidate. Dating from 1913, it also had a German connection as it was built by a German-born stockbroker called Gustavus Sidenberg (Theresa was his wife). It then operated a whites-only policy and was the tallest building in Harlem. After it was bought by a Black businessman in 1937, things changed.

It became known as the "Waldorf of Harlem," and it would be known as the high-profile destination for African American singers, musicians, writers, and civic leaders. Presidential candidates such as Dwight D. Eisenhower also came here in 1952, to try and secure the African American vote, but perhaps The Theresa's most interesting guest arrived in 1960—Fidel Castro. He came with the Cuban delegation to The United Nations. The Cubans had been kicked out of their first hotel after causing thousands of dollars of damage, partly a result of cooking chickens in their rooms.

On October 12, 1960, Senator John F. Kennedy gave a public speech here during his presidential campaign, which included the lines: "I am happy to come to this historic landmark. Behind the drama of Castro coming to the Hotel Theresa and Khrushchev coming to Castro is a great drama. It is the drama of a world in mo-

tion . . . We Americans should not fear Castro or Khrushchev coming here. We should not fear the world coming to Harlem . . ." The hotel later declined and closed in 1967.

Now cross over Adam Clayton Powell Jr. Boulevard, the view of the other side dominated by the soaring ㉙ **Adam Clayton Powell Jr. State Office Building**. This is the only building in central Harlem taller than the Hotel Theresa. It opened in 1974, its Brutalist design style influenced by African mask design. African Square below is the location of a striking statue of Powell.

This is where Nelson Mandela addressed a large crowd on his first visit to Harlem in 1990, shortly after his release from prison. Mandela made a big impact on New York, and particularly on Harlemites.

The building has divided Harlemites over the years. Construction halted in 1969 after locals protested against what was perceived as an unwelcome, white-dominated attempt at urban renewal.

Not far from here at the corner of 124th Street and Adam Clayton Powell Jr. Boulevard, once stood Rays—a restaurant owned by the legendary Harlem-based boxer Sugar Ray Robinson (1921-1989). In 1960 a young Cassius Clay, about to set off for the Rome Olympics, came here in a taxi to pay his respects to Robinson, his role model and hero. Robinson barely acknowledged Clay, who was deeply hurt. He later remarked, "I said to myself right then, 'If I ever get great and famous and people want my autograph enough to wait all day to see me, I'm sure goin' to treat 'em different.' On the same day, Clay also observed representatives of The Nation of Islam talking to passers by in Harlem. It would not be long before Clay would become the most famous sportsman on the planet, and—as Muhammad Ali—his own life story would be closely linked to that of Malcolm X and The Nation of Islam movement. Ali also stayed in the Hotel Theresa after his famous first win over Sonny Liston.

Head north up the Boulevard, passing on the left ㉚ **The Harlem Alhambra building** (look up for the "Alhambra" signage). This vaudeville theater opened in 1905 and could seat 1,650 people. This was a golden age of live entertainment before cinema changed everything.

Later, Billie Holiday, Bessie Smith and other stars performed here. There is also a loose Spanish and British connection. In the 1850s a music hall in London was named the Alhambra as it looked like the famous Moorish Alhambra palace in Grenada, Spain (Alhambra means "the red" in Arabic). The name was adopted by many other vaudeville theaters in Britain, and the trend later spread to New York.

Next on the left ㉛ look for the sign for **James Brown Way** at West 126th Street, recently named for the "Godfather of Soul," who recorded several live albums at the Apollo Theater. Historian Jacob Morris and the National Black Theater were involved in the campaign to rename this street. The artist's daughter, Deanna Brown Thomas, told the *Daily News* in 2004, "It [the Apollo] is where the eyes of

the world came to watch my father. If he was here he'd be thanking God for people loving him enough to put his name on that street."

Continue up the Boulevard, passing **No. 2190** on the left ㉜—the **Salem United Methodist Church**. Past members of this church include the poet Countee Cullen (1903-1946), prominent during the Harlem Renaissance and best known for poems such as "Incident." The groundbreaking opera singer Marian Anderson (1897-1993) also came here. Her talent endeared her to Einstein, Sibelius, and Toscanini. Anderson also battled racial prejudice, perhaps most notably when, in 1939, she was not allowed to play at a concert hall in Washington D.C. President Roosevelt, Eleanor Roosevelt, and others stepped in and Anderson ended up singing to a non-segregated crowd of 75,000 on the steps of the Lincoln Memorial, while millions listened on the radio. Listen to her version of "Deep River" if you have not heard her before.

You now walk a few blocks north, perhaps listening to some songs inspired by Harlem to get you in the mood. Perhaps Ella singing "Drop Me Off in Harlem," "Take the A Train" or "Holiday in Harlem," (the latter includes the cheerful lyrics:

"Up and down the avenue
You see faces old and new
With a smile that welcomes you
'Cause it's holiday in Harlem."

Just after West 131st Street you pass ㉝ the **"Tree of Hope" sculpture**, inspired by the elm tree that once stood outside the nearby Lafayette Theater. Performers such as Bill "Bojangles" Robinson would rub the tree for luck. The old tree was cut down when the road was widened in 1934. This sculpture was dedicated in 1972 and designed by artist Algernon Miller. A piece of the old tree can be found inside the Apollo where performers still rub it for luck.

Why was the tree associated with this area? The answer lies on the right, that is, east side of the sculpture. A modern building ㉞ (**No. 2227**, between 131st and 132nd Streets) occupies the site of the famous **Lafayette Theater** that operated here from 1912 to 1951. It was the first in Harlem to allow desegregated audiences—in 1913—and Duke Ellington made his debut in the city here in 1923. Orson Welles, then only 20, directed his groundbreaking *Voodoo Macbeth* at the Lafayette in 1936. Set in the Caribbean, it featured an all African American cast and caused a media sensation.

Directly next door, on the south side, stood Connie's Inn (No. 2221), a nightclub established in 1923 by German immigrants who made money from bootlegging. It attracted a mainly white audience who, during the glorious Jazz Age, ventured up to Harlem to see acts

such as Louis Armstrong, Fats Waller, and Wilbur Sweatman. Connie's Inn closed in 1934, a victim like many similar clubs, of the Great Depression.

From here take a detour left down West 132nd Street, to look at the exterior of ㉟ **St. Aloysius Catholic Church**, with its stunning Italian Gothic Revival style frontage. It dates from 1904 when the original congregation was principally made up of Irish, German and Italian immigrants. In 1935 it became a mission church to convert African Americans to the Catholic faith.

Retrace your steps to continue up the Boulevard, passing ㊱ the **Muhammad Ali Islamic Center** (203 West 133rd Street) one of many Islamic institutions and mosques founded in Harlem, mostly in the second half of the 20th century. Muslims first arrived in New York in the 17th century, part of the Dutch settlement of New Amsterdam. Now there are around 300 registered mosques in New York.

The east side of West 133rd Street was the original "Swing Street," and heart of the jazz world in the 1920s. There were around 20 jazz clubs there during the Prohibition years, including The Nest, Tillie's,

Hansberry's Clam House, and Bank's Club. Walk down here to stop at ⓷ **No. 148** on the right-hand side. At the time of writing, this is **Bill's Place**, which describes itself as "Harlem's only authentic speakeasy," and traces its roots back to the 1920s. It is named for sax player Bill Saxton who plays at the jazz club located here. There is a picture outside of Billie Holiday who sang here at the start of her career.

She would recall in *Lady Sings the Blues* (1956) how, as an impoverished 17-year-old in 1933, she "walked down Seventh Avenue from 139th Street to 133rd Street, busting in every joint trying to find a job. In those days, 133rd Street was the real swing street like 52nd Street later tried to be. It was jumping with after-hours spots, regular hour joints, restaurants, cafés, a dozen to a block." She entered a club called Pod's and Jerry's—"I was desperate. I went in and asked for the boss. I told him I was a dancer and I wanted to try out." She did not impress with her dancing and was about to be thrown out when the piano player asked if she could sing. The rest is history. When Prohibition ended in 1933, the clandestine speakeasies on 133rd Street were badly impacted, and "Swing Street" moved downtown.

Return to Adam Clayton Powell Jr. Boulevard and turn right. Walk a couple of blocks before turning right into West 135th Street. Stop on the right outside and look for the ㊳ **YMCA building** to your right (east). Dating from 1932 (and the one it replaced opposite, dating from 1919) was significant as many African American men at the time could not get into white-only YMCAs or hotels. Many prominent figures from the Harlem Renaissance period, including singer Paul Robeson, writers Langston Hughes and Claude McKay stayed here, as did Malcolm X when he was still Malcolm Little.

Continue up Adam Clayton Powell Jr. Boulevard, turning right into West 137th Street and walk down a short way where on the right is ㊴ the historic **"Mother Zion,"** or Mother African Episcopal Zion Church. It is the oldest African American church in the city, tracing its origins back to

Strivers' Row

1796. The congregation used a number of church buildings in the city before moving to Harlem in 1914 and then moved into this church building that dates from the early 1920s. It is the mother church of the African Methodist Episcopal Zion conference, which played an important part in the abolitionist movement and the Underground Railroad that helped escaped slaves. Harriet Tubman and Frederick Douglass were members of the AME Zion conference.

Continue up Adam Clayton Powell Jr. Boulevard and turn left onto West 138th Street, better known as ⑩ **Strivers' Row**. Part of the St. Nicholas Historic District, the houses along here and West 139th Street are regarded as some of the best examples of late 19th-century urban building in the city. David H. King Jr. (1849-1916) was the main developer, described as the Trump of his era. He aimed to attract white, upper-middle-class families, but the development had failed by the mid-1890s despite featuring designs by great architects such as Stanford White.

As many white residents abandoned Harlem in the early 20th century, many of King's houses were left empty, and African Americans

were only allowed to move in from 1919. It quickly became the desired location for many ambitious Harlemites, and the wealth, reputation or status of residents for the next few decades gave rise to the "Strivers' Row" nickname. Past residents include jazz pioneer W.C. Handy, Scott Joplin, "Bojangles" Robinson, Adam Clayton Power Jr., and the great heavyweight boxer Harry Wills. Today houses can sell for over $3.5 million.

The cultural and social significance Strivers' Row has inspired many artists, from Abram Hill who wrote the stage play *On Strivers Row* (1940), and Spike Lee, who placed one of his characters Flipper Purify, played by Wesley Snipes, in a house here in the film *Jungle Fever* (1991).

When you have had a look along Striver's Row, return to Adam Clayton Powell Jr. Boulevard. Cross over down West 138th Street to stop outside ⓴ **The Abyssinian Baptist Church** at **No. 132**. Its origins go back to 1808 when a brave group of African American men and women, including Ethiopian seamen living in the city, refused to accept segregated seating at their existing church so they decided to set up their own. They named it after Abysinnia, the ancient name of Ethiopia.

Under the leadership of charismatic figures such as Adam Clayton Powell Sr., and later his son Adam Clayton Powell Jr., it became one of the largest and most influential African American churches in the city. Its members were heavily involved in the Civil Rights fight, helping the poor during the Great Depression and providing a base for figures such as Clayton Powell Jr. to further their political and civic careers. The Neo-Gothic home of this "megachurch" is not that old, dating from 1923.

Adam Clayton Powell Jr. officiated at the wedding of Nat King Cole and jazz singer Maria Hawkins here in 1948—they had met at Club Zanzibar in Harlem. Three thousand people attended the wedding, including "Bojangles" Robinson and Sarah Vaughan.

Continue on, next turning right down Malcolm X Boulevard/Lenox Avenue, passing on the left the ㊷ **Salvation Army building**. The Salvation Army was founded by William Booth (1829-1912) in 1865, originally to help the poor of London. It arrived in the United States in 1880 and today assists 30 million Americans each year. Just past here is the ㊸

Harlem Hospital Center which traces its origins back to 1887.

In 1989 when misinformation about AIDS was still prevalent, Princess Diana visited the hospital and hit the headlines after hugging HIV-positive children. It endeared her to the public, although apparently not the Royal Family. The visit and aftermath is featured in the mini-series *The Crown*.

Continue along, passing ㊹ the **Schomburg Center for Research in Black Culture**, a research library of the New York Public Library. It contains a unique collection of materials relating to African American culture and history and emerged as a key institution during the Harlem Renaissance. Notable figures such as W.E.B. DuBois, James Baldwin, Paul Robeson, Eleanor Roosevelt, and Maya Angelou have taken part in programs here. Langston Hughes's ashes are buried under a medallion in the foyer titled "Rivers" from Hughes's poem "The Negro Speaks of Rivers."

The elegant building of the original library (just around the corner) dates from 1905 and has an Italian Renaissance design. The Center is named for Arturo Schomburg (1874-1938), a Puerto Rican with African heritage who built up a valuable collection that formed the basis of the library.

You can finish the walk here at the 135th Street Station.

INDEX

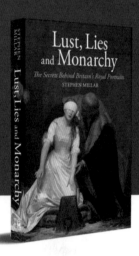